P9-DEY-261

TO BECOME A TEACHER

MAKING A DIFFERENCE IN CHILDREN'S LIVES

TO BECOME A TEACHER

MAKING A DIFFERENCE IN CHILDREN'S LIVES

WILLIAM AYERS, EDITOR

FOREWORD BY JONATHAN KOZOL

TEACHERS COLLEGE PRESS

TEACHERS COLLEGE
COLUMBIA UNIVERSITY
NEW YORK AND LONDON

Published by Teachers College Press, 1234 Amsterdam Avenue, New York, NY 10027

Copyright © 1995 by Teachers College, Columbia University

Chapter 4 copyright © 1995 by Nancy Balaban

All rights reserved. No part of this publication may be reproduced or transmitted in any form or by any means, electronic or mechanical, including photocopy, or any information storage and retrieval system, without permission from the publisher.

Excerpt from "A Poet's Advice to Students" reprinted from *A Miscellany Revised* by E. E. Cummings, edited by George J. Firmage, by permission of Liveright Publishing Corporation. Copyright © 1955 by E. E. Cummings. Copyright © 1965 by Marion Morehouse Cummings. Copyright © 1958, 1965 by George J. Firmage.

Excerpt from "View of the Capitol from the Library of Congress" from *The Complete Poems 1927–1979* by Elizabeth Bishop. Copyright © 1979, 1983 by Alice Helen Methfessel. Reprinted by permission of Farrar, Straus & Giroux, Inc.

"The Magic Flower" by Danny Marcus is from *MIRACLES: Poems by Children of the English-Speaking World*. Collected by Richard Lewis. © 1966. Distributed by The Touchstone Center, New York.

Library of Congress Cataloging-in-Publication Data

To become a teacher : making a difference in children's lives / edited
  by William Ayers.
    p.   cm.
  Includes bibliographical references (p.   ) and index.
  ISBN 0-8077-3456-X (alk. paper). — ISBN 0-8077-3455-1 (pbk. :
alk. paper)
    1. Teachers—United States.   2. Teaching.   I. Ayers, William,
  1944–   .
  LB1775.2.T6   1995
  371.1'02—dc20   95-10676

ISBN 0-8077-3455-1 (paper)
ISBN 0-8077-3456-X (cloth)

Printed on acid-free paper

Manufactured in the United States of America

02 01 00 99 98 97   8 7 6 5 4 3

This book is dedicated to the memory of Lillian Weber, founder of the Workshop Center for Open Education at the City College of New York, whose moral energy, social commitments, broad vision, and good work inspired generations of teachers.

Contents

Foreword

DAYS OF HEAVEN

When I was a child I preferred the company of grown-ups. Since I became a grown-up I have much preferred the company of children. The happiest years of my life as an alleged adult were, without question, the ones I spent in fourth and fifth grade as a teacher.

In one of the finest essays in this book, William Ayers speaks of the times "that are transcendent" for a teacher. I will, if I may, take that as the text for the foregoing sermon: There are many good reasons for becoming a teacher. Some do it out of love of subject matter, others out of a political and moral vision of a just society, and others still because they are intrigued and fascinated by psychology and learning theory. My own motive, at the start, was far more selfish and, I suppose someone might add, a good deal less mature. I became a teacher because children make me happy. They fill me with a sense of mystery about the goodness of existence, a feeling of magic, a feeling of amazement at the beauty of humanity before it has been soiled by the world's dirt.

Teachers-to-be will hear and read an awful lot these days about the obstacles they're going to face in bureaucratic principals, archaic texts, restrictive rules, and punitive exams; if they are to teach in inner-city public schools, they will also hear a lot about the social and economic problems that their students frequently will face. Much of this is absolutely true; and many days in many public schools will doubtless be sheer hell for many teachers. But the moments of transcendence, when they come, make up for almost everything.

Sometimes, as Ayers has written, these moments come "when a child responds with kindness to kindness," sometimes when a child's secret "hopes and fears can be expressed," and often simply when "minds are stretched," "connections are made," "horizons are expanded."

No matter what one reads in advance of why these good things happen under certain good conditions, they always strike a teacher as a bit miraculous. "When teaching is done well," as Ayers notes, "it resonates in the deepest parts of your being—it satisfies the soul."

To me, this is the heart of the whole matter: teaching as something that one does not because, when it's successful, one fulfills some arbitrary and external expectation, not because we hope to see our students pass another set of seemingly irrelevant exams, not because the skills they gain are "useful" to society, not because the business leaders in our cities will be grateful for an adult population trained to meet their mercenary needs and job-demands, but because it is a joyful way to spend one's life and because, when we feel satisfaction or exhilaration, we will often see it also in our children's eyes.

Contemporary press reports and government commissions rarely speak of happiness as having any valued or important place in education. Children are viewed less frequently as children than as future cogs within a postindustrial machine: little pint-sized deficits or assets, some of whom may be of no real worth to our society, others of whom may have some marginal utility. I hope that men and women going into classroom teaching will resist these ugly and dehumanizing measurements of failure or success. Childhood is something more than preparation for some later stage in life that many children in our inner cities will not even reach because so many, lost within the toxic miseries and illnesses that plague our cities now, will not ever live to be adults. Childhood has, or needs to have, a precious value in itself, for what it is, and not for what it's supposed to lead to.

Perhaps this is one reason why I have been drawn repeatedly to teaching children in the elementary schools and why I often feel quite sad when lively, cheerful, and amusing people in the schools of education tell me that they've been encouraged, sometimes even pressured, to think only about secondary education. I always try to steer the most ebullient and engaging teachers into teaching younger children because I believe that it is in the early years of school that liveliness, delight, a sense of magic in existence, beauty, laughter, whim, and a capacity for utter foolishness are most essential and, when they are present, most contagious.

This leads me to the other point I'd like to make—one prompted by the elegant contribution to this volume made by Maxine Greene. In recognizing, as she does, the deep despair that now confronts so many children in our urban schools—and perhaps almost all children who must grow up in one of the meanest periods of history that our society has ever undergone—she nonetheless selects some seeds of loveliness and hope out of the past in order to invent a more auspicious future. "I should like the unfinished conversations to be taken up again," she writes, "this time against the sound of blue guitars."

The metaphor of the "blue guitars," which comes from the poet Wallace Stevens, is so utterly unusual—so strange and wonderful and baffling to find within a book on education—that I just sat and cheered for "blue guitars" before I even had the time to figure out what it might mean. It is the kind of verbal magic one expects only from brilliant poets, charmingly eccentric children, and wise teachers.

I wrote in the margin: "What respectable scholar would ever use a phrase like 'blue guitars' to tell us about teaching?" And then I answered it: "A teacher who's been listening to children!"

A lot of college students write to me, after reading books I've written, to say they want to go into education so that they can help "to change an unjust world." Many are motivated by political convictions and write to me because my own books tend to be highly political. I write to encourage them because I think that teachers *ought* to be political, at least in the sense of being ardent and ingenious advocates for kids in all respects. But I also urge these students to look hard for something in—and not beyond—the act of teaching as a reason in itself, apart from politics, apart from "higher" purposes of any other kind. I urge them to be teachers so that they can join with children as the co-collaborators in a plot to build a little place of ecstasy and poetry and gentle joy.

From this point on, I think that I will tell them, "Listen for the sound of blue guitars." They probably will not know what I mean but maybe the phrase will stay within their minds. One day, in the midst of a chaotic lesson in which everything seems to be going wrong, a child who's never really opened up before may suddenly speak right from the heart and say something so beautiful and sad and unexpected that the teacher has to struggle not to smile and cry at the same time. Those are the moments when the blue guitars begin to play. If we listen, we will hear them.

I hope that this wonderful collection of wise writing by good teachers will lead many readers into lives lived joyfully among schoolchildren.

—Jonathan Kozol

(Jonathan Kozol's most recent book is *Savage Inequalities: Children in America's Schools*.)

Acknowledgments

Since teaching is always a search for better teaching, I am still in a fundamental sense becoming a teacher. I am stretching, searching, and reaching toward teaching. In my ongoing quest it has been my good fortune to have had many mentors and models, various colleagues and fellow travelers. Each of the authors whose work is presented in this book has nourished me as a teacher; each continues to challenge and guide me along my path.

Many thanks as always to Murray Korngold, fabled monk, raconteur, and sacred spirit; to Harriet Beinfield and Efrem Korngold, healers, river walkers, soul mates; to Michael Klonsky and Susan Klonsky, Mona Khalidi and Rashid Khalidi, Jeff Jones and Eleanor Stein, fierce fighters for justice, courageous thinkers, and friends.

Thanks, too, to Pat Ford, Faith Smith, John Ayers, Judi Minter, BJ Richards, Bruch McPherson, Sokoni Karanja, Bill Schubert, Ann Lopez, Coretta McFerren, Anne Hallett, Arnie Aprill, Allan Schwartz, Jamie Kalven, Adela Coronado-Greeley, Esther Lopez, John McKnight, Stan Hallett, Rick Ayers, Warren Chapman, Sunny Fisher, Carole Travis, Paddy O'Reilly, Kris Seiloff, Joan Jeter Slay, Aimee Horton, Vito Perrone, Norm Fruchter, Michelle Fine, Pat Carini, Esther Lopez, Deborah Meier, Linda Darling-Hammond, Ann Leiberman, Vivian Gussin Paley, Yvonne Smith, Denise Prince, Lucy Matos, Jane Andreas, Frank Tobin, Kim Day, Hal Adams, Susan Kilbane, Herb Kohl, Jose Lopez, Sarah Cohen, Alice Brent, Jonathan Kozol, and Jay Rehak. You continue to show me what good teaching can look like.

A special thanks to Ron Roszak, who typed the manuscript, kept me organized and on task, and anticipated and overcame a seemingly endless series of roadblocks and obstacles. His wit, wisdom, care, and commitment are embodied here as well.

And to Sarah Biondello, challenging and caring—much more than the word "editor" implies. She has been a coconspirator and friend for a long time.

With love and gratitude to my mom and dad.

To Bernadine Dohrn, as always, my deepest regard, respect, love.

And thanks, finally, to members of the North Dakota Study Group, Rethinking Schools, the Workshop Center, Democracy and Education, the Salmon River Community, Students for a Democratic Society, and the Bookies for nurturing and joining issues with me, and giving me a home.

William Ayers

JOINING THE RANKS

William Ayers

Because I'm married to a lawyer, I have an interesting window into how at least some of the rest of the world sees teaching and teachers. In a typical scenario I find myself at a holiday party in a fancy hotel with wall-to-wall lawyers. I look reasonably pulled together—coat and tie, clean shoes. While standing in a small circle of people, someone turns to me and says, "And what do you do, Bill?"

"I teach kindergarten."

The response: frozen smiles, wrinkled brows, looks that say, "But he seems so *normal*," or "He's a bit old for that." Looks of condescension and confusion mixed with pity. And then, following an awkward silence, one of the lawyers offers—hopefully—"Well, you must have a lot of *patience*." It is an attempt to be kind, I believe, a stretch, to say something "nice."

For years I endured this conversation quietly. But eventually I developed a reply that gave us teachers more credit and those lawyers something more to think about: "I teach kindergarten," I would say, "and it's the most intellectually demanding thing I've ever done." This always caused heads to snap as a disconnect registered between a commonsense view of teaching kindergarten and a description associated with higher pursuits. I would watch the wheels grinding behind the frozen smiles, the brows becoming more deeply wrinkled.

I had in mind the ways that teaching young children well—that is, taking their ideas and their questions and their interests seriously—can lead a teacher toward a deep and sustained inquiry into, say, penguins and popcorn and puddles, the production of chewing gum and cheddar cheese, the politics of playgrounds or the history of parks, the physics of hackey sacks or the chemistry of hotcakes. But more than this, I was thinking of the profound intellectual challenge every teacher faces: to see each student as a growing, dynamic, developing, stretching being—a fellow human creature—with specific needs and demands and hopes and desires and potentials. Teachers have to see each student in as full and focused a way as possible, responding to each fully and fairly and authentically— touching each life and reaching toward each soul. Now that is a staggering intellectual task, not to mention an awe-inspiring ethical challenge.

Of course, I rarely got to fully engage the lawyers in these questions. Typically, the response to my expanded reply was a more awkward, slightly longer silence, and then, even more emphatically, "Well, you *must* have a lot of *patience!*"

And so I amended my reply once more: "I teach kindergarten. It's the most intellectually demanding thing I've ever done. And it's also *ethical* work. I make decisions constantly, all day long, that impact the well-being of children and the direction their lives will take. It's really quite awesome. Say, maybe when you decide you've got enough money and want to do something really useful with your life, you might consider teaching."

Teaching is difficult, demanding, draining work. It is easy enough to mess up, to crash, to have a day when everything runs off the track again and again. The children become surly and argumentative, or, for no apparent reason, one day the students seem to take a collective step back from you, standing behind some invisible but resistant barrier. Or a project you developed and invested in finds no interest among the young, captures no one's imagination or commitment. Or you realize that you are in a rut, that no spark is generating from your efforts, that everything is becoming dull and ordinary, and that the students are bored and you are uninspired. And on and on.

But there are also times in teaching that are transcendent. There are moments when students are truly engaged in finding something out because it interests them and not because they are cringing in front of the grade book; instances when a child responds to kindness with kindness or to an appropriate challenge with a reasonable effort; spaces where the authentic voices of children can be heard, their hopes and fears can be expressed. Connections are made, minds are stretched, horizons are expanded—all this can create real exhilaration. When teaching is done well, it resonates in the deepest parts of your being. It satisfies the soul.

Becoming a teacher is risky. This is because—all the curriculum guidelines, layers of supervision, and connect-the-dots school improvement packages notwithstanding—there are no guarantees in teaching. In a world in flux, in transition, often in chaos, teaching is the least certain of professions. Every day in every classroom, a teacher's personality, preferences, capacities, judgment, and values are on display. When things are going well, it can feel personally rewarding; when things go badly, the cut is painful and deeply felt as well. Teaching, then, is highly personal. In big, impersonal, increasingly bureaucratized schools, the intensely personal nature of teaching can be temporarily obscured: "I haven't any control of curriculum"; "I just use the teachers' guidelines"; "I'm just following orders." But then, there you are in a classroom with kids who are real, living, breathing, dynamic, unique. And then these rationalizations *become* an expression of your values: following orders *over* taking this kid's needs seriously; using the boring teachers' guidelines *above* engaging kids in a project that grabs and propels them. To teach takes commitment, strength, struggle, a willingness to grow and develop. It is certainly not for the faint of heart. Becoming a teacher is hard work.

This is a book about possibility, about what could be accomplished in every public school in America if we only have the courage and vision and determination to do so. It is a book of implied (and sometimes explicit) criticism of a system that routinely turns students into passive consumers of curriculum and teachers into clerks in a bureaucracy, instructed to deliver the goods without much thought and without much care. It is a book filled with practical, concrete advice for new teachers (or experienced teachers who are rethinking their practices); advice on how to find allies in your quest for a better teaching practice; how to keep a vision of teaching as vibrant, dynamic, intellectual, and ethical work alive in a system that neither honors nor nourishes that vision; how to keep students at the center of your practice; and how to teach against the grain. It is a book for people who are swimming uncomfortably in a sea of habit and routine, of behaviorism and instrumentalism, and are hoping for something better.

Part I offers insights into teaching as a calling, teaching as an intellectual challenge, teaching as a deeply human enterprise. Part II draws our attention to the power of teaching, the responsibility, the kind of consciousness demanded and expected. Part III locates teaching in the real world of classrooms and schools and the larger society.

The authors gathered here are not idle dreamers. Each is a veteran of the school wars—reform movements, school improvement projects, restructuring efforts—of the past decades, and each chapter is grounded in practice and action. This is a dazzling collection of thinkers, teachers, and writers representing a wide range of backgrounds, interests, and experiences. They have been brought together here in their commitment to teaching as a calling with great humanizing potential, to the future lives of children and youth, and to an educational experience that will enable them to be bold, adventurous, creative, vivid, and illuminating—capable of exploring, understanding, and reinventing their classrooms and their world. The decision to join the ranks, to become a teacher, is a good choice, and I'm in awe. So let's work together to create a classroom, a school, and a world fit for all children—a place of peace and justice.

Part I

BECOMING A TEACHER

William Ayers

What makes a good teacher? When I ask college students this question, they typically come up with a wide and interesting assortment of qualities: compassion, love of children, sense of humor, kindness, intelligence. My own list includes passion, commitment, curiosity, a willingness to be vulnerable, authenticity. When I ask kindergartners the same question, they too have ready answers: a good teacher is fair, funny, smart, nice. They can tell us what they expect.

Generating a list of qualities that constitute goodness in teaching can be a revealing and important activity with students. It gives the teacher some insight into the standards students hold, and it makes conscious and collective for students their own goals and aspirations for the class. It is worth spending some time exploring how those standards might be applied to every member of the class—to the teacher, of course, and to each student, since we are all both teachers and learners in most classrooms—and what qualities complement one another and, added together, make a truly wonderful teacher (firm and fair, challenging and nurturing, saintly and tough). Perhaps most important, it is essential to operationalize each quality, to make it concrete and specific. How would compassion be experienced in the classroom? How would it be enacted, highlighted, rewarded, modeled, discussed, structured into the daily routine and environment? How would a newcomer to the group recognize it or see it embodied in the actions and interactions of class members? And so on.

The first and most fundamental challenge to teachers is to see each student in as full and complete a way as possible. Students are not inert pieces of clay to be molded by clever teachers, and learning is not primarily the passive ingestion of information. If this were the case, becoming a teacher would be simple indeed. But learning requires assent, desire, action; it is characterized by discovery and surprise. And students are learning all the time—experiencing the world, organizing, reorganizing, acting, sorting, constructing, and reconstructing knowledge. Of course they are not always learning what we intend. My lecture on insects may be a lesson in tediousness; another teacher's rules of behavior may provide clear instruction to some about hierarchy and their place in it. In any case, sprinkling information upon students' heads and then testing them to see what they caught has little to do with real learning or with teaching at its best. Teaching at its best requires knowledge of students, knowledge of the hopes, dreams, aspirations, skills, challenges, interests, preferences, intelligence, and values they bring with them to the classroom. Teaching at its best is first an act of inquiry, investigation, and research into the lives of children.

Seeing the student fully and well is harder than it might seem. This is only partly because each student is different, each a dynamic and complex and idiosyncratic fellow creature. This makes "seeing" hard enough, but layered over the obvious are a set of scrims or folding screens against messy reality. They block our vision and make seeing extraordinarily difficult.

One screen against seeing students is the toxic habit of labeling. When you look out into a classroom of students, you are *conditioned* to see categories: learning disabled, dyslexic, behavior disordered, gifted, special ed, EMH, TAG, NGG, and on and on. This way of talking and thinking about students has become the dominant language of schools, yet it does nothing to help classroom teachers teach. "James is BD," says the expert. All thought stops. James becomes a symbol, a group member, a one-dimensional insect fixed permanently in amber. Perhaps James is put into a special program where something mysterious goes on—a treatment done by specialists who are much smarter than you. Perhaps he goes to a special class or school. In any case, James is stuck, and so is the teacher.

Linked to this is the tendency to categorize students based on their deficits. Students are defined in schools by what they don't know and can't do. This is a shaky foundation on which to create the conditions for a robust or vital learning experience. The challenge, again, is to find out what students can do, what they enjoy, what engages their imaginations or energies. Seeing children "at promise" is the antidote for all the talk of children at risk. Assuming an intelligence in children—perhaps obscure, perhaps hard to access, but nevertheless *there*—is the only hopeful way to approach teaching.

Another screen against seeing is the institution of schooling itself. Schools can be places where the artificial but relentless press of time, the huge numbers of students, and the rational organization and scheduling of everything from bodily functions to creative expression are the norm. In these places, people often have difficulty being authentic. Whether pliant or resistant, sweet or surly, students are not always available, accessible, or truly visible in school. Think for a minute about yourself: There are lots of places in this world where you are considered smart, active, funny, generous, talkative, sexy, silly, friendly, wise, unique. The fact that most of those qualities are not apparent in classrooms is not because of *you*. The classroom doesn't call them out, it doesn't ask for them, and it provides no place for their enactment.

This, then, is the second fundamental challenge to teaching—creating an environment that challenges and nurtures the wide range of students who will pass through your classroom door. That is, the teacher must figure out how to create a space where students are *expected* to use their minds well, to derive knowledge from information, to invest thought with courage, to connect consciousness to conduct, and so on.

The teacher builds the context. For example, when I walk into some classrooms, they embody reading and writing and they tell me that reading is valued. I see books, magazines, comics; there is an author's corner and a cozy space to curl up with books; the walls are bristling with children's writing; an "author-of-the-week" is featured at one table. Other classrooms give other messages: Sit down and be quiet; face front because all knowledge is at the front; be obedient.

The point is that the teacher's ideas, preferences, values, instincts, and experiences are worked up in a classroom environment. As you set about building your own learning space, it is essential to reflect about what you value, to bring to awareness your expectations for children, and to construct a room that is an extension of those values. The dimensions you are working with are not just feet and inches but also hopes and dreams.

It may be helpful to think, then, about what you want your students to know about you and your intentions simply by walking through the door. Think about what atmosphere you want to project: is it a workshop for doing things or a trade show demonstrating dazzling and efficient stuff? Is it a quiet place to look but not touch or a formal garden for meditation? Is it an information desk, a video arcade, a laboratory, or a control room? Consider atmosphere when you build an environment for learning.

Think also about the quality of experience students are expected to have. Is it a group problem-solving experience, a sharing experience, or an individual-acting-alone experience? Is it public play, private reflection, or some combination? Is it browsing, finding your way, getting wet, having fun, personal space, or some combination?

Then there is the question of technique, or the means of delivering on an idea. For example, in your classroom, will the technique include sensory immersion, hands-on, group games, or observing? Will students be at the controls? How? Will your classroom involve scale shifts, such as building a huge heart to walk through? Why?

Finally, consider the question of voice. Will the teacher's voice be authoritative, impersonal, dramatic, informative, welcoming, comic, awesome, or some combination? Will the voice invite other voices into the conversation? How?

Seeing the student first and then creating the environment—these challenges are the foundation for becoming an excellent teacher. And still there is more. You need to find ways to take on the task of building bridges from each student to deeper and wider ways of knowing. You need to work to craft a learning experience that engages wider worlds, larger dimensions, even as it engages students' interests and preferences. You need to understand the social, historical, and political contexts of children's lives and find ways to participate there as well. You must continue asking yourself a basic question: what knowledge and experiences are of most value to this student at this time?

I was talking not long ago with an education writer about some of these ideas. He thought that he detected a "disdain for content" in my comments. No, I assured him, I feel no disdain for content. My problem is simply that I don't know how to decide which bits and pieces of information all kids should know at the same moment.

"That's ridiculous," he replied. "There are thousands of obvious things."

"Like what?" I asked.

"Well," he thought about it a moment. "Well, like every eighth grader ought to know the Bill of Rights. Simple and straight-forward."

"OK," I responded. "What's the Seventh Amendment?"

Silence.

It's not that I think knowing the Bill of Rights is unimportant. I think it's terribly important. And so is reading good literature, seeing plays, hearing concerts, attending dance performances, joining the chess club, being able to draw a map of Rwanda, Haiti, or Vietnam, and more. But all this is in the service of developing certain dispositions of mind—curiosity, intellectual engagement, creativity, and so on.

We never really agreed, but we moved on. He characterized my approach to teaching as inefficient. "Teachers can't be ex-pected to work that hard," he argued. "Teachers as a group aren't energetic enough, creative enough, or even smart enough. And why should they be asked to reinvent the wheel?"

Well, that's a good question. Of course, the phrase "don't reinvent the wheel" is an appeal to efficiency, control, and moving ahead, and these are often worthy qualities. But the problem with applying this aphorism to teaching is that it doesn't fit. In fact, in teaching, reinventing the wheel is necessary. Teaching requires invention and reinvention, dynamic involvement with growing and changing bodies of knowledge, complex connection of human beings making new discoveries with traditional ways of thinking and knowing. So reinventing is what we're about and where we begin.

CHAPTER 1

Letter to a Young Teacher

Joseph Featherstone

Dear Josie,

You asked me for some advice about starting out as a teacher, and what popped into my head first is an image of my grandmother. I never met her, but she remains a strong presence. She was the principal of a small, mostly immigrant elementary school in the Pennsylvania coal country. Like so many teachers then and now, the stories of her teaching got buried with her. She was one of many urban Irish Catholics who took part in the progressive educational and political movements of her day. I know that she was ambitious for kids' learning. The immigrant coal miners' children, whose families were often out of work, were to read high-class literature and poetry— she had a weakness for the English poet Browning. She also checked to see that kids brushed their teeth. She was a force in local and state politics, fighting for labor rights, pioneering in women's rights, and leading the movement to end child labor. She was the first woman elected to the state Democratic committee in Pennsylvania. I think she saw a direct link between politics and her practice in education: Both had as their aim the general progress of ordinary people. She was on the people's side, creating an expansive democratic vision of education based on the idea of a country that would work for everybody, not just for the rich.

This seems to me a perspective—a tradition, really—worth reminding ourselves about in a confused political time. Fewer teachers now put matters in terms of politics, although it seems to me that teaching in the United States today more than ever involves a political commitment. I would argue that, like my grandmother, you should think of yourself as a recruit on the people's side, working to build a democracy that doesn't yet exist but is part of the American promise. My grandmother would surely point out that there is important work to be done both in and out of classrooms, and that sometimes school matters get framed by wider social issues. I can hear her, for example, insisting that the biggest educational problem today is the growing despair of joblessness. And I'm sure that my grandmother would say that teachers today have a vital stake in a national health care system, for she always saw the connection between kids' learning and good health. Brushing your teeth and Browning were connected.

Her image reminds me that society and its schools are both battlegrounds, on which different sides fight for rival visions of America and its possibilities. The real basics in education, she would argue, flow from the kind of country you want the kids to make when they grow up. She was voting for a real, rather than a paper, democracy. And she thought that teachers had a role to play in helping the people become more powerful.

New teachers often don't realize that there are sides to take, and that they are called upon to choose. The old idea that education is above politics is a useful half-truth—it helps keep the schools from being politicized. But it conceals the essentially political character of choices we make for kids. Do we see the children we teach today as low-paid workers for the global economy, or as the reserve army of the unemployed? If so, why be ambitious for their hearts and minds? Alternatively, we can frame fundamental aims: that we are creating a first-rate education for everybody's kids, so that as grown-ups they can make a democracy happen. My grandmother and many in her generation would say that schools should offer what students need to take part in a democratic society and its culture—a complex package for everybody's children that would equip them for full participation in work, culture, and liberty.

This is clearly an ambitious goal, rarely achieved in world history, let alone in America. Schools alone can never accomplish it. Still, our sense of the purpose of education matters, and for a long while too many of our schools have not believed in educating the people. The old Greeks said that some were born gold and others brass, and they designed education accordingly. A slave or a woman would not get a free man's education. Over the centuries around the planet, a lot of the human race has agreed, establishing separate educations for rulers and ruled. Hewers of wood and drawers of water would not read Jane Austen in advanced placement English classes. In a democracy, however, the people are supposed to rule. They are, the old phrase has it, the equal of kings. So the people need an education commensurate with their potential political, economic, and cultural power. To give the children of ordinary people the kind of education once reserved for the children of the elites—to do this for the first time in history—is the dream of the builders of U.S. education like Horace Mann and my grandmother and thousands of others who triumphed and struggled and died in obscurity.

You are a newcomer to an historic struggle. Some of this you may have learned already, just by keeping your eyes open. You probably know that the United States has always been a deeply flawed democracy and that education has always mirrored the systematic inequality of society. There was no golden age when the United States did right by everybody's kids. This society still has vastly different expectations for well-off and poor kids. The gap seems to be growing, not shrinking. We are two educational nations. The schools for poor kids that you may visit and teach in will often look like schools in a desperately poor nation, not the world's most powerful country. Textbooks are old, the roof leaks, and there is a shortage of paper. People of color and women and immigrants had to fight their way into the educational feast and are still kept at the margins in many schools. But you also need to know that in each generation, strong teachers like my grandmother have worked with parents and communities to make democracy happen. Her ghost is silently cheering you on.

My grandmother was not alone in thinking that schools have a special responsibility for the progress of the people's culture. In taking a large, ambitious, ample—democratic—view of education's aims, she was opposing minimalist views that reduce children to tiny gears in the nation's great economic machine. She was opposing the oldest human superstition of all, the belief in fundamental inequality. She was also laying rude hands on the second oldest superstition, the belief that because there is never enough to go around, existing unfairness must be endured. My grandparents' generation had a healthy respect for policies that generate jobs for the people, but they never made the mistake of thinking that all of life is embraced by the equations of economists or the maxims of bankers and investors. The economy should serve human life and its needs, not the other way around. There is, the old progressives argued, no real wealth but life. Making a living ought to be a means to a wider end: making a life. And in fact, students educated to fit narrow economic grooves—management's view of what will suffice for today's workforce—will never be equipped to take part in debates and movements to change society and build a democratic economy in which everybody has a fair share and basic security.

The capacity to participate—in work, in politics, in the thought of the times—is really in the end a matter of cultural development. The key to the people's success will be the quality of their characters and their minds—the quality of their culture. It is this hardheaded grasp of the radical importance of culture that makes the progressives of my grandmother's generation worth listening to again today. Symbols and ideas and understanding have to become the property of the people if they are to ever gain any control over their lives and the lives of their children. Symbols and ideas and words and culture are no replacement for jobs or political power, but without them, people will easily lose their way. Many in my grandmother's generation admired Eugene Debs, who once said that he would not lead the people to the promised land, because if he could take them there, some other leader could convince them to leave.

Democratic teaching aims to make the people powerful in a host of ways, but perhaps most importantly in the realm of culture itself— the web of meanings we weave with language and symbols out of our experience and the heritage of the past. In a democracy, people should be educated to be powerful, to tell their stories, to make their own voices heard, and to act together to defend and expand their rights. Culture might be said to be a shorthand word for all the ways that people and their imaginations and identities grow—how we construct the world and make ourselves at home in it, and then re-invent it fresh.

Schoolteachers of my grandmother's era had an almost mystical reverence for the word "growth." This is how you can tell that, for all their toughness (my aunt Mary had my grandmother in the fourth grade and said that she was really strict), they were romantics under the skin. In tough times, against heavy odds, with huge polyglot classes, they kept alive an idea of democratic education itself as a romance. This language doesn't fit our current skeptical mood and circumstance. It has an extravagant and sentimental sound— it's the language of possibility, democratic hope. The old progressives believed in a version of true romance. Some got these ideas from politics, some from religion, and some from poetry, believe it or not. My grandmother mixed her poetry and her politics into a potent brew. One of her favorite romantic poets, John Keats, put the argument for a romantic, democratic view of culture this way: now the human race looks like low bushes with here and there a big tree; spin from imaginative experience an "airy citadel" like the spider's web, "filling the air with beautiful circuiting," every human might become great, everybody would grow to the full height, and humanity "instead

of being a wide heath of furze and briars with here and there a re-
mote pine or oak, would become a grand democracy of forest trees."[1]

A forest of oak trees: This democratic and romantic view of a
people's culture—articulated in the nineteenth century by poets like
Keats and Walt Whitman and practical dreamers like Margaret
Fuller, Elizabeth Cady Stanton, Margaret Haley, Jane Addams, W.
E. B. Du Bois, Eugene Debs, and John Dewey—insists that the goal
for which we struggle is a democratic culture in which everyone can
grow to their full height and take part in the world of ideas, books,
art, and music as well as work and politics. To hardheaded teachers
like my grandmother, this was a version of true romance—true, because they knew that no kid grows on a diet of dry academic splin-
ters and stunted expectations. If you teach kids just minimalist stuff—
isolated skills, for example—they never get to practice and enact the
real thing, culture itself. They get slices of the animal but not the
whole live hog. They lose what Emily Dickinson called the thing with
feathers—hope. In today's hard times, ruled by bastard pragmatism,
it is important to insist that beauty is a human necessity, like water
and food and love and work. The multiplication tables need memorizing. So do the French verbs. Not all learning is fun. But an idea of
learning that leaves out grace and poetry and laughter will never take
root in kids' hearts and souls. Education is in the end a movement
of the spirit. This is the realism behind the old vision of education as
true romance. Children require, finally, things that cannot be bought
and sold, accomplishments that last a lifetime. They are asking for
bread. Too many of our schools are giving them stones instead. From
our point of view today, the school culture of my grandmother's generation may have been too genteel—a white schoolmarm culture that
often ignored or disdained the experience of immigrants, women, and
people of color. It was a monochromatic culture, tied into the many
weaknesses of gentility. But what is impressive today about it is the
depth of its democratic aspirations: the assumption that everyone
can rise up on the wings of hope.

As today, Americans in the past argued over whose version of
culture to teach. The tug-of-war over today's (quite recent) canons
of literature and history is an inevitable aspect of being what Whitman called a people of peoples. I believe—though my grandmother
might disagree—that such tugging and pulling is a sign of cultural
vitality, part of a process of democratic change that Whitman described as "lawless as snowflakes." The arguments over whose version
of culture to teach will properly go on until the republic closes shop.
A democracy educates itself by arguing over what to teach the next

generation. But as grown-up groups struggle for each generation's balance of pride and recognition and representation and inclusion, we need to keep in mind how important it is for kids to be allowed to make and do culture, to participate in enacting live meanings and symbols. Opening up the school curriculum to the world's rainbows of cultures is a necessary step toward becoming a people of peoples, a real democracy. But it will not be much of a gain to substitute a new multicultural and multiracial orthodoxy for an older cultural orthodoxy. Nobody's version of the canon will matter if kids don't start reading real books sometime. Unless kids get a chance to make cultural meaning, and not passively absorb it, nothing will come alive. Anybody's version of culture can be delivered secondhand and dead. The real challenge is to help kids make cultural meanings come alive here and now, to act as creators and critics of culture, armed with the skills and discipline to—as Emerson put it—marry form and power. And what holds for kids surely holds for teachers too.

A romantic and democratic vision of human possibility may in the end be a practical thing for teachers—as real as radium, and even more valuable. Teaching is, after all, more like taking part in a religion or a political movement than anything else—the whole thing rests on what the old theologians called the virtue of hope. Its loss kills more kids than guns and drugs. The technocratic lingo of the educational managers and the boredom of today's colleges of education do no service to a profession that in the end requires true romance, the stuff that lights up the soul. Who would rise up on a cold, dark morning and go out to teach if the only goal were to raise the SAT scores? A democratic vision helps you not only in rethinking your purposes, in choosing the curriculum, for example, but also in making it through those February days when the radiators are banging and teaching school feels like the dark night of the soul. It says on the Liberty Bell, across the crack, that the people without vision shall perish. This should be a warning to us in an educational era dominated by dull experts, squinty-eyed economists, and frightened politicians. You will never survive your years as a teacher by listening to what passes for vision now in the United States.

The novelist Charles Dickens dramatized the basics—the fundamental democratic issues—in his novel about depressed times in nineteenth-century England, *Hard Times*. (Passages sound a lot like the United States in the 1990s.) Dickens introduces a capitalist named Mr. Gradgrind. Mr. Gradgrind, not at all coincidentally, runs a school for workers' kids. Gradgrind calls the kids by number, not by name, and insists on a curriculum limited to "facts, facts, facts." "You are not to wonder," he says to the children. Mr. Gradgrind stands for a minimalist and antiromantic political ideology that measures life by the profit margin and reduces humans to numbers. He is a utilitarian, like many of our current leaders in politics and education, for whom the bottom line is a religion. He believes only what can be measured and therefore misses out on human mystery and potential. To him, children are parts for the great economic machine. He sees a world composed of competing individual atoms. He fears the human imagination and the bonds of friendship.

Gradgrind wants kids and teachers to be passive recipients of the curriculum of "facts, facts, facts." They are not to wonder, because wondering makes trouble. Dickens argues that children's imagination is in fact a critical political issue, and that the imagination and the human heart require much more than calculations of profit and loss. He asks us to put true romance and human sympathy and the imagination back in our picture of education. Dickens is clear that Mr. Gradgrind's approach to education is a strategy of control: He wants passive labor, not active critical minds. Nothing could show more clearly the political implications of a minimalist, as opposed to an expansive and democratic, vision of culture.

Education is a battleground on which different visions of the future are struggling. Gradgrind offers a grim and colorless world of isolated, competing individuals in an environment whose skies are blackened and ruined by greed; he can never match the bright colors and laughter of communities of children.

Mr. Gradgrind is above all an enemy of the idea of culture for the people. He sees art and humor as absurd and dangerous frills. Children's imagination is a threat. He hates the circus, for example, which Dickens makes into a symbol of popular creativity. Mr. Gradgrind is not, alas, dead. He is everywhere today, in corporations, legislatures, governors' mansions, and central offices of school systems. I saw him on the evening news last night. He was wearing an expensive suit and was pointing to a wall chart. An hour later, he was flourishing a Bible. To fight today's versions of Mr. Gradgrind, teachers and the rest of us need to start imagining an expansive and democratic vision of education as true romance—not the romance of sentimentality and fakery and escape (the media have stuffed us all with too many such lies) but the true romance that knows that the heart is the toughest human muscle, the romance of respect for the people and what their children's minds are capable of.

To enact this true romance, we need to do many things. We need a democratic version of the humanities and the liberal arts from kindergarten through the university. At the university level, as in the schools, the older traditions of the "liberal arts" and the "humanities" and elite science and math are often preserves for privilege, crusted over with the practices and superstitions of human inequality. But the people's children deserve the best, and such subjects and traditions need to be rescued for them, not abandoned. Culture needs to be democratized, not abandoned. The people have a right to claim their heritage and take possession of what generations of leisure have given the privileged.

Underlying the daily work in schools, then, is the task of creating a democratic culture, a task that may take generations. Of course, a genuine people's culture, when it emerges, will look very different from the oily "people's cultures" concocted by the commissars in totalitarian regimes. To begin such work, teachers need to be able to see "culture" in its several meanings: what used to be called the "high" culture, the traditional symbols of academic learning, the great books and works of art and music; newcomers to the canon; and also the local webs of meaning and tradition arising out of the lives of students and communities. Today we want to interrogate the old "high" culture and ask who it included and who it left out. But in the end, we also want our kids to get access, to break into the old vaults as well as savor new treasures.

Instead of thinking of culture as a separate realm of "high" experience, an elite commodity, we want to show our kids the common continuum of human experience that reaches from the great works of art of all times and cultures to children's talk and imagining right now, to help students move back and forth from their experience to the experiences embodied in poems, artworks, and textbooks. Unlike my grandmother's generation, we want the visions of culture offered in our schools to be true rainbow bridges that the children crisscross daily in both directions—the home and neighborhood cultures on one end, and the wider worlds of culture on the other.

My grandmother had a vision of a teacher going forth to bring culture to the people. What we might add to that today is the image of the people and their children giving something back in a true exchange of gifts. Today we might be in a better position to see that culture making in the schools has to be a two-way street. The idea of culture embraced by the school must also reach out to embrace the cultures of the students and their families. As a Native American friend of mine says, you will be the children's teacher when you learn how to accept their gifts.

Gradgrind sees school as a small factory in which elite managers make decisions for the passive hands. This is also his model for politics. Does this sound familiar? Dickens, by contrast, sees education as taking part in a democratic community—groups of people who share imaginative participation. As a teacher on the side of the people, you need to make yourself a careful student of the care and feeding of small, provisional human communities, for these are where people learn to make cultural meaning together, to practice and create the people's culture. This is why John Dewey called schools "embryonic democracies" and why some of the old reformers called them "little commonwealths." Classroom communities require certain elements: learning to talk the talk, learning to listen respectfully, finding a voice, learning to make and criticize knowledge in a group, giving and taking, finding the blend of intellectual and emotional support that a good classroom group can provide, valuing the habits and skills of reading and writing that arise when speakers and writers and artists get responses from audiences and listeners and readers. The discipline that lasts comes from participation, and it is the discipline of freedom.

In practice, then, helping the people progress in cultural terms means the ongoing creation of provisional forms of community. In good schools, students are learning to make culture—the kind of broad, powerful, and purposeful meanings we associate with intellectual, artistic, scientific, and democratic communities—and to forge links between the kind of culture they are enacting in school and the cultures of their communities. In school subjects, they learn the discourse of many of the smaller worlds that make up the large world of culture, literacy, and the languages of math and science and the arts, as well as the logic of action required to go on making, re-making, and criticizing different kinds of community over a lifetime.

With her union background, my grandmother would warn you about Gradgrind's loneliness and the need for solidarity as an educational ideal. The Gradgrinds want you to stay isolated and to think of education and politics as mainly a matter of competition between individuals. Dickens and my grandmother tell you something different: that we are brothers and sisters, that we learn from one another, and that we will have to work out a common fate on a troubled and threatened planet. Not only that, but to the extent that we remain isolated, the Gradgrinds will prevail. Look at the way they have used the racial issue to divide the forces of democracy in the last 20 years.

Although individual students make the meanings, the business of taking part in culture always means participation in some kind of community, real or imagined. You are part of a music community, even when you play the guitar alone. Math skills and ideas have as their aim participation in the community of those who make, who "do," math. The old Greeks emphasized the communal side of math when they called it a performance art and—to our astonishment today—linked it with such communal arts as theater and dancing. They would be amazed to hear that we make kids study math solo, rather than reasoning together as a group.

I emphasize the community angle not to slight the individual— all education has to balance individual and social aims—but to stress the way that the individuality we prize so deeply in our students emerges from what they learn through community encounters with others, their families, peers, and teachers. Mr. Gradgrind doesn't get this. He preaches rugged individualism but is at bottom an enemy of true individuality. But students who haven't learned to listen won't have much of a chance of finding their distinctive voices; nor will students who have never spoken in class about something that really matters to them or made some significant choices at some important points about their own learning.

My grandmother's generation was in love with the idea of growth. It's easy to see the importance of growth for students, but how about for you? When you start teaching, you do not know enough, but you are also not culturally developed enough to be a model for your students. This might be particularly true if you come from a family that never had much access to "high" culture. Even if you got a lot of "culture," is it really yours, or is it a ragbag of secondhand experiences and unexplained views? How do you help your kids build the rainbow bridges back and forth? How can you sell them on literacy if you yourself don't read much and don't enjoy books? What about your identity as a teacher? What about the struggle for democracy? You might like the picture of the teacher going out to meet the people, but what do you really have to offer? This is a harsh question, but you have a big responsibility if you are signing up as a teacher. How do you start the lifetime work of becoming a practical intellectual who can help the people progress culturally?

The question of your own cultural development may in the end be the big question about your future as a teacher. With some attention, I think that you can begin to see how democracy is the underlying issue in our society today, and how education reflects a wider, worldwide struggle. It may be more difficult to see the democratic cultural challenge: to see that a lively discussion of *Frog and Toad* in the second grade is one step toward a people's culture. A vision helps, but it needs to come alive daily in your teaching practice. How can you start to become a practical intellectual who is able to bring culture to the people's children and able to accept their gifts back? This will never be easy. But don't despair, you aren't dead yet. There are lots of ways to begin expanding your own possession of culture, ranging from exploring your roots to developing your own literacies and your acquaintance with ideas, traditions, and symbols in a host of realms. My grandmother, with her message of solidarity, would urge you not to go it alone, to join up with other teachers and reach out to people in your community. Your own ability to nourish a learning community in your classrooms will be helped immeasurably if you yourself inhabit—and help create—genuine learning communities outside of class. The things you want for your students—the development of culture, interests, identities, and a voice—are all things that you need as a teacher. One or two genuine interests to share with kids are worth their weight in gold. Finding one or two ways to link your teaching to the wider struggle for democracy will show you the meaning of your work. Read Herbert Kohl's *Back to Basics* to begin to get a sense that history and democratic tradition are resources to draw on in the work of teaching. Learn something about your own history, because that can give you an important angle on where you stand in relation to culture making.

Culture is like—is another name for—growth and development and education itself. Like history, it has no end. Generations of thoughtful teachers have taken part in the long struggle. Now, just your luck, it's your turn. All the best.

Joseph Featherstone

P. S. I call you "Josie" because that's what W. E. B. Du Bois calls his student in his sketch of himself as a teacher in the rural South in *The Souls of Black Folk*. Josie has all the life and vitality of the people and craves a formal education, which she never gets, dying young. Du Bois was the young teacher going out to meet the people, and Josie was the people meeting the teacher. Both had something to offer in the exchange. The result for Du Bois was the complex educational goal in *The Souls of Black Folk*: to learn the ways and the powers of the wider culture represented by school learning and the classics, but to keep your soul and know your roots. Du Bois was the spiritual granddaddy of the civil rights generation—he died just as the 1963 March on Washington was taking place—but his vision of a democratic culture awaits our work. I know that the dreadful premature harvest of young Josies has not stopped, but I like to think that some are making their way into teaching, like you.

NOTE

1. This passage was quoted, significantly, by that romantic John Dewey (1934, p. 347) in *Art as Experience*, his great argument for a democratic approach to art and culture.

REFERENCE

Dewey, J. (1934). *Art as experience*. New York: Minton, Balch & Company.

CHAPTER 2

Taking Teaching Seriously

Suzanne C. Carothers

I grew up in Charlotte, North Carolina. During the summers of 1959 through 1963, as the nation around me endured record-breaking temperatures, hosted the Democratic and Republican National Conventions, experienced the March on Washington, and continued to maintain "separate but equal" facilities, I ran a summer school in my backyard for neighborhood children. From the time I was 9 until I was 13, my summer school was a neighborhood institution involving parents, other adults, and children who were just a few years younger than me.

There were many things I needed to do to get my school up and running and to keep it going through those years:

1. I made flyers and called and visited parents to tell them about my school.
2. I charged tuition—25 cents per child and 10 cents for each additional child in the same family—to support the work of my school.
3. I collected the end-of-the-year "throw outs" from teachers in my elementary school. Sometimes I would talk the teachers into donating unopened boxes of crayons and construction paper.
4. As the children needed a snack each day, my mother supplied a pitcher of water with ice cubes in it and some saltine crackers.
5. I hired my friend Beryl to teach at the picnic table under the other shade tree.
6. I planned field trips to the neighborhood library for the children.

Both my neighbors were teachers. Lil on the left taught fourth grade, and Aunt Minna on the right, a much older woman, taught math in junior high school. From Lil, I got back issues of *Instructor* magazine. It was a large magazine and had many more pages than either the *Highlights* or *Humpty Dumpty* magazines my mother subscribed to for me. As I turned the pages of *Instructor* magazine and read the suggestions for teachers, you could not tell me that I was not a *real* teacher.

In the afternoon, when my students had left for the day, Aunt Minna would invite me over to sit with her on the porch, where we'd eat ice cream. Inevitably she would ask, "Well, Suzanne, what did your little rascals do in school today?" So, with Aunt Minna, I had an opportunity to reflect about how the day had gone and what I might do differently on the next day.

I am sure that my family and neighbors must have had a pretty big chuckle behind my back, but my remembered sense of their response is that they took me seriously. So I really believed that I was a teacher, and in so being, I did what I needed to do to keep my school going: marketing the program, recruiting students, studying *Instructor* magazine to stay current, diversifying the curriculum to meet the needs of the students, talking with other teachers as a way to reflect about my own teaching, building in the support of a colleague to share in the teaching and learning process, and learning to be resourceful. All these are things that, in hindsight, I needed to do to have that school work well in my backyard.

Some of this hindsight reflection is applicable to what we teachers need to do now to plan for the students we teach, as well as for ourselves. We may need to:

- start where the students are—find out what our students' interests are, what they feel good about, and what concerns them;
- encourage our students to use writing as a tool for learning as they reminisce about things, inquire into new ideas, and confront different ways of thinking about issues;
- create opportunities for our students to learn in collaboration with others through small group work;
- dignify our students by the way we use language with them and the way we treat them as individuals who can take charge of their own learning;
- help our students assess their progress so that they can describe the ways in which they are growing and changing;
- stop teaching in a vacuum—find colleagues of like minds who

talk about their teaching and work at rethinking ways to become better at it;

- read articles about teaching and learning and discuss them over lunch with colleagues; and
- visit one another's classrooms and engage in discussions about what we have noticed.

Doing all these things won't make perfect teachers. Participating in these activities, however, will enable teachers to chart new directions to reach those whose education we are responsible for.

At the urban public college campus where I now teach, a third-year engineering student came to my office recently to inquire about "picking up some courses" in early childhood education. I invited him to talk. I asked the young man to tell me about himself and his interests. During his lengthy discussion about both topics, not once did he mention anything about children of any age or about teaching. He certainly did not mention the familiar refrains, "I want to make a difference" or "I am concerned about what's happening in public schools" or "I want to give something back."

When I asked why he wanted to teach and, more specifically, why he wanted to teach young children, the young man quickly responded. "Oh, I've always heard that it's good to pick up some teaching credits. The early childhood education program looked doable [easy enough, I quickly interpreted] with my engineering courses. Anyway, if all else fails," he continued, "I could always fall back on teaching."

I then said, "Do you like children? What about children between the ages of 3 and 8?"

"Well they're OK," he replied. As an afterthought he added, "It couldn't be *that* difficult to teach young kids."

As a keeper of the gate in the interest of children, learning, teaching, and schooling, I felt compelled to tell this young man to find another insurance policy and not to use teaching as his fallback position. What may be in his best interest as an aspiring engineer may not be in the best interests of young children and their families. There are too many people currently teaching who have entered the profession from this fallback position. Rather than encourage yet another, I suggested that the young man shop elsewhere and look into law or medicine.

How I wish that this young man's story was an exception. Much to my dismay, however, I have heard variations of this story throughout the years of my own journey to becoming a teacher. Now, as a professor, I actively question prospective and practicing teachers about what's motivating their choice to teach. Why do they want to teach? Why are they teaching? These are important questions that we need to ask our future teachers, questions that each person must thoughtfully engage, questions whose responses they must carefully hear. What's motivating a person to teach has far-reaching implications. It influences whether or not a person makes a commitment to children, to families, and to the teaching profession. It determines whether she or he is willing to work relentlessly, seriously to become effective in creating classrooms and planning for the students who enter them.

I encourage all teachers to take teaching seriously. The decision to teach should not be an afterthought if one intends to become an outstanding teacher. It must be a primary thought. In teacher education, we need to renew the spirit of teaching by inviting prospective and practicing teachers to invest in themselves and their preparation as they seek to invest in others.

Thoughts of September and early fall recall a time of major contradiction and transition. It is a time of year that ushers in new beginnings as it beckons us to say good-bye to the lazy, carefree days of summer. September is filled with familiar images: back-to-school sale signs; freshly sharpened yellow pencils; bright new book bags; notebook dividers with multicolored see-through tabs separating the still untouched clusters of notebook paper; shiny plastic lunch boxes yet to adopt the smells of sandwiches and fruits; and, of course, new clothes—trousers, dresses, skirts, shirts, and shoes. Fall is the time of apple picking, the first dew, shorter days, longer nights, expected yet regretted temperature drops, and the digging out of warmer clothing. Yes, giving up summer to go back to school is met with mixed emotions, whether you have had many years of schooling or very few.

The mere mention of school strikes an immediate chord. If we were to call up images of school or to tell stories about our experiences there, it would be difficult to do so without talking about teachers we once had—those we liked, those who didn't like us, those who were tough on us, those who let us slide by, those we can barely remember. Reflecting about our own moments of learning in classrooms would reveal that none of us has escaped the impact of teachers' actions and behaviors in schools. Some propelled our learning forward, others cast doubt about our ability to learn. These lessons can be bittersweet, but whether positive or negative, we carry these stories for a long, long time.

Teachers can use these stories and this knowledge to reflect about their own teaching beliefs and practices. Given the many classrooms I have occupied, what lessons will I bring to life for my students? What stories will they tell about me, their teacher, when they move on? How will I be remembered?

Each school year offers both teachers and students an opportunity for a new start, a fresh beginning. In order to take fresh beginnings seriously, consider these questions: What do teachers need to know? What do teachers need to think about in planning for the needs of learners of all ages? What do teachers need to do to plan for a successful year for their students and themselves?

As teachers, we need to know a few things about ourselves as learners before we set out to plan for the learning of others. Maybe the primary question to ask here is, what led you to teaching in the first place? The reasons are familiar. I teach because I get the summers off. I teach young children because they are not as intimidating as older ones. I teach content, not students. I teach because my grade point average was too low for nursing. I teach because I needed a job. I teach because, well, just because. Or I teach because I love teaching. I teach because I love kids. I've always wanted to be a teacher. Nothing is better than being a teacher.

We have come to teaching from various and sundry locations— not always sure how we have gotten here or what we will do now that we are here. But teachers need to know what motivates them to teach. If you really believe that you teach because you *can't* or are not skilled enough to do anything else, or if you believe that teaching is easy and will not require much from you, please don't teach. I encourage you to find other work. Surely there is something more fulfilling that you *can* do.

Teaching is hard work. Choose teaching because you *want* to teach. Teach because you *believe* that the human spirit is capable of learning at any age and you strongly *desire* to be part of the dynamic interactions that characterize positive learning—total engagement of the mind, body, and spirit in an inquiry about those things that are known as well as those that seem distant and impossible. No matter how long a person has been teaching, being a good teacher is no excuse for failing to become an even better teacher.

As teachers, we experience the unknown, help students take risks, develop high expectations of them, create a challenging environment in which learning can take place, and struggle to be sensitive to the ways in which people learn differently, discovering when to push harder and when to relax a bit. My years of teaching have suggested to me that a student's success is strongly linked with good teaching

—teaching that is engaging, innovative, respectful of differences, and challenging—rather than the inability to succeed because of "perceived," "expected," or even "actual" limitations of the student.

The footing on which you start often significantly impacts the footing on which you land. When your students enter your classroom, what is the implicit message that extends an invitation to them? What says, "this is your classroom, you are expected to be actively engaged in the learning process here, and you are responsible for your own learning"?

Once, as I was thumbing through a book on my shelf, I ran across a bookmark with a quote on it: "Who will teach me what I must shun? Or must I go where the impulse drives?" The quote is from Goethe. After making several inquiries and being somewhat persistent in my determination to find its source, I learned that it was from *Faust*, his most dramatic story-poem. Off to the library I went to look at different translations of *Faust* to find the quote. The poem is based on the medieval legend of a man who sold his soul to the devil. However, it speaks to us in modern times as we seek to address alienation and the need to come to terms with the world in which we live. The themes of estrangement and fulfillment explored in *Faust* are of particular interest to me and, I believe, to us as educators. Are we estranged by our in-school learning or fulfilled by it? The quote can be found early in Part One. They are the words of Faust. The translation I liked best was:

> Who teaches me? What should I shun?
> That urge I feel—should I obey?
> Both what we do and what we suffer to be done,
> Alas, impedes us on life's way. (Goethe, 1976, p. 16)

Far too often, classrooms become alien places in which students shun—they reject, avoid, ignore, or disregard the lessons of the teacher as well as the possibility of clearing impediments on life's way. In such classrooms, the teachers' lessons may be planned without regard for the learners' engagement. The learner may then be left to consider, must I go where the impulse drives—to follow that urge, maybe an urge to self-discovery?

I was observing a group of 4-year-olds and saw up close what following urgency can mean, as well as the consequences of such a journey. A teacher who was licensed in art but had been assigned to a preschool class for the year was conducting a lesson on money with an alert, active group of 4-year-olds. As I sat in the back of the classroom—a class I had been in and out of many times during the year—the teacher began her lesson. She stood behind a child-size desk that became the holder of her props as the children began to gather, to be bunched together, in a small space on the floor. The desk, of course, provided a natural barrier between the teacher and the children. The teacher then held up a piece of cardboard, half the size of a sheet of notebook paper, on which she had mounted a real penny, nickel, dime, and quarter. My attention was drawn to one child who had not quite made it to the small space where he was expected to be seated on the floor. With a puzzled look on his face, the boy stared at the teacher, then cast his eyes on the children bunched there on the floor whose limbs could not avoid touching. He calmly announced, "I'm going to go build with blocks." Although it seemed to be a perfectly logical decision to me, the teacher reprimanded the child for "not following the directions."

Following your own impulses in classrooms, where the locus of power is unevenly experienced between those who teach and those who are taught, can lead to unfortunate consequences for learners. It can lead to silencing the active imagination of the mind and restricting the physical need of busy bodies to move. So, as Goethe suggests, "both what we do and what we suffer to be done" to us in classrooms *can* hinder or obstruct us on life's way. Although this may be an unorthodox reading of Goethe, it can shed light on ways of looking at and understanding possible outcomes of classroom practices. What may be instructive for us as teachers is a simple reminder: It is critical to plan thoughtfully, carefully, and even lovingly for the students we teach as we make them the center of our planning.

What should teachers consider in planning to meet the needs of all learners? They may wish to think about where they stand when students enter their classrooms, and what they say as they greet them. They should take a good look at the way the classroom is set up. Does the arrangement of desks and chairs say, "I, the teacher, am in charge"? Or does the placement of the furniture encourage the students to interact with one another, enabling many voices of authority to emerge in the classroom, ensuring that each person's voice is expected to be heard? Teachers need to question how the things to be learned in their classrooms are connected. They should consider planning the curriculum in a way that encourages the students to learn the basic skills of reading, writing, math, and science in a context. After all, bread is bread, but when you put peanut butter between two slices of bread, you no longer have just bread, you have created a sandwich. It's the sticky stuff of the peanut butter that holds the bread together. Teachers need to ask themselves: What is the sticky stuff, the peanut butter, in my curriculum on which skills can be applied and learned? Perhaps for modern teachers, the metaphor is not peanut butter but Velcro. The question remains: Where's the sticky stuff?

For example, in learning grammar and punctuation, are students memorizing the rules of capitalization? Or is the class writing letters to merchants in the community, asking them to display posters the students have made pointing out the importance of recycling? If the latter approach is used, the teacher can explain to the students that starting sentences with capital letters and ending them with some form of punctuation is necessary so that when the merchants read the letters, they will know when one idea has ended and another has begun. Curriculum viewed from this perspective affords the actual practice needed to learn a thing well.

A friend of mine told me a story about her group of 7-year-olds. This year's class had gotten off to a good start. My friend had spent considerable time thinking about her second graders and planning the room arrangement. She created a meeting corner by utilizing carpet remnants that were about to be tossed out. She carefully selected a wonderful array of books that reflected the children's interests and concerns, and when the kids looked inside the selected books, they saw children who looked like themselves. She made a variety of reading and math games to individualize the work for the children. Each morning when the children came to school, they seemed eager and happy to be in the class.

Some weeks into the year, one child in the class said something most unpleasant to another child, who was saddened by the remark and went into a corner to sulk. After talking to the sulking child privately, my friend seized upon the opportunity to reaffirm the values of a caring community in the class. The children were asked to gather on the rug for an important meeting. "In order for this to be a community in which people in our classroom feel liked, special, and important, we really need to think hard about the words we use to help each other feel this way, rather than have people in our room feel disliked, not special, and unimportant," said my friend. When she asked the class whether anyone had ever been hurt by being called unpleasant names, heads began to nod up and down. It was the unanimous opinion of this group of 7-year-olds that being called unpleasant names *can* hurt your feelings.

My friend continued by asking the children, "What names do we not want to hear each other called in our classroom—those names that will not help people feel good about themselves?" The children sat quietly and listened attentively. One child broke the silence, "booty scratcher," she quietly called out. "Yes!" agreed another child, as my friend wrote her words on the chart paper. The next child said, "Bitch, that's not a nice thing to say." "Bum ain't either," said a fourth child. When the next child added, "the F word," all the children nodded in agreement. One child waved her hand frantically to be recognized. When called upon she said, "MK!" When everyone looked puzzled and could not quite figure out what she meant, my friend suggested, "Do you mean MF?" The child thought for a moment and responded, "Oh yea, that's it, that's it." When "buck tooth beaver" and "fart face" were called out, they too were added to the list. Finally, "DH" concluded the list when the last child said, "No one should ever call anybody a dumb head."

Although this may be an amusing story to us, there was absolutely *no* laughter in this group of 7-year-olds when this discussion occurred. Indeed, the ideas and concerns of this group of second graders were taken seriously, and they took their discussion seriously as well. They were discussing issues that truly mattered to them, that mattered to their quality of life in that classroom. When the meeting ended, the children went back to work. The child whose feelings had been hurt by the unkind words smiled as he went back to work.

What were the teacher's goals for having such a meeting? How did she feel about the discussion that ensued? What might she do to follow up with it? All of my friend's responses to these questions were important, but the one that seemed to undergird them all was this: In order for learning environments to have integrity and to be places of fairness and trust, learners need to know that they are safe within them—that they will be protected from physical as well as emotional harm. Although as children we all chanted, "Sticks and stones may break my bones, but words can never hurt me," the reality is that the scars of verbal hurts can last forever. Teachers need to create learning environments where how people feel is as important as what they think. What we do and how we use language with our students matter deeply. Both are critical in setting the tone for learning. Establishing and maintaining caring environments make engagement in learning possible.

Although I had been in school for 4 years, Mrs. Maxwell was the first *real* teacher, and the very best teacher, I ever had. She is still very much a part of me, as she was in 1985 when I wrote her a long letter. I was teaching a course in language and thinking, and I asked my students (who were incoming freshmen) to write letters to their former teachers about who they were now as learners and how they had come to know what they know. My letter reads as follows:

Dear Mrs. Maxwell,

As I thought of those first 12 years, your name, face, and classroom sprang forth out of a sea of nameless faces and classrooms bare. Though I did not know it then, your classroom would be one that I would return to many, many times in years to come. No, I have not returned physically to the room, but my memories of you and your classroom are very vivid to me. The way you looked, the things we did, and the things you said still stand out for me.

I believe that you helped me to see learning as the desire to know and you showed me how to make knowing happen for myself. For the 2 years you were my teacher, we actually learned by doing in that fifth- and sixth-grade class. I remember you had such a way with words. Words sang out in your classroom. Language was full, rich, encouraged, and enjoyed. You read to us, we to you. We wrote and produced plays. During the 1960 gubernatorial campaign, we gave campaign speeches right at University Elementary School standing in front of our makeshift podium. We wrote poetry. You loved language in every form. We made books, bound them, and on each page made a border using a potato on which we had cut a design. The books were quite pretty. They were very colorful. In retrospect, these must have been very simple words and ideas, but, written in those books, they felt important. I remember you called us authors of our books and put our books on the shelf with the real books.

You believed that children can learn, that each child is special and has something special to give. But as you remember, in the late 1950s when I was in elementary school, they called kids like me "late bloomers." This label explained why those like myself did not do well on the California Achievement Test. I was never in the "Blue Jay" or "Cardinal" reading groups. Funny thing, in your class, I don't remember sitting in those dumb reading groups. Reading was all over the classroom and beyond its four walls. It was in the stories and plays we wrote, the campaign speeches we gave, the choral speaking we did, and the newspaper articles we read. See, you taught reading, but not like any teacher I had had before. Your idea of "learning to read" was connected to the world that I knew and the one that I began to discover.

You valued the knowledge we brought to school with us. You

taught us that learning begins with desire—the desire to want to know more and the willingness to dig and find it. You seemed to understand that the process of digging to find out was not easy. The day that Chauncy threw the chair at you because he became angry when he could not do the long division problem, the whole class quaked with fear. What would happen next? we thought. You calmly walked over to Chauncy and said, "Learning to do long division is hard, but you can do it. Once you know how, you'll be able to do so many things with it. Now get the chair and put it back under the desk." Some of your exact words I may have lost over the years, but I will always remember the feeling of what you said and the way you said it. We all saw Chauncy go over and get the chair. He settled back to work, and so did we.

Had you ever read Dewey? Did you know about progressive education? How did you know those things? Who was your teacher?

You understood the notion of holistic learning—that good learning happens when the left and right brain complement each other. For you, intellect was not a book to be read, an author to know, or a thing in the abstract. Rather, from the way that you taught, it seemed that intellect was a matter of thinking, questioning, and charting one's own course to knowing. You provided many tools. You awakened a deep curiosity in each of us and helped release the confidence buried within us.

I never had an opportunity to tell you these things because you died long before I finished high school, before I ever understood that I would want to say these things to you, before I even knew what I know. In the classrooms where I now travel, I take you with me.

Love,
Suzanne

As we begin to take teaching seriously, I encourage each of us to become a Mrs. Maxwell for those who will enter our classrooms.

REFERENCE

Goethe, J. W. V. (1976). *Faust* (Walter Arndt, Trans.; Cyrus Hamlin, Ed.). New York: Norton. (Original work published 1808 and 1832)

CHAPTER 3

I Just Want to Be Myself: Discovering What Students Bring to School "in Their Blood"

Lisa Delpit

When my daughter Maya was 3 years old, she surprised my dinner guests and myself with a particularly insightful comment. Maya was playing under the table while we were eating dinner, and I decided to try a strategy that I had found useful when working with pre-schoolers professionally. "Maya," I said, "if you wanted to be a big girl, you would sit in the chair and eat your dinner like Uncle Larry, Mommy, and Aunt Joyce." Maya came out, stood up, and said, "But Mommy, I don't want to be a big girl, I want to be *myself*. I just want to be Maya, the only Maya in the whole wide world." Then, with dramatic arm gestures and a louder voice for emphasis, "Mommy, *I just want to be myself!*" Needless to say, we sat in stunned silence. None of us knew how to respond, because, indeed, what response could there be? Maya understood the importance of being her 3-year-old self, despite the pressures of the adults around her that she be otherwise.

I'm thankful that I have been given a child at an age when I am old enough to begin to forget the miracle of childhood but young enough to remember that I wanted what I was losing. I now feel that I have a chance to relearn, and that this child—even when I've felt like wringing her neck—has taught me more than I can say. Maya understands, "I just want to be myself."

Having worked with children of color over the years, I am struck with the difficulty that many of our children have "just being themselves" in institutions designed to coerce them into being someone else: 8-year-old African American Randall was punished by his principal with no recess for the rest of the school year because he would not allow into a game a white classmate who insisted on calling African American children "nigger"; 14-year-old Duane's mother was shocked to learn that his teachers believed him to be a nonachiever and "from a bad family" based on his haircut. I've known too many African American children to count who have been placed in special education as a result of their energy levels rather than any lack of intellectual prowess.

My realization of the predicament of many of our children was captured in a metaphor of doors when I was a student teacher in an alternative school in an urban area of the Northeast. The principal purposely maintained a racial balance: 60% of the children were from poor African American families from the South Side; 40% of the children were from the upper-middle-class white families of Society Hill. The school was located just on the border of those two communities. The front door opened onto Society Hill, and the back door opened onto the South Side. The problem is, the back door never opened. It was permanently locked. All the African American kids had to literally and figuratively leave their community in order to come to school.

I came to understand that the doors of the building were a telling metaphor for what happened inside. Just as the school opened only to Society Hill, what happened inside was in great part an expression of Society Hill culture. This may have been why there was such a long waiting list for white children to enter the school but no waiting list at all for African American children, who sometimes had to be recruited. On their trip every morning to the other side of the building, the South Side children were asked to leave what they knew and who they were behind, and to become someone else. They were not asked or expected to be themselves, but rather some permanently inadequate version of the white Society Hill children.

This struggle to maintain a sense of self in an institution designed to make you into someone else has always reminded me of one of my favorite sayings by e. e. cummings:

> To be nobody-but-yourself—in a world which is doing its best, night and day, to make you everybody else—means to fight the hardest battle which any human being can fight; and never stop fighting

I write here about the ways our institutions of education try to force children of color—and parents and teachers of color as well—

to be "everybody else." The real question that we must answer is, What happens when the power to define oneself, to determine the self one should be, lies outside of the self or outside of one's referent community?

We live in a society governed by power. And those in power are typically not oppressed people of color. Oppressed groups in this society are inevitably assessed differently from the white mainstream by virtue of their skin color. Here are some typical examples:

- The assumption that an African American professor in an exclusive high-rise apartment building near the university is a maid.
- The assumption that an Asian college student will have difficulty with English, even though he was born in New Jersey.
- The assumption by the Educational Testing Service that the test scores of Jaime Escalante's Latino students in East Los Angeles were falsified because they were too high.

This false assessment plagues both teachers and students of color in our educational system, but not because the educational system is *especially* biased. The problem is that the educational system is as *typically* biased as *any* institution in a society stratified by race.

What happens when the self is defined and determined by others? In education, as in the larger society, you will find that there are assumptions of inferiority and deviance about oppressed minorities. Further complicating the matter, there are misinterpretations of behavior and misjudgment of academic competence stemming from the tendency we all have to assume that the way "we" do things is the right way, the only way. When one "we" gets to determine standards of appropriateness for all "we's," then some "we's" are in trouble.

For example, this story about Anthony and Carolyn illustrates what can happen when ethnic stereotyping enters the classroom. Carolyn is a young Irish American kindergarten teacher who has been teaching for 5 years. She has taught at a predominantly white middle-class school in a quiet neighborhood in Cambridge, Massachusetts. Because of recent redistricting, the school population now includes children from a housing project not far away. These children are almost exclusively poor and Black. Thus, Carolyn and the other teachers in the school are newly faced with a population of children with whom they are completely unfamiliar. I am working in a research project with Carolyn. She has asked me to observe a little boy named

Anthony, a 5-year-old Black boy from "the projects," whom she has defined as a child with behavior, learning, and language problems. She wants to use the results of my observations to "get him help."

In my observations of Anthony in the classroom, I have noticed that he gets almost no positive feedback during the course of a day; instead, he receives a tremendous amount of negative attitude and commentary. I have taken Anthony out into the hallway several times to talk and play privately so as to get a better idea of his actual abilities. The following dialogue is taken from a transcript of a conference with Carolyn about my observations. I am attempting to point out some of Anthony's positive points to her:

LISA: Anthony told me that he liked school and that his favorite thing in his class was group time.
CAROLYN: That's amazing, since he can't sit still in it. He just says anything sometimes. In the morning he's OK, after nap he's impossible.

LISA: He's really talking more it seems!
CAROLYN: He's probably never allowed to talk at home. He needs communicative experience. I was thinking of referring him to a speech therapist. He probably never even got to use scissors at home.

LISA: He told me about his cousin he plays with after school. It seems he really does have things to talk about.
CAROLYN: It's unfortunate, but I don't think he even knows what family means. Some of these kids don't know who their cousins are and who their brothers and sisters are.

As a result of living in this society, Carolyn makes big assumptions about Anthony, assumptions that blind her to what's directly in her path. What you have here is a teacher who, because of the stereotypical attitudes she has developed about African Americans who are also poor, is incapable of really seeing this child. She sees his actions, words, family, and community as a collection of pathologies.

Here is another, related example. Charles is a 3-year-old African American boy who likes a little white girl in his nursery school. Like most 3-year-olds, his affection is expressed as much with hugs as with hits. One morning when I dropped Maya off, I stayed for a while to make sure she was settled in. I noticed that Charles had been hovering around Kelly, his special friend. He grabbed her from be-hind and tried to give her a bear hug. When she protested, the teacher told him to stop. A short time later, he returned to her table and tried to kiss her on the cheek. She protested again, and the teacher put him in "time-out." I commented to the teacher with a smile that Charles certainly seemed to have a little crush on Kelly. She frowned and replied that his behavior was "way out of line." "Sometimes what he does just looks like lust." I was shocked. I tried to tell her that children often imitate what they see on television, that I didn't think she could attribute adult emotions to this 3-year-old's actions. Clearly, she was unimpressed with my explanation, and I left pondering the fate of our African American boys when such devastating stereotyp-ing starts in nursery school.

Courtney Cazden (1988) reported on a project that studied nar-rative styles. In her study, a white adult read on tape the oral narra-tives of Black and white first graders with all dialectal markers re-moved. Educators were then asked to listen to the stories and comment about the children's likelihood of success in school. Researchers were surprised by the differential responses of African American and European American educators to an African American child's story. European American adults were uniformly negative. Their typical comments included: "terrible story, incoherent"; "not a story at all in the sense of describing something that happened."

This child's story was told in a style referred to as associative, which, according to Michaels and Cazden (1986), is more typical of African American children's stories. The style referred to as topic-centered is more typical of white children's stories. Asked to judge the child's academic competence, all the white adults rated her be-low children who told topic-centered stories. They also predicted difficulties with the child's school career: "This child might have trouble reading." One white adult indicated that this child exhibited language problems that would affect school achievement: "Family problems or emotional problems might hamper academic progress."

By contrast, African American adults found the story "well formed, easy to understand, and interesting, with lots of detail and description." All five African American adults mentioned the "shifts" and "associations" or "nonlinear" qualities of the story, but they didn't find this distracting. Three of the five African American adults selected this story as the best of the five they heard. All but one judged the child as exceptionally bright, highly verbal, and potentially suc-cessful in school.

When the interpretation of narrative differences can produce such differential results in teachers' attitudes toward Black and white children, clearly those children who are different from the teacher and from the mainstream may be in serious trouble.

In still another example, in my first-grade class, Howard couldn't do the simplest math worksheets. The best conventional school knowledge recommended special education assessment. I agreed until I got to know his life outside of school. I discovered that his mom was afflicted with drug problems and that his 3-year-old sister had cerebral palsy. Howard got both of them up every morning, dressed his sister, and got both of them on the bus. He had to do a good bit of math figuring simply to get the right amount of money for the bus. Howard also did the family laundry. He had to keep track of his change for the laundromat and had to keep from being cheated when he bought detergent. Still Howard couldn't seem to do a simple math worksheet on coins: 5 pennies = 1 nickel, or 2 nickels = 1 dime.

This story illustrates two concepts of an African American child's difficult struggle to be himself. First, it shows the multiple negative assumptions we make on the basis of school behavior without adequate data on out-of-school behavior. Second, it reveals the limited means by which we seek to assess competence. Whereas Howard found it difficult to perform in a decontextualized paper-and-pencil setting, he was superior in a contextualized real-life setting.

When I think about the narrow scope of much of the instruction provided in schools, and the potential negative effect on many children, I wonder what it would look like if schools were responsible for teaching African American kids to dance. Rather than have the children learn from one another in real contexts, the school would have each particular dance broken down into 200 mastery-learning units. Kids would have to complete a workbook and pass paper-and-pencil tests on each unit before moving on to learn the first half of the first hand movement of the first dance. By the end of a year we'd have a slew of remedial African American dancers!

Several years ago I conducted interviews with Native American teachers. These teachers poignantly expressed the pain of living and teaching in a world that expected less of Native Americans. Here, a Native Alaskan teacher is talking about her teacher-training experiences:

> I must have heard this so many times, that Native kids are low achievers. It used to frustrate me to hear that, and here I used

to think, *what they don't know*. What I thought was that these "educators" have never really been out there. They just went by what they learned from books.

I had a hang-up about this for a long time. I used to try to strike back without realizing what I was saying. Finally I started to say to myself, "In order to get through this thing, I have to pass this course, even though they're talking about *me*."

This is happening in my graduate classes right now. They're talking about Native kids and I relate it to me—low achievers, high drop-outs, they don't function well academically. We are labeled right from the beginning, although I didn't know that when I was growing up. We were never labeled that way. I never saw that I was a low achiever. I never saw myself as "at risk." It kind of shocked me to hear these things about my people. I was succeeding, you see. But then I hear these things about my people and I get so frustrated.

Several interviewees criticized professors, students, and the curriculum for perpetuating stereotypes about people of color. This kind of discrimination is exemplified by the comments of a Native woman who objected to a fellow student who declared in class that one could not expect Native children to speak in a classroom "because they're just not like that, they're very silent." The people from her region, she counters, "are *very* vocal, and children are taught to be vocal, too." She continued:

I resented those kinds of stereotypes about Native children. I remember in a reading class there was a discussion. The generalization was made that Native children coming from a village are a lot slower than white children living in town, and that you've got to expect this and you've got to expect that. And really, when everybody knows the clout of teacher expectations, people who say that really burn me up. They develop a very narrow view, a stereotype of how a Native child is. They don't really look at that child as a person, but as a Native. That was one thing I struggled with as well, people supposing things about me before getting to know me.

Another Native teacher said that "reading all those studies about 'the plight of Native students' made me feel like part of a group of people who were failures and I was the one exception. Why do they do that? I guess that's one way for a dominant culture to maintain dominance—not to recognize any of the strengths of another group." It is sobering to realize that most of what concerns these teachers was probably added to curriculum in an attempt to address issues of cultural diversity.

A final story of how differences are interpreted as deficits by schools in which children of color reside has to do with parental behavior. In a predominantly Puerto Rican school in Boston, the non-Latino teachers were frustrated with the parents because even though the school had requested that parents drop their children off in the school yard and then leave, these Latino parents insisted on bringing their first-grade children to their classrooms up to 30 minutes before the bell rang every day. It got to the point where teachers locked the doors and parents threatened to go to the school board. The teachers failed to realize that in many Latino communities, 6-year-olds are thought of as babies in need of a mother's protection. The parents' perspective was that these teachers did not even attempt to protect their children, so the parents took up the responsibility. The parents were particularly distressed because teachers are thought of as surrogate mothers, and these teachers did not act that way. The teachers not only did not protect the kids in the school yard (where paraprofessionals were left in charge) but they tried to prevent parents from doing so. The parents concluded that these teachers did not care about their kids and could not be trusted to supervise them. Rather than trying to understand the problem, teachers merely assumed that the parents were uncooperative, stubborn, and intent on creating problems in the school. The widespread misinterpretation of behaviors and misjudgment of competence or intention can grow and develop when there are basic assumptions of inferiority and deviance.

Another way that people of color are not allowed to define and be themselves is through the invisibility of their histories and themselves in teachers' minds and in the school curriculum. Whether we are immediately aware of it or not, the United States is composed of a plethora of perspectives. I am reminded of this every time I think of my friend Martha, a Native American teacher. Martha told me that one year she got very tired of being asked about her plans for Thanksgiving by people who seemed to take no note that her perspective on the holiday might be a bit different from their own. In her frustration, she told me that when the next questioner asked, "What are you doing for Thanksgiving?" she would answer, "I plan to spend the day saying, 'You're welcome!'"

If we plan to survive as a species on this planet, we must certainly create multicultural curricula that educate our children to the differing perspectives of our diverse population. In part, the problems we see exhibited in school by African American children and children of other oppressed minorities can be traced to this lack of a curriculum in which the intellectual achievements of people who look like themselves are represented. Were that not the case, these children would not refer to doing well in school as "acting white." Our children of color need to see the brilliance of their legacy, too.

Ellen Swartz (1992) notes that in typical American textbooks, statements like this go unchallenged: "Most cotton planters in the South believed their way of life depended on slave labor." What about the perspectives of the enslaved? "Depended on" implies that slavery was natural and inevitable, even though slavery was a choice the planters made. Contemporary textbooks continue to include sympathetic, apologetic accounts of slave owners like the one above. But notice the difference in this perspective: "Most cotton planters in the South prospered from the forced and free labor of millions of African American men, women, and children. Even though the white planters' way of life created misery for so many people, they were not willing to give up the profits made from slavery."

I must point out, however, that merely changing the textbooks and creating a more inclusionary curriculum are insufficient. Great damage can still be done to children of color when the attitudes of teachers or school administrators are less than sensitive. Attitudes are all-important. The new multicultural textbook or the new multicultural curriculum will do as much harm as good if the real adults of color connected to the children's *everyday* lives—their teachers and parents, the school's paraprofessionals, the other adults with whom children regularly have contact—are not respected and recognized as being valuable to the school and to the community. Furthermore, if administrators and teachers do not really believe that these children can excel in the same way that the personalities they read about have, this message, spoken or unspoken, will be heard loudly and clearly by the students.

When we were in another city for an extended period, my daughter Maya attended a child-centered, progressive preschool. It was predominantly European American children and teachers, but there were a number of African American "grandmothers" hired to help in each class. A deliberate attempt was made to be multicultural. I was happy to see that, unlike at the nursery school Maya attended in Baltimore, there was a great emphasis placed on Martin Luther King, Jr.'s birthday. There was a special whole-school assembly led by one of the teachers, Robert. At the assembly, videos of Dr. King were shown, and songs of the freedom movement were sung. There was a serious discussion of segregation.

At first I couldn't figure out why I felt so uncomfortable about all this. Finally it hit me. All this information was being provided for children—both Black and white—by Robert, a white man. Although the African American "grandmothers" had lived through everything that was being presented, they were not asked to lead, or even participate in, the formal assembly. Even with the best of intentions, children were still being given the subtle message that white men had all the knowledge—even (or especially) about Black people—and were the only ones competent to speak.

I realized that what I was feeling was my own child's heritage being taken from her. We must be constantly aware of this. It reminds me of what Ken Haskins (personal communication, 1987) calls the "Star Trek" model of multiculturalism: "one of everything with a white man in charge." It's quite possible to have a great curriculum and send overt as well as subtly negative messages.

A young teacher I know taught Black history through literature. She spent much time in libraries searching for the right books. She even did a special unit on Gwendolyn Brooks with her first graders. But the way she handled discipline undermined and overturned everything else. For example, she would say to children who were not sitting still, "You'll never be like Gwendolyn Brooks or anybody else we've studied in this classroom. You better learn how to behave. You just don't appreciate what I'm trying to do for you."

When this class and a neighboring class taught by a culturally aware and child-sensitive teacher got together to watch Bill Clinton's inauguration, the children were asked, "How many of you think you could be president?" All the children in the sensitive teacher's class raised their hands. None in the other teacher's class did so. It turns out that her attitude was more important than any Black-history-through-literature curriculum.

Even with well-intentioned educators, not only our children's legacies but our children themselves can become invisible. Many of the teachers we educate, and indeed their teacher educators, believe that to acknowledge a child's color is to insult him or her. In her book *White Teacher*, Vivian Paley (1979) openly discusses the problems inherent in the statement that I have heard many well-intentioned teachers utter: "I don't see color, I only see children." What message does this statement send? That there is something wrong with being Black or Brown, that it should not be noticed? I would like to suggest that if one does not see color, then one does not really see children. Children made "invisible" in this manner become hard-pressed to see themselves as being worthy of notice. Of course, the noticing must be in the context of noticing their strengths, their beauty, and their heritage, and not in noticing the screens of stereotypes through which we are prone to see children who are different from ourselves.

In order to begin to address the problem, we must overcome the narrow and essentially Eurocentric curriculum we provide for our teachers. At the university level, teachers are not being educated with the broad strokes necessary to prepare them properly for the 21st century. We who are concerned about teachers and teaching must insist that our teachers become knowledgeable of the liberal arts, but we must also work to change liberal arts courses so that they do not continue to reflect, as feminist scholar Peggy McIntosh (Keohane, 1986) says, only the public lives, exploits, and adventures of white Western men. These new courses must not merely teach what white Westerners have to say about diverse cultures, they must also share what the writers and thinkers of diverse cultures have to say about themselves and their history, music, art, literature, politics, and so forth.

If we know the intellectual legacies of our students, we will gain insight into how to teach them. For instance, Jaime Escalante repeatedly calls upon the Latin American heritage of his poor Latino students as he successfully teaches them advanced calculus. The movie chronicling his work, *Stand and Deliver*, reenacts a scene in which Escalante tells his students, "You *have* to learn math, math is in your blood! The Mayans discovered zero!" In another case, Stephanie Terry, a first-grade teacher I recently interviewed, breathes the heritage of her students into the curriculum. Stephanie teaches in an economically strapped community in inner-city Baltimore, in a school with a 100% African American enrollment. She begins each year with the study of Africa, describing Africa's relationship to the United States, its history, its resources, and so forth. As her students learn each new aspect of the regular citywide curriculum, Stephanie connects this knowledge to aspects of their African ancestry: While covering a unit about libraries, she tells them about the world's first libraries, which were established in Africa; a unit on health presents her with the opportunity to tell her students about the African doctors of antiquity who wrote the first texts on medicine. Stephanie does not replace the current curriculum; rather, she expands it. She also teaches about the contributions of Asian Americans, Native Americans, and Latinos as she broadens her students' minds and spirits. All Stephanie's students learn to read by the end of the school year. They also learn to love themselves, love their history, and love learning.

Stephanie could not teach her children the pride of their ancestry and could not connect it to the material they learn today were it not for her extraordinarily broad knowledge of the liberal arts. However, she told me that she did not acquire this knowledge in her formal education. She worked, read, and studied on her own to make such knowledge a part of her pedagogy. Similarly, were it not for his knowledge of their culture and history, Jaime Escalante could not tell his Chicano students that mathematics was "in their blood."

Teachers must not merely take courses that tell them how to treat their students as multicultural clients, that is, those that tell them how to identify differences in interactional or communicative strategies and remediate appropriately. They must also learn about the brilliance the students bring with them "in their blood." Until they appreciate the wonders of the cultures represented before them—and they cannot do that without extensive study, most appropriately begun in college-level courses—they cannot appreciate the potential of those who sit before them, nor can they begin to link their students' histories and worlds to the subject matter they present in the classroom. Thus the children are hampered not only by being unable to be themselves now but also by being unable to be what they could be in the future.

The final issue I wish to raise about the difficulty people of color have in being themselves in a system designed for others is just that—the system is designed, and continues to be redesigned, for someone else. One of the problems with much educational research, for example, is that it purports to tell us what is good for all children while being "normed" on predominantly white children.

Even when children of color are included in norming samples, the effects specific to them are usually washed out in the final results. Recently some researchers, particularly researchers of color, have begun investigating the effects of specific strategies on specific groups of children. They are finding that there can be dramatic differences between groups in what was previously considered true for all children.

Harry Morgan (1990), a psychologist, compared African American and European American children's behavior in class and found that Black kids move more than white kids, and boys move more than girls; that is, Blacks and boys display greater activity, collaboration, and physical contact.

Allen and Boykin (1991), comparing the effect of background music on African American and European American kids when learning new tasks, found that the African American kids learned and recalled new information better *with* background music. European American children did not.

I have written about differences in children's home lives that enable them to bring different abilities, skills, and knowledge to classrooms. For example, classrooms that focus solely on "discovery" learning may be giving some children the opportunity to show what they have learned at home through more explicit teaching from their parents but handicapping other children who have received no such explicit instruction; this refusal to explicitly let them know what other kids already know keeps them out of the circle of knowing.

For example, I watched a middle-class father picking up his daughter from nursery school. In this Montessori classroom, there was a tree trunk into which the children were happily pounding nails. The father walked over to the tree trunk with his daughter, who wanted to show him her nail, and said, "That's wonderful, sweetheart! Do you remember what those circles inside the tree trunk were called? . . . Right, rings! And do you remember what those rings could tell you? . . . You don't? They can tell you how old the tree was when it was chopped down. Let's count the rings together to see how old this tree was." Clearly, this is a child who will appear to "discover" a lot about trees (and counting) in a student-centered classroom of the future. But what she will actually be doing is recalling the direct instruction her father gave her at home.

I also notice with my own daughter that I, like many other middle-class parents, take every opportunity to connect her sound play to the knowledge that she will need when she begins to read. When she goes around singing "m-m-m Maya," I join in saying, "That's right! And m-m-m mommy! And m-m-m milk! And what else goes 'm-m-m'?" Again, when Maya appears to discover the connection between sounds and letters in her literacy-rich kindergarten, much will be made of how bright she is, when in reality, she will only be replaying what she has learned at home.

In too many classrooms, teachers think that the children who "get" the discovery lesson are truly discovering rather than exhibiting previously learned knowledge. They then find other children to be remedial before they're ever taught anything because they aren't "discovering."

So what can we do to make the struggle to be themselves in our institutions of education easier for children of color? Solutions are not easy to come by, for they involve fundamental changes in attitude.

We must begin to acknowledge, to paraphrase Pat Carini's 1986 presentation at the North Dakota Study Group, that people are the authors of their own lives. We must set more places at the tables where educational policy is created. We must make sure that parents, teachers, communities, and children of color have a voice in determining their educational needs. We must attempt to rid ourselves of the stereotypes society pushes on us about certain groups of people and be willing to do battle when we encounter those stereotypes among our colleagues or supervisors. We must reconsider how we conduct research to allow a focus on specific groups, so that we come to understand that what is good for one child or one group of children is not necessarily good for all. We must find the humility to learn from children and communities, and we must realize the fundamental connection that exists between ourselves and the children we teach.

We must, finally, come to the realization that the children we teach are the gifts we give to the future. And whether those gifts will be prized or spurned is in our hands. An older African American nursery school teacher brought this home to me when I visited her class. She pointed to a little boy and said, "You see that little boy over there? He's either going to grow up to be my doctor or hit me in the head and steal my purse. My job is to make sure that he's my doctor!"

I close with a slightly modified verse of Kahlil Gibran's poem, that has meant so much to my parenting and my teaching:

> We are the bows from which our children
> As living arrows are sent forth.
>
> The Archer sees the mark upon
> the path of the infinite,
> And he bends us with His might
> That His arrows may go swift and far.

My wish for us is that we allow ourselves to be bent so that all our young arrows find their marks in the future.

REFERENCES

Allen, B., & Boykin, A. W. (1991). The influence of contextual factors on Afro-American and Euro-American children's performance: Effects of movement opportunity and music. *International Journal of Psychology*, *26*(3), 373–387.

Cazden, C (1988). *Classroom Discourse: The Language of Teaching and Learning*. Portsmouth, NH: Heinemann.

Keohane, N. O. (1986). Our mission should not be merely to "reclaim" a legacy of scholarship—we must expand it. *The Chronicle of Higher Education*, *32*(5), 88.

Michaels, S., & Cazden, C. (1986). Teacher-child collaboration as oral preparation for literacy. In B. Shiefflen (Ed.), *The Acquisition of Literacy: Ethnographic Perspectives*. Norwood, NJ: Ablex.

Morgan, H. (1990). Assessment of students' behavioral interactions during on-task classroom activities. *Perceptual and Motor Skills*, *70*, 563–569.

Paley, V. (1979). *White teacher*. Cambridge, MA: Harvard University Press.

Swartz, E. (1992). Emancipatory narratives: Rewriting the master script in the school curriculum. *Journal of Negro Education*, *61*(3), 341–355.

CHAPTER 4

Seeing the Child, Knowing the Person

Nancy Balaban

Understanding children is every teacher's challenge. The elements that foster this knowledge include self-awareness, recognition of how children grow and learn, familiarity with educational theories, time for reflection, and comprehension of how and what to observe and record. This chapter describes how teachers can "see" their children as they are and thus develop plans for their learning. It explores meanings inherent in self-reflection and reveals that theories of development can be both aids and barriers to "seeing" children. It stresses teachers' written recordings and questions as the link between knowing children and developing programs for children's learning.

Possibly the most treacherous aspect of teaching occurs "when teachers face themselves" (Jersild, 1964). Critical to truly seeing and understanding the children we teach is the courage to reflect about ourselves. Facing our biases openly, recognizing the limits imposed by our embeddedness in our own culture and experience, acknowledging the values and beliefs we cherish, and accepting the influence of emotions on our actions are extraordinary challenges.

If we are to see children as they are, "from the inside out" (Cohen & Stern, 1983, p. 5), we need an antibias viewing lens. Bias is "[a]ny attitude, belief, or feeling that results in, and helps to justify, unfair treatment of an individual because of his or her identity" (Derman-Sparks & A.B.C. Task Force, 1989, p. 3). Bias has many sources. It may spring from experiences growing up in a specific family or community, from experiences with people different from oneself, from hidden messages in the media, from unquestioned tenets of society.

Teachers often have feelings about children whose ethnic, racial, or cultural group differs from their own. Sometimes teachers deem particular behaviors acceptable for boys but unacceptable for girls. Negative or fearful reactions to children in wheelchairs, to children who cannot see or hear, or to children with other physical disabilities are familiar to teachers. Opinions about gays and lesbians are sometimes projected on to children or children's parents. Bias is at work when a teacher describes an inquisitive boy as "bright" and an inquisitive girl as a "chatterbox."

Biased attitudes can cause teachers to make incorrect decisions about children's capabilities and potential for learning.

> A teacher of 7-year-olds disliked the way Tim followed her and whined "teacher, teacher" many times during the day. The teacher was particularly repelled when Tim picked his nose and rolled the mucus into balls.
>
> One day the teacher brought in some sand and fine-, medium-, and large-mesh screens for the children to explore. She recorded the activities of a small group, including Tim, as an exercise for a course she was taking. The record contained Tim's words: "Hey, the sand comes out faster when the holes are larger!" Reading the record aloud at the course, the teacher disregarded this statement until several members of the course called her attention to Tim's discovery. The teacher's prior judgment about Tim had prevented her from seeing the child's achievement.[1]

In addition to personal preferences, embeddedness in one's own culture can interfere with seeing children objectively. Familiar cultural customs, even the way we phrase what we say, can stand in the way of understanding or appreciating what others mean by their behavior.

> An Asian American author, writing about a black boycott of Korean grocers in Brooklyn, was shocked to hear a black resident comment that "'The Koreans are a very rude people. They don't understand you have to smile.' Would she have reacted differently," the author continues, "had she known smiling at strangers just isn't part of the Korean culture? . . . [That] they equate being solicitous to being insincere. The Korean demeanor is the absence of a demeanor. Koreans have a name for it: 'mu-pyo-jung.' It means 'lack of expression.'" (Kang, 1990).

Caucasian teachers sometimes tell Latino children to "look at me when I speak to you," misunderstanding that in the child's culture, looking down is a sign of respect. How can we step outside our own culture in order to learn other meanings for familiar behaviors? Teachers can ask themselves, Why did I do it that way? What did the child really mean?

Normally, teachers are so busy teaching that they are unable to take time to reflect on how their own backgrounds affect what they believe about children and what they think children should learn. The accumulated experiences of childhood; family membership; participation in the larger social, economic, and political community; and the critical involvement in school forge beliefs and values that shape the way teachers look at children. Yet every day teachers unconsciously make decisions based on these beliefs and values that influence their choice of program content, materials available for children, and arrangement of the physical environment. Such reflection contributes significantly to teachers' philosophies and their ideas about how children learn. Listen to a kindergarten teacher reflecting on the influences of her childhood in a large family in Ireland, her professional education, and her teaching experience:

> Education was important to my parents, and we were expected to work hard and to achieve good results. . . . My philosophy of teaching has developed as a result of these experiences and has been strongly influenced by studying as a graduate student at Bank Street College of Education and by my experience as an assistant teacher with a master teacher. My philosophy is child-centered. I believe children are motivated to learn. I believe that children learn by doing, by experiencing. By providing the materials and the opportunities for experiences that foster the child's self-esteem and independence, the teacher can use the child's natural curiosity to explore and learn. (Foote, Stafford, & Cuffaro, 1992, p. 74)

Sometimes feelings and emotions of the moment may override a teacher's commitment to stated beliefs and values.

A teacher grew tense when an unexpected incident caused the whole class of 5-year-olds to go out of control and begin racing around the room like a pinball machine gone amok. She raised her voice to a pitch unfamiliar to the children. In their shock, they stopped in place. She apologized to them, explaining that she feared for their safety.

One of the teacher's values, a calm and safe environment, was threatened by the children's actions and her own emotional behavior.

Is it possible for teachers to think about what they are doing, *while* they are doing it? Donald A. Schön (1983, p. 50) refers to this capability as "reflection on knowing-in-action." Teachers' practice of this technique can provide a method of becoming self-aware and thus opening doors to seeing the child.

Theories of development are critical in guiding teachers' understanding of children's motivation, in focusing on the different abilities and interests of children of different ages, and in helping teachers relate materials and program content to children's capabilities. Developmental theories help teachers understand why extensive paper-and-pencil desk work is troublesome for 4- and 5-year-olds, why 2-year-olds are uncomfortable leaving their parents, and why 6- and 7-year-olds need concrete learning materials.

Knowing a specific theory may help sharpen a teacher's observational acumen and see a child's thinking and learning in process.

> Seven-year-old Helen takes apart a triple-layered three-dimensional puzzle but does not know how to begin to put it together. She is sitting at a table with a number of adults. Grace points out that the outside edges of the puzzle are smooth. Together they find those pieces. While holding two pieces next to each other, Grace points out that each succeeding layer of the puzzle is thicker. Helen begins to put the pieces together with Grace's guidance. When they get to the third and top layer, Helen says, "Let me do this one by myself." She does the puzzle twice more. Each time less scaffolding assistance from Grace is necessary. Finally Helen takes the puzzle to Joan, one of the other adults at the table, and, using some of Grace's techniques, teaches Joan how to do it.

In this anecdote, Grace based her supportive behavior on what Vygotsky (1978) calls "scaffolding." In Vygotsky's theory, scaffolding refers to the way the adult guides the child's learning via focused questions and positive interactions. Grace's participation enabled Helen to do a task that at first she was unable to do alone and that later, with practice, she was able to teach to someone else. Vygotsky refers to this increasing independent ability as occurring within the child's "zone of proximal development." Using Vygotsky's theory, Grace was able to help Helen move to a higher level of competence and become familiar with Helen's ability to think, her style of learning, and her persistence.

However, a theory can sometimes act as an obstruction to seeing children's individuality and capabilities. For example, cognitive developmental theory has taught many early childhood teachers that because preschool children are egocentric they have a limited ability to see another's point of view. The effect of this theory is that when children tell one another "You can't play," teachers often tend to uphold the individual rights of the player to choose playmates. Yet in her kindergarten, Vivian Paley (1992) thought that preserving this position was detrimental to children's development. She instituted a new rule, "You can't say you can't play." She tested and demonstrated her own theory that, as a result of the rule, children became more aware and considerate of the feelings of their peers.

Do teachers have the wisdom to see that although a particular theory may not hold for the children in their group, it may hold for the children in another teacher's group? Theory tells us that 6-year-olds, for example, have many physical skills. Yet although all the 6-year-old children in Mr. Young's classroom were experts at double Dutch rope jumping, none of the children in Ms. Quigley's classroom could jump double Dutch. Is the fact that Mr. Young's children live in an urban area and Ms. Quigley's in a rural area powerful enough to account for the differences? Are the urban children unusually talented? Are the rural children slow? Does the setting in which a child grows up play a role?

When teachers fit a child to a theory, they run the risk of ignoring the context of development and leaving the individual out of the picture. When teachers cautiously fit applicable theory to a child, they can enhance their insight.

Asking thought-provoking questions can help teachers understand their children. Knowing how a child arrived at the answer to a specific question or what the child's own questions are is more useful to teachers than the child's "right answer." In fact, "wrong answers" frequently supply a key to understanding the child's thinking. Open-ended questions also elicit this kind of information. "How do you think this fountain works?" will provide an interesting basis for investigating water pressure and pumps. Answers to the question will give the teacher some clues about children's knowledge and speculations. "What will we see when we go to the firehouse tomorrow?" is a question that can reveal how much 4-year-olds know or don't know. One teacher made a list of children's answers to this question: a fire truck, a big hose, a firefighter, fire, a monster, the chief. She learned how fearful some children were and was able to reassure them beforehand. After the visit, she reread the list with them, and they revised it.

When teachers are open to the clues that children give in an atmosphere that allows them to speak their minds freely, children emerge as the whole people they are.

A first grader was building a one-story supermarket with a large, flat roof. A ramp extended from the block shelf to the roof.

Ms. H.: What is this ramp for?
ANNA: That's where the trucks bring in the food.
Ms. H.: How does the food get from the roof inside the store?
ANNA: They throw it down near the door and carry it in.
Ms. H.: Suppose the truck brings eggs.
ANNA: Could you please go help somebody else?

Later on, Ms. H. saw Anna pushing a truck to the front door, calling, "Food coming in, food coming in."

It is seldom possible for teachers to think as children do. Children's thinking is not *lesser* than adults', rather it is qualitatively *different*. Although it is not surprising to hear a 3-year-old, after seeing *The Wizard of Oz*, ask, "Can you really grow up to be a tin man?" no adult would entertain such a thought. Teachers profit from asking themselves: How did the child think about this action, problem, or event? How might I have thought about this situation when I was a child?

Is it possible for teachers to recall their own 3- to 6-year-oldness? Remembering one's own childhood questions and confusions helps one understand how serious children's questions and observations are. Constructing the world is hard work. A first-grade teacher recalled her own 6-year-old thought:

> I was riding in the car with my parents, approaching the George Washington Bridge. From the road, I could see the whole expanse of the bridge, including the cables and the roadway. I focused on the cables. When my parents told me that we would soon be crossing the bridge, I began to scream in terror. I thought that our car would have to balance on the cables.[2]

It would be easy to label this child "overanxious" without finding out what she was thinking. It would also be unlikely for any adult to conceptualize such a bridge crossing. Asking the question, without judgment, brings the teacher closer to the child's individual way of figuring out the world's mysteries.

Teachers often forget how literal young children are and that they sometimes misinterpret adult language with their own private meanings.

> Four-year-old Jorge, at the water table, was soaking wet. He complained to the teacher, who said, "Don't worry, I'll change you." "Change me? Into . . . ?" sobbed Jorge. "I mean," the teacher explained, when she understood his fear, "I'll change *your clothes.*"[3]

Observing children's behavior and their answers to pertinent questions is only part of what is needed to be an effective teacher. It is critical to complement observations with ongoing, systematic, written recordings of both individual children as well as the whole group or subgroups in journals or logs or on note cards (Cohen & Stern, 1983). Written material concretizes those observations that teachers make every day. Records prevent the fade-out of important information about children's lives in the classroom. Written anecdotes enhance teachers' reflections. Accompanied by children's own work, these recordings form a basis for thorough and focused parent conferences. Furthermore, written anecdotes, collected over time, help teachers recognize which children they have neglected to record. Why has this girl or that boy been left out of the anecdote collection? What is there about those children that prevents their capture in the teacher's eye and pen?

Writing down what teachers see and hear is the handmaiden of curriculum planning and assessment.[4] There is a strong relationship between how a teacher sees and knows the children and the program the teacher develops for the children's learning and growth.

> A teacher of 3-year-olds heard several children discussing going to the doctor. She invited two of the children's mothers, who were pediatricians, to visit the class and demonstrate how they make an examination. The visit was a source of great interest, especially to some children who were unaware that women could be doctors. Following the visit, there were several discussions with the children about what doctors do. The teacher read books about doctors. Some children began to play doctor, so the teacher helped them set up a doctor's

office and a waiting room, complete with phone, pads of
paper, pencils, stethoscope, white coat, and an array of plastic
pill bottles. The play went on for several days before their
interest waned.

The principles of observing, expanding on children's interests,
and providing materials and time, which were used by this teacher
of 3-year-olds, are the same principles to be used by teachers of
6- and 7-year-olds. In the following anecdote, a second-grade teacher
provided concrete experiences to enhance the children's understanding of immigration and math in a piece of integrated curriculum.

Several of the children in this particular class had immigrated
from other countries. The whole class had done research
about these countries and had interviewed some adults from
these areas. As a follow-up activity, the teacher divided the
children into small groups to pretend that they were taking a
boat from one of the countries to the United States. She asked
them to (1) make a list of all the items they would need for the
trip and (2) limit the weight of the items to 50 pounds.
     At a meeting to discuss their lists, the children discovered
that a wide array of items had been selected, including books,
blocks, food, water, a quill, compass, flashlight, four steaks,
pencil, and paper. When the teacher encouraged them to
explore their reasoning for their choices, she enabled them to
become more realistic about the appropriateness of certain
objects.
     She also discovered that they had little knowledge about
the weight of things. Some wrote "blankets, 4 pounds; food,
2 pounds; pillows, 3 pounds." One child asked how much
people weighed and was uncertain about her own weight. The
teacher made a plan to bring in a variety of scales along with
many of the articles on the children's lists in order to chart
their weights. She planned for them to record their own body
weights and chart those as well.

Observations reveal where children's interests lie and what con-
fuses them. Observations uncover what children bring to school from
their homes and streets. This information is a potent source of early
childhood program content. It is the teacher's task to choose from
this information in designing meaningful curriculum that fosters
children's long, complex task of constructing their world. When ob-

servations are transformed into written history, then seeing becomes knowing.

Acknowledgment

I wish to acknowledge the contributions of Nancy Nager and Harriet Cuffaro of the Bank Street Graduate School of Education to this chapter.

NOTES

1. Communication from Dr. Leah Levinger. The names in this anecdote, and in all those following, are fictitious.
2. Anecdote related in a class taught by Nancy Balaban; student unknown.
3. Anecdote supplied by Harriet Cuffaro.
4. There are many articles and books about alternatives to standardized testing for young children that emphasize the use of teachers' own recorded data.

REFERENCES

Cohen, D. H., & Stern, V. (with Balaban, N.) (1983). *Observing and recording the behavior of young children* (3rd ed.). New York: Teachers College Press.

Derman-Sparks, L., & A.B.C. Task Force. (1989). *Anti-bias curriculum: Tools for empowering young children.* Washington, DC: National Association for the Education of Young Children.

Foote, M., Stafford, P., Cuffaro, H. K. (1992). Linking curriculum and assessment in preschool and kindergarten. In C. Genishi (Ed.), *Ways of assessing children and curriculum: Stories of early childhood practice* (pp. 58–93). New York: Teachers College Press.

Jersild, A. T. (1964). *When teachers face themselves.* New York: Bureau of Publications, Teachers College, Columbia University.

Kang, K. C. (1990, September 8). Koreans have a reason not to smile. *New York Times.*

Paley, V. G. (1992). *You can't say you can't play.* Cambridge, MA: Harvard University Press.

Schön, D. A. (1983). *The reflective practitioner.* New York: Basic Books.

Vygotsky, L. S. (1978). *Mind in society: The development of higher psychological processes* (M. Cole, V. John-Steiner, S. Scribner, & E. Souberman, Eds.). Cambridge, MA: Harvard University Press.

PART II

THINKING
AND TEACHING

William Ayers

Teaching demands thoughtfulness. There simply is no way to become an outstanding teacher through adherence to routine, formula, habit, convention, or standardized ways of speaking and acting. Thoughtfulness requires wide-awakeness—a willingness to look at the conditions of our lives, to consider alternatives and different possibilities, to challenge received wisdom and the taken for granted, and to link our conduct with our consciousness. Hannah Arendt (1958, p. 5) challenged us all to "think what we are doing."

It is hard to think what you are doing all the time, to challenge, to reflect, to demand all the time. Why am I going to class? What are the alternatives? Who says class should be 3 hours long? Why should certain readings be required? Why should I drive on the right-hand side of the street? What might I do after class besides pick up my kids and take them home for a snack? That kind of questioning all the time could make you crazy.

It can be overwhelming as well to try to think what you are doing in a classroom of 30 students, embedded in a school of several hundred (or thousand), situated in a town or city of several thousand (or million). Each of your students has her or his own needs, skills, capacities, hopes, and dreams. The school has its own goals and plans to attend to. And society makes its own demands as well. Who am I to question the bell schedule, the curriculum, the sorting and ranking of students, the patterns of success and failure?

And yet, that is what teachers must do if they are ever to rise above being petty functionaries. Make no mistake about it: All the testing, sorting, credentialing, certifying, and supervising that aspiring teachers endure reduce teaching to clerkship and turn teachers from thinkers to bureaucrats. To break with that requires strength and courage—the strength to think in a time of thought-lessness, the courage to care in a culture of carelessness.

Teaching is intellectual and ethical work. It requires the full attention—wide awake, inquiring, critical—of thoughtful and caring people if it is to be done well. Although there is always more to learn and more to know as a teacher, the heart of teaching is a passionate regard for students. With it, mistakes and obstacles will be met and overcome; without it, no amount of technical skill will ever fully compensate. The work of teaching involves struggling to see each student in as full and dynamic a way as possible, to create environments that nurture and challenge the wide range of students who are actually there in classrooms, and to construct bridges with each learner from the known to the not yet known.

Learning to teach well involves a deep engagement with the surrounding social and historical environments. It involves, as well, knowledge of various literacies—ways human beings have described and understood their worlds. And it involves knowing oneself well, one's attitudes, beliefs, values, and prejudices as well as one's underlying conceptions of knowledge and knowing.

Teachers need to engage questions of immediacy and urgency from their classrooms: What is teaching? What is learning? How do we know what we know about teaching? What is the evidence? How does it compare with other things we know? Who is being served in schools, and how? What the hell is going on in our classrooms? What does it mean for the teacher? How are the kids experiencing it?

There are also broader questions of great importance. What knowledge and experiences are most worthwhile (for you, as students of teaching, as well as for students in your classrooms)? How can students best have access to that worthwhile knowledge and those valuable experiences? There is no easy answer; the unknown always outweighs the known.

This does not mean that teachers are powerless, nor that becoming a (better) teacher is mysterious, fated, or somehow outside the self-activity of teachers themselves. There are countless action steps that anyone can take right now to seize control of the process, direction, and tempo of becoming a teacher. And self-activity is essential in teaching. If you wait for someone else (the board, the superintendent, the union, the principal, the parents, the university, the professor) to get it right *before* you do the best you know how to do for children, you will wait a lifetime. Similarly, if you postpone doing what is best in the belief that there will be a future free of constraint, postponement will become a way of life, and you will forget what you had once planned as original (and maybe even subversive) in favor of something resembling obedience and conformity. No, the only way to go is to take control of yourself and your corner of the world now, to build alliances with students, families, and like-minded teachers over time, and to justify your actions on the basis of doing what is best. The time to begin is now—to struggle to be heard in your college classes, for example, or your union, or your staff meetings; to take your own growth and development into your hands; to consciously choose to be the teacher you are becoming.

You could, of course, decide that each year you will take a certain number of workshops or classes offered to teachers by the board, the union, or a university. This is one way to stay in touch with current educational issues and to take seriously your own professional growth and development. It is a relatively easy step, straightforward and obvious, and that is both its strength and its weakness. Workshops are accessible, but they are often simple-minded, unchallenging, and silly. You need to be selective, deliberate, and critical as you work through the world of teacher workshops.

Perhaps you could commit yourself to staying alive and challenged as a thoughtful, inquiring person—to being an intellectual. This might mean continuing some kind of formal study through a university, museum, or other cultural institution. In part, this is done in recognition of the need for teachers always to know and understand more, to continually become smarter and more competent (for finite beings in an infinite, expanding universe, there is *always* more to know and understand). But it is also done in part to honor the need of teachers to be self-conscious students of learning and of teaching—to live actively and consciously in the role of one who does not know and to reflect on the process of learning and acquiring skills. To study archaeology, chemistry, philosophy, geometry, early feminist history, the folk art of Haiti, Native American mythology, comparative religions, modern Chinese film, the photography of Robert Mapplethorpe—

or anything at all—is to expand your world and your consciousness at the same time that you participate at your own adult level
in a process that is at the heart of your work. You might come
away from the experience a little more informed, a little deeper
and broader, and you might also come away bored stiff or confused or alienated. In any case, the encounter may allow you to
harvest insights into the world students inhabit, and that—with
reflection and action—could make you a better teacher.

You should also hang on to and pursue your own projects and
passions (and if you haven't any, think about and challenge
that)—quilt making, amateur astronomy, sketching, button
collecting, hiking, and so on. Projects can be a rich source of
insight and understanding. They can inform your teaching directly
(building kites with students and branching off into culture and
history, geometry and physics) or indirectly (noting the sense of
accomplishment and satisfaction associated with gardening and
figuring out how to offer kids a range of ways to engage in physical labor, or vowing never to undertake a lesson or unit that
doesn't involve students in reaping what they sow).

You should think deeply about what you want for youngsters—your hopes and aspirations for your students—and then
examine your own life for evidence of those hopes realized. For
example, most teachers want students to read better, to read more
often, to read widely, to read a range of materials for a variety of
purposes. If this is one of your goals, then ask yourself this: Do
you read the daily newspaper? Do you read for pleasure? Do you
read novels or biographies? A simple action step—entirely in your
power—is to begin now to read a newspaper every day, a novel
every few weeks, a biography or history or other book of nonfiction every month. You might ask a few friends to join you in a
book group—dinner once every other month, perhaps, followed by
discussion about an agreed-upon book.

Similarly, if you want students to be good citizens (a common
goal), are you active in your block club, community organization,
political club, environmental or other advocacy group? If you
want them to be cooperative, do you participate in a co-op or
community-building effort? If you want youngsters to be critical
thinkers, are you part of any arts organization or project? These
and similar connections are necessary if teachers are to move
beyond espousing simple slogans and well-worn clichés and to
take their goals for students as urgent and personal.

You might also investigate and contact networks of teachers who can nurture your hopes and dreams as a teacher, or challenge you to rethink what is stale or failing in your teaching. There are often local networks—caucuses in unions, discussion groups, curriculum projects. (Appendix B offers a host of other opportunities.)

It is important that teachers fight the atomization, isolation, and alienation endemic in teaching. Teachers typically find themselves alone in classrooms with too many children and too little time. When teachers talk to other teachers, it is usually a brief encounter at lunch or during a break, and the talk is rarely about the content and conduct of their work. The isolation is sometimes defended as a precious and guarded autonomy, but it can easily turn to disconnection and burnout.

The most successful teacher development projects I know do not rely on university people, curriculum specialists, gurus, or outsiders of any kind. Rather, they are teacher-run, small, informal, and personal. They are teachers talking to teachers about teaching. They are often conducted over coffee or dinner—time carved out of busy lives after school or on weekends.

In Chicago, several networks now exist called Teacher Talks. Some are based at a particular school; others are cross-city and involve teachers who share a common view of their work; still others focus on a specific aspect of teaching—for example, a Teacher Talk on alternative assessment, a Teacher Talk on building literature-rich classrooms, a Teacher Talk on developing schools within schools. Each network is focused, small, and teacher-built.

These networks are promising because they require no special expertise or equipment or package. They are built on the needs, experiences, and collective wisdom of teachers themselves. They are close to the realities of classroom life and promise, therefore, no pie in the sky. And yet, by focusing on teachers' own concerns collectively and publicly, they assume that good teachers are always in search of better teaching practice. They allow for scrutiny, self-reflection, criticism, and support in the difficult task of becoming outstanding teachers.

The focus of Teacher Talk is curriculum, instruction, and evaluation—the content and conduct of teaching. This is itself remarkable. School staff meetings are so dominated by procedure and organization (announcements of regulations, reports of committees) that a visitor to such a meeting would have no idea what the enterprise was about. By contrast, Teacher Talk is only about students and teaching.

One way to structure this kind of gathering is to hold each meeting in a different classroom on a rotating basis. The host teacher might provide snacks and lead the session by describing the environment for learning—the goals she or he has organized and embodied here in this space, this routine, this school—and then presenting to the group a detailed observational portrait of a particular student, or perhaps a specific teaching challenge to begin the discussion.

These are merely some of the steps you might take on a pathway to teaching. Nothing will automatically meet the challenge of becoming an outstanding teacher. That is a lifelong pursuit. Each of these steps can be thought of as dynamic and open-ended, leading (if you choose) to further activities, engagements, and commitments—further steps of your own invention and your own desire. What is critical is this: Only you can create a life that does not make a mockery of your values. Only you can be this particular teacher who touches that particular life, and that one, and that. Only you can work to leave your own unique footprints in the earth.

REFERENCE

Arendt, H. (1958). *The human condition.* Chicago: University of Chicago Press.

CHAPTER 5

Choosing a Past
and Inventing a Future:
The Becoming of a Teacher

Maxine Greene

Reaching back over the years, seeking the themes of my becoming, I try to find contact points between my story and the stories of those who are teachers-to-be and teachers today. We have in common, I want to believe, the notion of teaching as a project. A project turns us forward; we choose it as a way of gearing into the world, of reaching beyond what is to what might or ought to be. We choose it also as a way of shaping our identities, of making something out of what we have been made (Sartre, 1963, p. 91). We may have in common, too, a sense of connection between what happens in our classrooms and what might happen in the society around, with all its flaws and deficiencies. There must be links, after all, between what we are trying to make of ourselves and what we are striving to make possible in the lives of those we teach; and, yes, there must be consequences in the larger order of things. I cannot divorce the idea of shaping the future from the practice of teaching; nor can I abandon the notion of context, the many facets of life to which we respond. Thinking this way, I recall the phrase Hannah Arendt (1963) borrowed from Kafka: "between past and future." Nor can I stop thinking about its relevance for our understanding of the choices we are attempting to make in what are undeniably "dark times" (Arendt, 1961, p. viii).

It seems to me that we live in what we experience as an interlude between a lived past and what we conceive to be some future possibility. Depending on our location and, in large degree, on our gender, class, and what is now called ethnic identity, we interpret the historical as well as our personal pasts contingently. What we see and how we interpret are deeply affected by our situations, by our memberships, and by the kinds of intelligence we use in reading the landscapes spreading around us and extending back in time. They are focally affected as well by the way we view ourselves in relation to the many manifestations of power, how we define ourselves with regard to what Foucault called "the eye of power" (1980, pp. 146–165), the degree and quality of freedom we think we can achieve as we live.

Considering the schools and their history in our country, we may be highly likely to view them as primarily agents of normalization, oriented to the reproduction of an inequitable, consumerist, stratified culture. We may look upon them even today as reflectors of a society bent on manipulation and exclusion, concerned primarily with private gain. A reform movement linked to anticipations of a highly technologized future seems to do little to diminish the hegemonic impact of schooling. What Jonathan Kozol (1992) calls "savage inequalities" continue to shed an ironic light on the presumed guarantees of "Education 2000." If this is our perspective, we are likely to acknowledge (with more than a little weariness) that deeplying economic and social changes may be necessary before we can begin to think of educational projects that release people for growth and critical questioning, that allow them to learn what is required to effect far-ranging transformation. Yet this is a period when there exists not only what Dewey (1927/1954) called "an eclipse of the public" but also the kind of cynicism or hopelessness that makes it difficult to imagine collaborative actions of any kind in the name of the humane and the just.

In contrast to this view, there remains in many quarters a stubborn confidence in a kind of forward movement in American history, a movement toward democracy that may be in some manner advanced by the public schools. Every effort to restructure or reform seems grounded in a faith that, for all the flaws in our society, education can indeed be transformed. Much of that faith centers on teachers and what may occur when their potentialities are at last released. We find communities taking shape in diverse schools; we foster teacher research; we work toward active learning; we devise what we call measures for "authentic assessment"; we talk of treasuring "diversity" as we work for dialogue and mutuality. It is, very often, as if we are reawakening the promises of the 19th century: initiating newcomers into a welcoming community, providing the skills needed for lives lived usefully, noncompliantly, and in freedom. Repressing images of darkness—of violence and hypocrisies, like those on the riverbanks in *The Adventures of Huckleberry Finn* (Twain 1884/1959); the underground refuge of the "invisible man"; the "vast, vulgar, meritricious beauty" in Jay Gatsby's American Dream; the marigolds that did not grow in Toni Morrison's *The Bluest Eye* (1970) —we open ourselves to untrammeled possibility. We are, in some of our moods, like Fitzgerald's Gatsby, with his; "extraordinary gift for hope." And, perhaps like Gatsby, we will turn out all right in the end: "it is what preyed on Gatsby, what foul dust floated in the wake of his dreams" (Fitzgerald, 1922/1942, p. 2). Some of us are beginning to see that if we do not take heed of that "foul dust," the myth of the public school becomes a void.

There are, clearly, multiple visions, multiple readings; and we who are striving to be teachers ought to take several perspectives as we construct what we think of as an educational reality. Integrating them if we can, orchestrating the various themes, we need to confront the darkness as well as the light, the radiance of the always receding dream. Situating ourselves in the interlude "between past and future," we may be able to make meanings where there were few meanings before.

From my vantage point, two significant moments shine forth in the backdrop I choose as my past. Both happen to be associated with the history of Teachers College, but that is largely because so much of my own career has been spent there, and I could not avoid (because of personal experiences and indirect encounters) seeing them as somehow intrinsic to Teachers College's changing and sometimes paradigmatic tale. The first moment was one in the 1930s, the time I read about when I was trying to make sense of the contexts surrounding my own growing up. That meant the Roosevelt period, the New Deal, the Works Progress Administration, the trade union movement, the sounds of collective action and of communities in the making. And, yes, it was the period when the Nazis were seizing power, when fascism was moving from Italy to republican Spain, when cities (perhaps for the first time) were being bombed. For all that, it was a moment of hope, of confidence in what were called "the masses," of trust in the mind, the active mind, the group. There was belief in protest too—in marching for peace and then against fascism, in demonstrating for social spending, in carrying banners spelling out one or another version of Carl Sandburg's phrase: "the people, yes!"

Teachers College was not the only educational center that resonated to the messages of the New Deal and the struggle against "economic Tories" or "royalists" or financiers. But Teachers College was the place where the *Social Frontier* was published, where John Dewey was using the language of democratic socialism, where George Counts wrote "Dare the Schools Change the Social Order?" Young people like me, reading all this, projected a new and startling "progressivism" into the pedagogical dialogue. What some of us read, what some of us heard, made us find a mode of resistance in the very activity of educating, especially if we had taken seriously the accounts of the injustices, the false pieties, the indifference of the existing social order. Reading some of the literature of the 1930s, we could be convinced that the way of thinking it seemed to embody might well turn aside the manipulative and ideological forces that made so much of what happened in public schools miseducative.

The second significant moment has a greater immediacy for me, because it was the moment when I began teaching at Teachers College, near the close of the 1960s. There were the protests at Columbia; there were the antiwar vigils and marches; there was the civil rights movement and what came after; there were Freedom Schools in the neighborhoods during a teachers' strike; there was music, always music. And yes, like a great dark blood spot in the middle of it all, like some awful herald of what was to come, there were the three assassinations (not to mention the deaths of the innumerable nameless ones) to remind us that the "greening of America" could never be guaranteed. The 1930s had ended in war, leading, eventually, to Hiroshima and Nagasaki; the 1960s ended with the sound of gunfire too, and another war still going on.

They were two quite different periods, raising different questions, each one leaving different questions still aching, still unresolved. Each carried a hope, an insistence that things could be better—and that education might have something to do with repairing what was wrong. I am sure that such an insistence fed my own desire to try to become a teacher; I would like to believe that it lives below the surface cynicisms in many practitioners today. In many respects, the 1930s seem incredibly distant, and the talk of reform that marked that decade appears, at first, to have little relevance for today. When we listen more carefully, however, we hear talk about poverty, health care, women's rights, youth, unemployment—issues that depended on a kind of solidarity among men and women of different classes and different professions that is scarcely dreamed of in these times. Forestry projects, arts projects, murals in the post offices, low-cost theaters in the cities, folk schools for mountain people and the poor: They did not last long, but they offer us exemplars even today. They suggest what can be done when what Dewey (1927/1954, p. 184) called "an articulate Public" begins to come into being out of an ever-deepening and ever-expanding association of human activities. That public was in eclipse, Dewey said, when he wrote about it more than 60 years ago. It is certainly in eclipse today, taken over by consuming audiences, by those who watch the talk-show hosts and the televangelists and (because of a need for comfort, a need for answers) let their own voices be silenced under the drumbeat and patter of certainties and packaged truths. In its very absence, however, it calls out for presentness, for remaking, even as the value of solidarity calls out for reincarnation once again.

Still struggling to become a teacher, still trying to find ways of opening spaces in which learners can choose themselves as they pose their questions and learn to learn, I still find the notion of persons coming together to transform, to change, compelling. As Maurice Merleau-Ponty (1967, p. 443) suggested when writing about freedom, everything depends on the ways in which individuals *experience* what lies around them. It is not a matter of conceiving the surrounding society as a system of impersonal or invisible forces working upon them, raising the obstacles, determining from outside what they can do. It is rather a way of being in the world as someone reaching toward community, trying to understand, feeling interest and concern. And it may be part of the practice of a teacher to open the door to this way of being in the world. With some exceptions (as in the case of certain parts of the feminist movement), the last decade and a half has been devoid of the kind of social commitment that sets people moving. The intensity, for example, that drove individuals to organize and come together during the civil rights movement is seldom felt. To reawaken memories of the 1930s may arouse teachers to ponder ways of relating what they do in classrooms to what might be done and should be done in neighborhoods and open spaces. Literacy may come to signify more than technological skill. Learning itself may have as much to do with bringing about changes in a locality as it does with preparing for the upward climb to whatever constitutes success. Perhaps it is time to try to revive such images as those of the trade union leader Joe Hill; of John Steinbeck's (1939) Tom Joad; of Harriette Arnow's (1954) Gertie Nevels, mother and "dollmaker"; of Andre Malraux's (1936) Kyo Gisors, fighting for a decent life for the suffering Chinese; of Ralph Ellison's (1954) "invisible man," striving to achieve his own visibility; of Virginia Woolf (1938/1966), challenging the daughters of educated men to form an Outsiders' Society to battle the iniquity of dictatorship in all conceivable forms.

Again, trying to become (even today) a teacher who can awaken people, who can make a difference, I try to heed those forgotten voices of the 1930s, try to create myself and construct a reality that demands a mode of thought and action that reaches beyond the private sphere. Perhaps the issue is one of deciding to fight what Albert Camus (1948) called "the plague"—meaning the indifference of injustice or random suffering. Perhaps it is a matter of turning life in classrooms to the formation of "sanitary groups" now and then. "These groups," says the narrator, "enabled our townsfolk to come to grips with the disease and convinced them that, now that plague was among us, it was up to them to do whatever could be done to fight it. Since plague became in this way some men's duty, it revealed itself as what it really was; that is, the concern of all" (p. 121). For "plague" we can substitute homelessness, AIDS, the violation or neglect of children, exclusion, prejudice. Reaching back to significant moments in the past of memory and story, how can we choose our projects once again with the need to repair, if not to heal, in mind?

There was, of course, the other moment in the past that still sheds light, sometimes a flickering light, for me. The anniversary of the 1963 March on Washington summoned up many people's memories, many kinds of nostalgia. Many of us are sickened by the helplessness we have felt in the face of the Bosnian tragedies, the massacres in Rwanda, the terrible events in Angola and Armenia and other afflicted places on the globe. We think back (how can we not?) to a time when we truly believed that we could indeed "overcome" if we held on to one another and kept the dialogue and the singing going, that things could really be otherwise. There seems to have been in the 1960s, for all the mistakes, for all those who were left out, the discovery of a personal sense of possibility. Of course the sufferings were multiple, as were the frustrations. There were false hopes; there were instances of romantic self-indulgence; there were extremes of addiction, of risk taking. But there were radiant instances of commitment and self-sacrifice, along with the carnival and the violence, along with the charging of what Mailer called "the armies of the night."

When I think back to those days in my continuing quest for transformations of teaching, for a "reflective practice" (Schön, 1983) fired by an involvement with a cause, I remember our shared horror at the police crackdown on the Columbia campus. A community seemed to stem from the burst of moral outrage; for many, it was the first time there had been such an effort to define what was decent and humane, what was simply inhumane and wrong. There was the sound of guitars in the halls at Teachers College; there were "liberation classes" announced on all sorts of posters and placards; there were ongoing conversations; there were hands squeezing hands. Certain leaders of the Columbia University protests came and spoke in the Teachers College courtyard. They used phrases like "articulate public" and "participatory democracy"; for a while, there were startling echoes of John Dewey and the progressives around them. There were strands being woven between the 1930s and the hectic, wonder-struck 1960s. But now there was a peculiar, stark concreteness about the evils that had to be contested: napalm, cluster bombs in villages, bureaucratic dominion, the artifices of language, racism, abstractness, numbness, dread banality. For some, as we went on choosing our projects, the very point of teaching had to do with arousing persons to name all this, to come together, to renew.

Looked at from this distance, it may have been the best of times as well as the worst of times. There were the Johnson reforms and the promises of the so-called Great Society, many of them shattered by the demands of an unjustifiable war. And there were the killings at Kent State and Jackson State, the tragic circus at the Chicago convention. As in the case of the 1930s, it was as if potential social frontierspersons, potential Reverend Kings and Fannie Lou Hamers and Dorothy Days and Daniel Berrigans, were cut off in mid-sentence. Worse, the fabrics of the incomplete conversations and explorations were torn apart and apparently forgotten, and far too few tried to pick up the threads.

The ostensibly romantic accounts of what education might become, the neo-Marxist and humanist and Deweyan critiques of what it was, were drowned out before long by talk of competencies, behavioral objectives, controls, and a peculiarly arid notion of accountability. We know all too well the acquisitiveness, the privatism, the business ethic, the neglect of cities, the misty mystifications of the era. They diminished and in some manner trivialized the work of public schools; they rendered hard and sterile whatever thinking went on with regard to becoming a teacher. Also, we cannot forget the "Great Satan" against which this nation was expected to define itself —the so-called communist threat. Nor can we forget the use of that threat as rationale for murders and tortures and invasions in Central America and other places in the world. Too frequently, the self-definitions that were attempted took the form of a Rambo, a Dirty Harry, a vacuously smiling white father intent on defending individualism, efficiency, power, free markets, and (when convenient) authoritarianism in countries East and West.

How can we identify ourselves as teachers in the midst of all this?

Can we go back to dreams of the Great Community, to a faith in intelligence and scientific method, to a belief in the inalienable dignity of (almost everyone would say) "man"? Can we summon up images of vastness once again: dams and irrigation projects and national parks as emblematic of a progress in which we could all believe? Can we imagine the men and women in overalls, once battered by economic depression, finding themselves in solidarity, moving arm and arm toward something better as far as the social order was concerned? With the 1960s intervening between such a Whitmanesque view and the multiplicities of the present, we are bound to ask how many voices were unheard in those days, how many faces were obscured. Invisibility and "nobodyness" throws hundreds and thousands of women and minority groups into the shadows. The shapes of miners, sailors, farmers, factory workers appeared in the foreground oftentimes, but we did not pay heed to the differences among them, to the wonders and complexities of diversity. There was talk of "man," "humanity," "the people." There was little talk of particularities, little attention paid until the 1960s.

That was when we heard the cries for recognition on the part of African Americans. That was when we were bound to attend to students asking to be viewed as human beings and not "IBM cards." In the midst of all that, the power of feminism was released in novel ways. Teachers' attention, as well as attention throughout society, had to be drawn to distinctive ways of knowing, to new conceptions of rationality and connectedness, to fresh perspectives on reciprocity and responsibility, on the meanings of community, the meanings of care. At once, fascinated as many of us were with activating what we thought of as the "public sphere" (Arendt, 1961; Dewey, 1927/ 1954), we had to think of breaking through the barriers between private and public. For almost the first time, we began to ponder seriously the importance of infusing the public space with values such as compassion, so long limited to the wholly private sphere. The old separations, the old alienations began to give way.

Children, too, so long pressed down by bureaucracies and impersonality in the schools, became visible in unprecedented ways. Writers of the 1960s exposed coercion and what it meant, as Paul Goodman (1960) saw it, to grow up "absurd," or, as Jonathan Kozol (1967) put it, to experience "death at an early age." Like others, in trying to appropriate aspects of that historic moment, I have struggled to stay in touch with the integrity, energies, fragility, and wonder of children rather than submerging them in a classroom crowd. Of course there were unforgettable crimes and duplicities in the 1960s, but the road was opening to a vast range of human possibility, to new modes of communication, new modes of argument and protest and critique. And then, as most of us realize, it was as if the road was closed, or as if a sudden curtain of fog blocked the way ahead.

Hannah Arendt begins her book *Between Past and Future* with a recollection of French poet Rene Char, who wrote of a "lost treasure" when he remembered the days of the French Resistance, in which he had played a part. Those who joined the Resistance, he said, found themselves. Each one found himself or herself going beyond insincerity, "stripped of all masks—of those which society hands to its members as well as those the individual fabricates for himself in his psychological reactions against society." They found themselves visited by "an apparition of freedom, not . . . because they had acted against tyranny and things worse than tyranny—this was true for every soldier in the Allied armies—but because they had become 'challengers,' had taken the initiative upon themselves and therefore, without knowing or even noticing it, had begun to create that public space between themselves where freedom could appear" (Arendt, 1963, p. 4). After the liberation and the return to the ordinary, Char talked of a "sad opaqueness" of private life centered upon nothing but itself, about the ways in which people wear masks and disguise the authenticity they discovered in the unprecedented public space they made during the war.

There is no way of comparing a teacher who is always in the making with a freedom fighter in the Second World War, but there is something recognizable about the feeling of a "lost treasure," particularly when I think back to some of the excitements of the 1960s and what was held before us as social possibility by those who emerged from the 1930s. I yearn for—and want others to yearn for—the feeling of outraged affirmation experienced when we are striking out for our humanity. If we were to view ourselves in an interlude between certain moments in the past and the open future, we might think of our lives in terms of narrative at the intersection of multiple social and economic forces. Writing, shaping our narratives, we perceive our lives in terms of quest. We turn our faces to some conception of what we believe to be right and good, and we orient ourselves to their pursuit. That may be what Char meant by a "treasure." It is surely something that teachers, in a not always hospitable world, might seek at some moments to hold in their hands.

There can be no repetition of the past, not even a full recapitulation of it. But there may be a way of making our own remembered lives part of what we view as history in a way that gives that history

meaning it might not otherwise have. We might think of the emphasis on social inquiry and social intelligence in the 1930s, for example,
from the vantage points of the many modes of teaching educational
research with which we are now involved. We might think of it as
grounded, as it hardly would have been without the perspectives
opened up in the 1960s.

It would be difficult, for instance, to justify much of our research
today without considering what Cornel West (1993) calls "race matters." West has also looked at the kinds of solutions for contemporary problems rooted in the New Deal and the Great Society. He has
talked about the need for the debate to go beyond the tension between 1930s liberalism (or the liberalism of the 1960s) and the new
conservatism. Structures and behavior are inseparable, of course, but
West went on to remind us that culture is as much a structure as
economy and politics, and it is rooted in our institutions. He wrote
about the "waters of despair and dread that now flood the streets of
black America." In earlier times, the days of slavery or segregation,
Black people's rage and pessimism were muted because of fear of
retaliation.

> The major breakthroughs of the sixties—more psychically than politi-
> cally—swept this fear away. Sadly, the combination of the market way
> of life, poverty-ridden conditions, black existential *angst*, and the less-
> ening of fear of white authorities has directed most of the anger, rage,
> and despair toward fellow black citizens, especially toward black
> women who are the most vulnerable in our society and in black com-
> munities. (West, 1993, p. 18)

Terrible poverty, crime, and, worst of all, what he refers to as "the
unprecedented collapse of meaning" due to the betrayal of the 1960s'
hopes characterize much of the Black community today.

West talks in a way that I have to recognize as a teacher, a citizen, someone absorbed in literature and the arts. He is talking in a
way that we have to recognize and resonate to as we struggle to decide the kind of persons we desire to be. The arts cannot but help. I
have been remembering Jacob Lawrence's journey paintings—the
people on the railroad waiting to go north, the smoke against the sky.
I think of Toni Morrison and those journeys from the south to the
north, of the marigold beds and the loss of Pecola Breedlove (who
wanted desperately to have blue eyes), of the ties between the lost
mother, the "Wild Woman" in the southern woods, and the women
moving through Harlem on their high heels, in their thin coats (Mor-

rison, 1992). It is difficult to imagine research today that ignores this kind of psychic suffering altogether. It is hard to imagine research that ignores inequalities or the problems of second languages or the problems of desolate homes.

The time may have come again for the painting of murals, for the defining of new visions of social possibility. The time may have come for new experiments with apprenticeships, mentoring arrangements, workshops, storefront schools, playgrounds, gardens, charters, coalitions never seen before. And surely it is a moment for fresh engagements between those who are teachers and those who are newcomers, parents and children, and for tapping their perspectives on the problematic world of schools. It is a time as well for extending whatever dialogues we can open beyond our classrooms and institutions into the areas (crowded or not) where people truly live. And surely it is a time for breaking through the "sad opaqueness" of our own self-concern as well as through the self-concern of those around us.

Perhaps we can invent a future that will make whatever past we appropriate as our own part of a narrative with sense and purpose, and with the pulsating meanings for which we are all in search. Perhaps, like our predecessors in the 1930s, we can respond to a consciousness of crisis with a social intelligence attuned to the lived lives of diverse men and women, girls and boys, to their needs and their demands. Perhaps, like those who came before us in the 1960s, we can seek out the many modes of necessary liberation as we contribute to the overcoming of invisibility and silence, as we try to release the thwarted voices and open more and more situations in which people will be able to choose together and for themselves.

Becoming, for me, entails opening many windows so that those around me, like myself, will be able to see beyond the actual to a better order of things. It entails enabling more and more people to come to understand one another, whether or not they differ, to participate reflectively and passionately and cooperatively in spaces where democracy (like the marigolds) will someday take root and grow. They may be spaces where imagination can play in all its dimensions, where language can be various and vivid and clear, where automatisms may be interrupted, where freedom can appear. The becoming I have tried to describe may at length become a communal becoming, a movement where we can walk hand in hand.

I would like the unfinished conversations to be taken up again, this time against the sound of blue guitars. Poet Wallace Stevens speaks of a blue guitar as a metaphor for imagination, the blue guitar that does not play things as they are, the guitar that surprises anyone who dares to pay heed. "Things as they are," says the guitarist, "are changed upon the blue guitar" (Stevens, 1964, p. 165). Indeed, that is the task of imagination: to enable us to look at things as if they could be otherwise; to provoke us to transform.

There is another sort of music from Elizabeth Bishop's poem about the Air Force band called "View of the Capitol from the Library of Congress." She writes of the blue-uniformed members of the band playing hard and loud, but finding their music blocked by the giant trees that stand between them and the library.

> I think the trees must intervene,
>
> catching the music in their leaves
> like gold-dust, till each big leaf sags.
> Unceasingly the little flags
> feed their limp stripes into the air,
> and the band's efforts vanish there.
>
> Great shades, edge over,
> give the music room.
> The gathered brasses want to go
> *boom—boom.*   (Bishop, 1983, p. 61)

"Want to go," she writes; they are intent on going, on breaking through the blockade of trees. We might attend to those gathered brasses as we call on our own shades to edge over while our narrative takes shape, while we struggle hand in hand to become.

REFERENCES

Arendt, H. (1961). *Men in dark times.* New York: Viking Press.

Arendt, H. (1963). *Between past and future.* New York: Viking Press.

Arnow, H. (1954). *The dollmaker.* New York: Avon Books.

Bishop, E. (1983). *The complete poems: 1927-1979.* New York: Farrar, Straus & Giroux.

Camus, A. (1948). *The plague.* New York: Knopf.

Dewey, J. (1954). *The public and its problems.* Athens, OH: Swallow Press. (Original work published 1927)

Ellison, R. (1954). *Invisible man.* New York: New American Library.

Fitzgerald, F. S. (1942). *The great Gatsby.* New York: Viking Press. (Original work published 1922)

Foucault, M. (1980). *Power truth.* New York: Pantheon Press.

Goodman, P. (1960). *Growing up absurd.* New York: Random House.

Kozol, J. (1967). *Death at an early age*. Boston: Houghton Mifflin.

Kozol, J. (1992). *Savage inequalities*. New York: Crown Publishers.

Malraux, A. (1936). *Man's fate*. New York: Modern Library.

Merleau-Ponty, M. (1967). *The phenomenology of perception*. New York: Humanities Press.

Morrison, T. (1970). *The bluest eye*. New York: Washington Square Press.

Morrison, T. (1992). *Jazz*. New York: Knopf.

Sartre, J. P. (1963). *Essay on method*. New York: Knopf.

Schön, D. A. (1983). *The reflective practitioner*. New York: Basic Books.

Steinbeck, J. (1939). *The grapes of wrath*. New York: Viking Press.

Stevens, W. (1964). *The collected poems*. New York: Knopf.

Twain, M. (1959). *The adventures of Huckleberry Finn*. New York: New American Library. (Original work published 1884)

West, C. (1993). *Race matters*. Boston: Beacon Press.

Woolf, V. (1966). *Three guineas*. New York: Harvest Books. (Original work published 1938)

CHAPTER 6

A Teacher's Awesome Power

Mary Anne Raywid

Teachers don't see themselves as powerful, and in some ways, they are sadly correct in this assessment. In other ways, they are often tragically wrong. They tend to see themselves as relatively power-less—in relation to the negative external forces against which they must struggle, and in relation to the internal authority exerted over them by the system. Teachers know that many students come from homes that aren't particularly supportive of education, or where the youngsters receive little support of any kind. They realize that it is difficult to sustain much academic momentum and effort in children who are hungry, or who return daily to a physically unsafe environ-ment, or who are emotionally starved or otherwise abused. Under such conditions, efforts to educate are an uphill struggle, and it is not surprising that teachers feel powerless.

Moreover, within schools and school systems, the teacher oc-cupies the subbasement of the pyramid. Department chairs, grade-level chairs, principals, supervisors, superintendents, test makers, textbook authors, parents, and other community members, as well as legislators and governors and city council members, can all shackle, shape, or coerce teacher behavior. From the teacher's un-enviable perspective, he or she stands vulnerable on the none-too-sturdy bottom rung of the power ladder.

Teachers certainly have justification for perceiving themselves as relatively powerless. Yet there are also grounds for seeing things in a very different way—a diametrically opposed way that makes the teacher an awesomely powerful figure. This is the teacher in rela-tion to the child. Even though the teacher may be weak vis-à-vis the socioeconomic environment and the educational system, he or she is often virtually all-powerful vis-à-vis the student. A lack of awareness of this has made tyrants out of people who never intended to function that way and may not even realize that they are doing so.

Teacher power is awesome with regard to establishing and controlling the social environment of the classroom. It is the teacher who determines the roles of every person in the room and the expectations that will govern every interaction. It is the teacher who decides whether the general tone of the classroom will be relaxed and informal, friendly and supportive, brisk and businesslike, essentially competitive or cooperative. And this decision has profound implications for students and what is expected and required of them. A teacher who distributes multipaged sets of classroom rules on the first day of school makes quite different demands on students than the teacher who spends the first week having students become acquainted and helping them develop class rules. But *both* of these teachers are dictating classroom personae for the students.

It is the teacher who decides whether students will be treated as persons deserving of respect or as a group to be structured and controlled lest it get out of hand. And it is the teacher who decides what kind of power students will possess: to what extent and in what degree they will retain the power to express themselves within the classroom. Which kinds of dress and speech and decorum will be permitted and which rendered taboo? Over what matters will individuals be able to exercise choice and some control for themselves? Over what matters will there be joint and shared control such that students in effect collaborate in policy determination for the classroom? It is the teacher who decides all this. As one insightful analyst summed it up, it is the teacher who writes the constitution for the classroom, determining not only what the rules and regulations will be but also how they will be arrived at (Sarason, 1990).

Not surprisingly, then, it is customarily the teacher who unilaterally decides throughout the day what will and will not be discussed—in short, what's worth talking about. It is also the teacher who decides how matters are to be addressed—not just by whom and in what order, but the fundamental rules governing the conversation. For instance, it is the teacher who determines the extent to which negative biases and prejudices can be vented, or indeed what constitutes bias and prejudice and what does not.

The results of all these discrete decisions are powerful and ongoing. In setting the tone of the classroom climate, the roles and expectations of all, and what the conversation will be, the teacher has determined who will be the winners and who the losers, whether the classroom will represent a comfortable or an artificial environment to students, permitting unself-conscious operation or requiring guardedness and self-monitoring. And since these decisions determine which children are rewarded in school and which will succeed and thrive there, they have a profound emotional impact on youngsters, both immediate and long term. Moreover, the teacher not only has the power to reward some behavior and punish departures from it; he or she is also in a position to provide the explanations for lapses and to proceed accordingly. The teacher's role gives her or him the power to decide, for instance, that Johnny's just trying to get attention, or that Susie is emotionally troubled, or that Sam is just mean and nasty and determined to make trouble for everybody else. This means that the teacher has the power to provide the crucial explanations that guide and justify decisions: to read students' intentions and assign motives to their behavior. The power to act on such formulations can be far-reaching indeed, so far as a child's future is concerned.

To cite yet another sort of power: We are aware of the vulnerability of young children, and we recognize the power teachers can have over them when youngsters accept the teacher as a fount of knowledge and as always right, or as a figure to be emulated. What we are sometimes less aware of is the emotional impact teachers can exert on youngsters of virtually any age. One important reason is the enormous authority teachers possess within the classroom, serving as rule maker, assessor, judge, and jury in relation to their students. Another reason is that youngsters are often unaware of protections and protest procedures, and there may be no place to turn despite how bad things get. School is required. A lot of time may pass before a child is even capable of formulating a grievance or perceiving it as remediable or as the fault of someone other than himself or herself. It is this kind of naïveté, plus the imbalance in the way the resources are distributed between child and adult, professional and client, that makes youngsters so impotent and vulnerable and that transforms the teacher's considerable formal authority into power that is awesome.

One image I will always retain is of a tiny 6-year-old Filipino boy hopping around his classroom, repeating, "My teacher say I stupid. My teacher say I stupid." I have often thought of the costs that probably attached to the unforgivable comment or behavior that prompted that child's grotesque little dance around the room. The teacher's power remains, however, even after youngsters have become more aware and sophisticated. For instance, a recent study found that fifth graders actually believed that they had become more intelligent once their teachers ceased scheduling them for remedial instruction. "I used to be dumb," they said, in effect. "But now I'm just as smart as anybody" (Vosburgh, 1993). Consider, then, the enormity of the emotional impact of a teacher's fairly routine decision to enroll a student for remedial work—and of the later decision to declare such enrollment no longer preferable.

In reality, however, the youngsters who believed that their intelligence had been altered by a teacher's assignments are not totally wrong. A teacher's power is such that judgment about a child's ability, whether accurate or not, determines the kind of work laid out for and expected of that child. Thus the decision that a youngster is intellectually limited will probably restrict that child's assignments to simpler, less challenging material, which puts the teacher in the position of fulfilling his or her diagnosis. A child treated that way long enough may never be able to catch up. Such a child actually becomes intellectually limited, whether he or she started school that way or not. Through the making of such decisions, a teacher has the power to decide who will be tomorrow's leaders and professionals and who will be the laborers with far lesser rewards.

We tend to think that by adolescence many youngsters are relatively impervious to their teachers, but even those who appear most indifferent are not necessarily so at all. Indeed, one prominent theory about why students reject school—either through disruptive behavior or by dropping out—is that it is their only way to protect themselves: Their failure forces them to choose between their own self-respect and self-esteem, on the one hand, and school, on the other. The price of sticking it out in school and deferring to teachers' rules and assessments is their own positive conceptions of themselves (Gold & Mann, 1984). Under such conditions, it may well be that dropping out is the emotionally healthier response.

We know that people of any age may reject learning from an individual they dislike. It is also the case that they may reject learning from an individual they perceive to dislike them. One of the most frequent explanations dropouts give for having left school is non-caring teachers. This helps explain why some observers insist that many dropouts are really "pushouts" instead. It means that teachers, through expressions and behavior that convey indifference or hostility, have the power to make a youngster want to leave school. And once that departure has occurred, the youngster's life chances have been seriously compromised—opportunities related to employment, income, job satisfaction, and lifestyle. Thus, the emotional impact teachers have on adolescents as well as on younger students can set up a chain of events with enormous consequences. The teacher's power is indeed considerable.

We have not yet mentioned the teacher's power over the content of a student's mind. This, too, is far more substantial than we typically imagine. We know that young people are exposed to a number of powerful influences outside school—family, neighborhood, and peers, not to mention television. But it would be difficult to overrate the significance of the teacher in shaping the intellects of the youngsters in their classrooms. By the time a student graduates from high school, he or she has spent in the neighborhood of 14,000 hours under the tutelage and direction of teachers—in the only institution that is officially charged with mind and person shaping, and the only one (except, periodically, the armed forces) where the individual's attendance and participation are required by law. And it is through the role and person of the teacher that "the rubber meets the road"— that is, through whom all this authority is immediately brought to bear.

Consider that within the classroom, the teacher selects and presides over the conversation, deciding what is relevant in the first place and determining the quality of those responses and entries deemed pertinent. The teacher is also the arbiter of meaning within the room, stipulating the designation not only of words but also of gestures and actions. Moreover, it is the teacher who assigns significance and value to each of the meanings thus established. The teacher determines, for example, whether a student's brilliant insights outweigh the crude and impertinent way he sometimes presents them; or whether grammar is more important than substance; or whether in doing math and science, process is more important than product, or vice versa; or whether the possession of factual knowledge is more or less important than what one can do with it.

Perhaps even more fundamentally, it is the teacher who selects the level of discourse for the classroom and, in determining the conceptual level at which business will be conducted, sets limits on the cognitive growth likely to ensue. It is not only as content chooser that the teacher exercises power over what learning is to occur, but also as arbiter of content treatment. If material is always presented and handled in its most concrete form and application, then students are not learning to generate and deal with abstractions. But if the teacher consistently pushes beyond fill-in-the-blank questions to more intellectually demanding queries, students' capacity to cope with the world in more realistic and flexible ways is being nurtured.

The teacher's handling of content also determines students'

understanding of the way in which new knowledge should be screened for credibility and acceptance. One teacher's analytic framework may prompt her to ask of any statement that is a candidate for belief, Whose idea is it? If accepted, who would it benefit and who harm? Another teacher's analytic framework might instead recommend, With which knowledge and beliefs is this idea consistent, and with which incompatible? Yet another may be modeling questions such as, What psychological dynamics would prompt an individual to advance such an idea? The point is that the teacher's mind—his or her own analytic framework for testing and accepting knowledge— is constantly being set before the students. Inevitably it figures prominently in the way a teacher assesses student statements, and it may well be internalized by some students not as the teacher's orientation but as part of the way the world is.

Moreover, the way in which a teacher goes about his or her work, and stimulates students to go about theirs, generates particular habits of mind and of work. The teacher for whom neatness is first in importance will doubtless implant in some students the assumption that this is simply one of the world's qualities. The teacher convinced of the importance of critical mindedness and a degree of skepticism in one's comportment may implant and develop that too.

The cultivation of ideas such as these within students' heads is perhaps the most long-lasting and pervasive of teachings, because they tend to become internalized in such a way as to function as "givens," the typically unquestioned assumptions undergirding what we think and do. It is this sort of learning that prompted the most defiant—but perhaps also the most sophisticated and insightful— student rebels of the 1960s to admonish their teachers, "Don't walk through my head with your dirty feet." It wasn't so much content learnings that they were objecting to but the unconscious imbibing of orientations and perspectives too subtle and indirect for recognition, hence rejection. Certainly it is within the teacher's power to implant such learnings.

What, then, does all this mean? What does it suggest for teacher behavior? Teachers' awesome power seems to impose heavy obligations. Extensive moral responsibility flows from the power to benefit and to harm. One who has little such power has minimal responsibility to others. Conversely, one with the awesome power that teachers exert has enormous moral responsibility to those over whom he or she exerts it. Here are some of the things that such power and responsibility seem to recommend.

First, a teacher's obligations extend to all the youngsters in the classroom—not just to the eager and attractive and cooperative ones, but equally to those who appear least responsive and appealing. Indeed, because the least successful and least "worthy" student may be the neediest—and the one whom the teacher has the greatest capacity to help—such children may be precisely our most compelling moral obligation.

Second, since we know that children and adolescents—and perhaps even adults—need teachers to care about them, it appears that teachers have an obligation to at least try to establish personal relationships with their students and to cultivate appropriate ways of extending positive affect to them (Bryk & Driscoll, 1988; Noddings, 1984).

Third, perhaps teachers have an obligation to share their power. Given what we know about the role of power in eliciting the interest and engagement essential to learning, this may be necessary to teacher effectiveness and student accomplishment. As Sarason put it:

> When one has no stake in the way things are, when one's needs or opinions are provided no forum, when one sees oneself as the object of unilateral actions, it takes no particular wisdom to suggest that one would rather be elsewhere. (1990, p. 83).

And one who feels this way about school is unlikely to be an achiever. Those cast in the role of "pawns" manipulated by others are simply not likely to be effective learners (DeCharms, 1977). Thus, the teacher's obligation to enable students to succeed may in turn obligate the sharing of power with them.

Fourth, beyond the objective of enhancing teaching and learning, there is another reason that the teacher ought to deliberately devolve some of his or her power to students. Doing so is a prime way of helping them learn major lessons and acquire vital truths about the conduct of human affairs. As Sarason put it:

> the teacher should accord students the right and responsibility to participate in . . . [forging] . . . the constitution of the classroom . . . not [primarily] to come up with rules but to begin to comprehend the complexities of power in a complicated group setting. (1990, p. 85)

This lesson is crucial, say democracy's devotees, not only to citizenship education but also to peaceful coexistence in any human assemblage of any size.

Finally, and perhaps most fundamentally, the teacher's possession and constant exercise of such awesome power impose an obligation of continuing consciousness of it. The nature of the situation, with the enormous power imbalance between student and teacher, requires that if teachers are to avoid inflicting considerable harm, they must understand the inevitable asymmetry of power. An ensuing awareness of their capacity to damage other human beings must never be far from consciousness. And they can never allow themselves the luxury of what has been called "compassion fatigue."

The teacher's power is truly awesome. He or she is in a position to function as the most terrible of tyrants. Unfortunately, to the long-term detriment of children, there are teachers who consistently do so.

REFERENCES

Bryk, A., & Driscoll, M. E. (1988). *The high school as community: Contextual influences, and consequences for students and teachers*. Madison, WI: National Center on Effective Secondary Schools.

DeCharms, R. (1977). Pawn or origin? Enhancing motivation in disaffected youth. *Educational Leadership, 34*(6), 444–448.

Gold, M., & Mann, D. W. (1984). *Expelled to a friendlier place: A study of effective alternative schools*. Ann Arbor: University of Michigan Press.

Noddings, N. (1984). *Caring: A feminine approach to ethics and moral education*. Berkeley: University of California Press.

Sarason, S. B. (1990). *The predictable failure of educational reform: Can we change course before it's too late?* San Francisco: Jossey-Bass.

Vosburgh, K. L. (1993). *Remedial pullout programs: Student perceptions*. Unpublished doctoral dissertation, Hofstra University, Hempstead, NY.

CHAPTER 7

Get Ready, Get Set, Teach!

Patricia Redd Johnson

So you want to be a teacher? Well, although it may not always be an easy job to do, it can be one of the most rewarding experiences of your life. You will have the opportunity to make a powerful, positive difference in the lives of young people, who may then go out into the world to try to make it a better place.

In my experience, it is crucial that you find a mentor early in the school year—sooner if possible. Your mentor can help you think through the questions and problems that emerge in any classroom and will lessen the stress of starting a new year.

You'll probably need to know:

- Who is the assistant principal who can help organize and set up my classroom?
- Who will review my lessons?
- Who will observe me and evaluate my teaching?
- How do I learn the grading system?
- How do I design a test that will indicate how much the students have learned?
- How do I organize preparation time?
- How do I build in free time?
- Whom can I confide in when I need a solution to a persistent problem?

These are pretty straightforward, but there's much more to do to get ready.

Before you go into the classroom, you need to practice being a teacher, in the same deliberate way that an actor prepares for a role. When you were a student teacher, you always had someone in the classroom with you. Now, because you will be by yourself, you need to practice teaching with anybody you can find—a neighbor, a family member, a church or synagogue companion, or just a good friend. You can practice in front of a mirror if you like. Observe your quirks and mannerisms and decide how you can improve. In this way, you will become polished and will look pulled together in the classroom.

Students lose patience when they are struggling with a concept they do not understand. Enlist the help of other students in the class: "Who can help me explain this?" Often students will be able to connect with one another on their own terms, guiding and supporting the learning process. An added bonus is that this collaborative effort helps boost the self-esteem of students. As a teacher, you don't have to feel threatened because you and the students are engaged in the process of being both teachers and learners.

As a teacher, you'll have to learn how to improvise and be spontaneous in the classroom, based on what the students need. Allow youngsters to do the thinking; classes can be student centered, not always teacher centered. You are guiding them, but you don't need to provide all the answers. Let them struggle, take the risk of being incorrect; support them through this process. Provide a safe space for learning: Never allow students in your class to address anyone as "stupid" or "dummy."

Even with a successful group learning effort, students need one-on-one attention. I meet with students before class, during lunch, or after school. After a number of individual sessions, I establish groups of four to five students with varied learning styles to help teach one another.

Collaborative learning can be a useful way to help students overcome school fears, including the typical anxiety some kids have about taking timed tests such as the SATS. Initially, I ask students to work as a group on the individual questions without being timed. Gradually, I introduce them to answering questions under a timed deadline. Eventually, they become less intimidated and learn to relax while taking a test under a timed deadline.

A common fear is that you won't know how to answer a question. Kids know when you don't know the answer, and they'll get on you when they know that you're hedging a response. When you don't know something or you've made a mistake, admit it! Be a real risk taker and say, "I don't know the answer, but I'll try to find out for you," or, "Let's explore that together." Your students will respect your honesty; kids are less critical and judgmental when you become more human to them.

What's key to your success as a teacher is not only lesson plans and theories of learning but also how you view your profession. You start by dignifying and respecting yourself.

I have a strong sense of pride about being a teacher. In the community where I grew up, teachers were greatly respected, and they took their jobs seriously. No one ever thought to apologize for "just being a teacher." Today you hear, "Those who can, do—and those who can't, teach." This is a prejudiced statement by a misinformed public; your job is to work hard in spite of that misconception and lack of respect.

Nor should you underestimate the wonder of young people. They are too often maligned in our society when they should be appreciated and valued. When your expectations for them are high, children can perform well; when your expectations are low, children live up (or is it down?) to those expectations. Let's challenge our children to go forth and serve because our expectations for them are high. You have the awesome responsibility of being accountable to many impressionable young minds. You can make a vast difference in all our futures because you can help in the development and maturation of responsible citizens who will make their own unique contributions. By dignifying students, we dignify all our lives.

CHAPTER 8

Reconstruction Alternatives: Opening the Curriculum

Monroe D. Cohen

Welcome aboard, fellow voyagers in the moral enterprise called teaching! As you move forward in your quest to become a teacher, all of you will soon be actively involved with examining alternatives to traditional systems of schooling. For a long time I have been engaged in a similar journey—parts of which I want to share with you here.

Historically, the consideration of educational alternatives has gone in several major directions: the reconstruction of existing schools, the creation of new schools free of the present system, and, above all, the expansion of schools into the world. At various times, all three have been spotlighted by would-be educational reformers. I have remained most concerned with the first direction, the reconstruction of existing schools.

In the varied professional roles I have enjoyed through the years —as classroom teacher of children and later of adults, as editor of an educational journal, and as overseas consultant—I have witnessed a welter of proposals and counterproposals for the reform of American schools. Recently I had occasion to revisit some of the writings of Charles Silberman, a man who was once considered something of a prophet for his searing critique of our schools and of their programs of teacher preparation.

Silberman, in his book *Crisis in the Classroom* (1970), related the results of a 3½-year study compiled by him, his wife, and an extensive staff. They cite example after example of "intellectually sterile and esthetically barren" (p. 10) classrooms and of a lack of civility on the part of teachers and administrators. "Education," Silberman says, "should prepare people not just to earn a living but to live a life—a *creative, humane, and sensitive life*. This means that the schools must provide a liberal, humanizing education" (p. 114). Out of such schools, he predicted, will come the humanized future educators, those who believe with Alfred North Whitehead that education is the "acquisition of the art of the *utilization* of knowledge" (Whitehead, 1929, p. 6).

Silberman not only documents ways that many of our schools fail dismally but also gives examples of schools that succeed. Especially he points to experimentation in the British infant schools and to American schools based on their model. He makes a strong case for so-called informal education, or what soon came to be called "open" education. To a large extent on the basis of Silberman's recommendations, many school boards, principals, and teachers jumped on the open education bandwagon. That troubled me back then, over 20 years ago. It still troubles me, although I personally came to *favor* the informal school idea in general and the British schools in action (more about that soon). What bothered me, in essence, was the indiscriminate rush to a new educational fad or label as a quick, convenient way to solve our problems. American educators have seen a number of such instant panaceas come and go, such as programmed instruction, team teaching, nongrading, educational television, and computer-based interactive technology.

I remember well a conversation with Roy Illsley, onetime headmaster of Battling Brook County Primary School in Leicestershire, who was much in demand as a conductor of workshops in the United States based on methods used in his British classes. Illsley spoke of the 25 to 30 years of experimentation that preceded the development of informal education programs in England and expressed his dismay over the *oversimplification* that often greeted him in his workshop classes.

Just what was it that all the zealots meant by open education? To some, open education referred to openness of space, so it was often characterized by informal physical arrangements—perhaps removing walls or replacing desks with tables. Some suburban communities moved quickly to demonstrate new learning places they called "open classrooms." To others, open education meant primarily openness of prescribed curriculum content, so they interpreted it as requiring a greatly increased amount of "stuff"—concrete materials, some prepackaged and expensive, most simple and inexpensive. Open education was occasionally viewed as organizational change: a varied mix of ages or increased flexibility of schedule or emphasis on individual rather than group activity.

But too often, open education did not move beyond the adjective and noun stage. Once, in my "Over the Editor's Desk" column in *Childhood Education*, I addressed this point and suggested that we might do better if we thought more in terms of verbs: *opening* education, *doing* education, *making* education. Alas, column space ran out before I could amplify on these points. I ask your indulgence as I seek to pick up where I left off.

By referring, in a very personal way, to some of my own experiences in schools in this country and abroad, let me suggest to you that all the world's children need the following kinds of learning if we are truly to open up education. They need to:

learn by laughing
learn by playing
learn by meditating
learn by forming
learn by modeling
learn by communing
learn by exploring various ways of knowing

I would like to touch briefly on each of these points.

First, children *need the opportunity to learn by laughing.* Of all Silberman's criticisms of the schools he saw, perhaps the most damning was his description of their "grim joylessness" (1970, p. 10). In classroom after classroom, solemn-faced teachers and solemn-faced children appeared to be serving time, without zest or interest.

Laughter breaks up old molds of fear and incapacity. How many times have we said, as we rocked back with a good laugh, "That breaks me up!" "Stop," we plead, "my sides are splitting!" What would happen if we really put our minds to making classrooms centers of joy and festivity? Let's be clear that this question is not asking how to revive teacher fun in the classroom: fun with numbers, fun with Dick and Jane. I believe it was John Holt who wisely observed that children quickly learn that when adults say that they're going to like something, they're going to have to do it whether they like it or not.

To do a bit of homemade action research on this topic, I asked my youngest son, Jem, to help with the problem. About all he could come up with was, "Maybe we could tell jokes and riddles once in a while—I mean, not just at recess." But I remember his enthusiastic descriptions of the teachers he most liked. "Miss Morse, she's always kidding around. Mr. Carter, the science man, he's always making puns. Miss Stewart, the physical education teacher, she sings the jump-rope rhymes right along with us, and Mrs. Logan read us *A Rocket in My Pocket* with all those funny poems."

I remember another teacher who decided to bring the underground press idea above ground by encouraging his children to write their own humorous reports to parents of what was happening in the classroom. The first edition was known as *The Strain on the Brain News,* the next one *The Knock-Kneed News*. Folks could hardly wait for the third!

Some years later, during my stint as an educational consultant on a Teachers College, Columbia University team in Afghanistan, laughter served my family and me well when we found ourselves struggling with strange-sounding and strange-feeling customs. The first time my wife and I walked into a bazaar, a marketplace in Kabul, it was like being transplanted back across centuries, back to scenes that could have come from the Bible. Everywhere were bearded men of all shapes and sizes with turbans and long, striped, collarless coats. We were surrounded by unfamiliar sounds and smells and sober looks. It was frightening. And then a child smiled at us, and we smiled back. Then more smiles came our way, from every direction, from men who moments before had appeared so fierce. To this day, when I think of an Afghan bazaar, I think not just of rugs and pistachio nuts and fat-tailed sheep and artistic piles of pomegranates. I think of white teeth in bushy black beards and of a remarkably independent, robust, and laughing people. Once we were able to laugh, we were able to learn about places and peoples and ways of living that were drastically different from our own.

Only about 10 of every 100 Afghan children attend schools of any kind. Their learning by laughing comes from rich tribal traditions. They enjoy, for example, a wonderful folk simpleton named Mullah Nasrudin, who helps them relax from their serious concerns, their never-ending search for *naan,* the precious flat slabs of whole wheat bread that provide their major sustenance. Most Afghan schools that do exist are dreary and solemn places, but I knew of one warm, wise teacher who frequently brought Mullah Nasrudin stories into his classroom and enlivened the days with the sweet balm of laughter.

What examples can *you* provide—or have your children create—to help children learn by laughing?

Point number two is that children *need to learn by playing*. Today's revived interest in Piaget, in "whole language" and "constructivism," is helping to give rational support to the overwhelming importance of play experiences in children's concept building.

Political scientist Karl Deutsch (1971), of Harvard and MIT, used to speak of Thorstein Veblen's description of the ethics of the kindergarten, "where joy and sharing and cooperating reign" (p. 235). Deutsch himself characterized kindergartens as places where combinative play contributes to processes of "strategic search" and "strategic simplification," which feed into later scientific learnings. It is intriguing to know that the great Frank Lloyd Wright ascribed his interest in architecture to his days playing with blocks or "gifts" in a Froebelian kindergarten. But with notable exceptions here and there, the blocks and the sand and the water pans that still thankfully appear in many nursery schools and kindergartens are disappearing from the first grades up, to reappear if at all in engineers' and architects' graduate schools.

Children also can gain much by what may seem like inaction. Children *need to learn by meditating*. For the next image, I take you on a visit to a British infant school. My whole family (my wife and three sons) had been invited to accompany me on a trek to the famed Sea Mills School in Bristol. The event remains vivid in my consciousness, thanks to a little 8-mm film made by my oldest son, Adam, an aspiring filmmaker.

While there we saw a dance performance, an astonishing fairytale mime put on by a group of 30 children, with absolutely no adult direction. We had glimpses of a host of other small group and individual activities, from counting eggs in the school's own hen coop, to bird-watching, to seashell sorting, to "maths" explorings. Here the blocks and sandboxes and water pans had not disappeared. They were everywhere in sight and in use. But my favorite memory is of a sunny-haired girl of 6 or 7 sitting in a little rocker in a corner alcove, with a book in her lap. The book lies open, but she is not looking at it. Instead, she is rocking gently to and fro and musing, with a quizzical smile on her face. No other child is near. No teacher is near either to urge her on to the next page or the next lesson, to ask why she is wasting time. To me, she seemed clearly to be making time—if you will, to be *making* her education.

Again I ask, what can we do in our classrooms, not in some unforeseeable future, but *now*, to help children learn by meditating? How do we loosen up space and time and content to allow it?

That leads us to point number four. Children *need the opportunity to learn by forming*. The late Harold Rugg gave us a credo to print on flying banners: "I say what I feel with form" (often cited in his "Education and Creative America" classes, which I attended at Teachers College, Columbia University, in the fall of 1949; for amplification, see Rugg's seminal book *Imagination* [1963], especially Chapters 6 and 7).

My mind's eye shifts to Salvador da Bahia, the graceful colonial-style capital of a huge state in eastern Brazil. There you will find the Escola Parque, a kind of educational park, where four huge Quonset huts house centers to which children from four slum feeder schools come to spend half of every day and participate in a variety of activities. Not 2 or 3 but 30 or 40 options are provided—many forms of physical exercise, singing, dancing, weaving, painting, cooking, even shoe making. Murals flow over the walls. Music saturates the atmosphere. And everywhere is the sound of children laughing. These Bahiano children were once written off as nonachievers, as ne'er-do-wells, in the way that too many children throughout the world continue to be written off by schools that do not move out to meet them where they are.

Children also *need to learn by modeling*. For a parallel to my experience at the Escola Parque, I ask you to join me on another swing around the globe, this time to Tashkent, Uzbekistan, showcase city of the central Asian republic of the former Soviet Union. We will pass by the model school that I was allowed to visit under the close supervision of an Intourist guide. But far more impressive were the after-school, extracurricular sessions in a nearby Pioneer Palace. Again an unbelievably rich program unfolded, offering a broad spectrum of experiences in art, dramatics, model building, radio programming, and movie making.

You may say that we can easily match these activities in any of a number of our neighborhood recreation centers. But something special was happening in the Pioneer Palace in Tashkent. In every group, a special person—a special model, if you will—was brought before the children. Heading the radio laboratory was one of the leading engineers from a nearby research institute. In the dramatics workshop was an honored actress of the Tashkent Art Theater. And commanding the full attention of the roomful of lovely young aspiring ballerinas was the prima ballerina of the municipal ballet company.

To be sure, everywhere were paintings, photos, busts of Lenin. But the immediate "people" environment provided much more than political propaganda. It provided an opportunity for identification with sympathetic guides who represented high qualities of dedication and achievement, along with the ability to relate responsively.

Children need such relatedness, and they *need to learn by communing*. The dictionary defines "to commune" this way: "to converse or confer together; to take counsel, to converse intimately, to hold spiritual or confidential intercourse." If we were to use the term "commune" loosely, many of the experiences just described could be considered communal sharings—the bazaar visit in Afghanistan, the sea of sharings at the Escola Parque in Bahia, or the Tashkent Pioneer Palace. The fantastic 4-day-and-night spectacle of the Carnival in Rio is perhaps the world's most spectacular example of a group communal rite.

During my second year of teaching, I had a couple of memorable experiences with learning by communing. After a year of teaching children in a fancy upper-middle-class community in Westchester County, New York, I had moved to Corpus Christi, Texas, where I was assigned to work with a fifth grade of Mexican Americans. I told my new charges, "Look, I'll make a deal with you. I may know a little about New York City, but I know nothing about Corpus Christi. If you'll teach me some things about Corpus, I'll teach you some things about New York." That led to a series of lively after-school excursions. We proceeded to make visits to an oil rig, to a fleet of shrimp fishermen, and to see real cowboys (at the million-acre King Ranch). And then through slides and movies and books, I shared scenes of the Empire State Building and Times Square and Yankee Stadium. These close-up sharings provided an invaluable bonding between the youngsters and me.

Later we were able to extend this communing when we viewed a remarkable film called *People Along the Mississippi*. It was about a Native American boy named Robert Bigras who lived on an Indian reservation in Minnesota, near the headwaters of the Mississippi River. The movie depicted him launching a little wooden boat he had carved and sending it on a journey down the river, toward New Orleans. At the suggestion of one of the fifth graders, we wrote to Encyclopaedia Britannica Films to find out if we could get Robert Bigras's address. To our delight, they put us in touch with him. We then wrote to him with a proposition: "We'll tell you about Corpus Christi if you'll tell us about your life and your people there in Minnesota." What followed was another series of sharings. Our class designed a huge "postcard" with many pockets into which went their stories and poems, paintings and carvings, and sand and seashells from the Gulf of Mexico. Soon after, Robert Bigras sent us similar memorabilia from his life on the reservation. The terms "Indian" and "Native American" took on very personal meanings for all of us.

I am pleading, however, not just for such dramatic, large-group sharings but also for a narrower, deeper sense of communion: "to converse intimately"—child with fellow child, child with adult, adult with adult, one human being with another, and also with oneself.

Finally, children *need to learn by exploring various ways of knowing*. Through the years, one of the most powerful approaches to opening the curriculum has been to focus on interdisciplinary learning. The traditional academic disciplines can be regarded as distinctive strategies of inquiry, which can productively be related to one another in thematic studies.

I have been privileged to see vital applications of this "learning across boundaries" at the Louis Armstrong Middle School in East Elmhurst, Queens, New York. There, a team of teachers representing seven disciplines (history, literature, linguistics, science, mathematics, music, and video arts) has been collaborating with other teams of teachers and students to make connections that have expanded the prescribed curriculum of sixth- and seventh-grade classes. Utilizing some of the "multiple intelligences" theories of psychologist Howard Gardner (first presented in his seminal 1983 book *Frames of Mind*), the team has pursued themes designed to develop a range of ways of knowing that acknowledge students' diverse learning styles and cultural backgrounds.

For example, the team selected the theme of the village and launched a series of investigations that engaged students in using strategies often employed by professionals—historians, mathematicians, linguists, ethnographers, and sociologists. Groups of children conducted oral-history interviews, did extensive library research, and then made decisions about the locales of their imaginary villages, taking into account such factors as climate, flora and fauna, and other natural resources. Making use of computer technology, they produced newsletters to share their findings. Other groups invented original languages and number systems, composed myths and chants, experimented with herbal medicines, developed museum exhibits, and performed a pageant for visiting classes. In the second year of the program, the focus shifted to such themes as the election process and a many-sided recreation of colonial life.

In the same school, an itinerant poet-in-residence, Richard Lewis, has been working for a number of years with teachers and students in exploring other thematic studies (the sea, the sky, the earth) that emphasize the nurturing of the imagination and result in an amazing flowering of projects in the arts. Sometimes Mr. Lewis brings other poets and storytellers into the school to make presentations that focus on the current theme. Special events often include excursions—to the Metropolitan Museum, the American Museum of Natural History, the Center for Inter-American Relations, the Asia Society, the Aquarium for Wildlife Conservation, and more. A celebration of the birthday of the sun, for example, featured a reading of the sun myths of the Aztecs, a viewing of sundials in the Shakespearean Garden in Central Park and in the Brooklyn Botanic Garden, and a dance-music drama "The Sun." Festive culminations of the year-long projects have included original theater pieces, dances, and exhibitions in the school museum of the art and writing of the children who participated.

As I think of the various approaches to learning cited above, I am brought around full circle to the beginning of our discourse. Of all the alternatives proposed above for the reconstructing of our schools, I share the spreading conviction that the informal education or open education approach offers particular hope of enlarging the scope of children's learnings. And the integrated day, family grouping concepts appear to be built around the cornerstone of our basic premise that the child must be helped to make his or her own education, to *do* education rather than wait passively to *be* educated. The child is inventor, not invention.

So all the nouns—the informal physical arrangements of many of these schools, the amount of materials (learning stuff) they contain, the individual as well as group activity, perhaps above all the respect for the model provided by teachers who are free to commune on their own terms in their own way—could provide lessons to be treasured if we keep clearly before us the underlying assumptions about what children are like and how they learn.

I heartily endorse a dusting off and careful reperusal of the justly famed (though too seldom read) Plowden report on the British primary school, which affords a beautifully lucid statement as the basis for its recommendations: "At the heart of the educational process lies the child" (Her Majesty's Stationery Office, 1967, Vol. 1, p. 7).

For those who ask for more extensive measures of the success of these methods, much of the evidence is already in. One needs to look not just at test scores but at the absorption of children in their work, the high demands placed on them to produce to their utmost capacity, the nature of their talking, the quality of their writing, the richness of their painting. Harder to measure but clearly present is enlargement of their capacity for initiative and responsibility.

Teaching and learning, process and product, are inextricably linked. The job of a teacher is to further the process of growth, to remove shackles that might restrict the learner from pursuing exploration that can bring about experimentation, discovery, and self-discovery. Teachers should be free-ers.

REFERENCES

Deutsch, K. (1971). Relating and responding: The adult. *Changing Attitudes in a Changing World*. New York: Bank Street College of Education.
Gardner, H. (1983). *Frames of mind*. New York: Basic Books.
Her Majesty's Stationery Office. (1967). *Children and their primary schools* (2 vols.) (Report of the Central Advisory Council for Education [England]). London: Author.
Rugg, H. (1963). *Imagination*. New York: Harper and Row.
Silberman, C. E. (1970). *Crisis in the classroom*. New York: Random House.
Whitehead, A. N. (1929). *The aims of education and other essays*. New York: Macmillan.

CHAPTER 9

Building a Safe Community for Learning

Mara Sapon-Shevin

Visiting my students in the field, I have the opportunity to go into a lot of classrooms. I get to absorb little snatches of conversation, notice what hangs on the walls and how the room is arranged, observe a wide range of lessons and management strategies. And always, if I allow myself to notice, I have feelings about what I see and hear. I enter one classroom and am immediately struck by a feeling of gloom —tension, uneasiness, silence or bickering, a sense that all is not well in the world. The teacher is yelling, threatening, brow furrowed and intense, unhappy with this stance but somehow resigned to it. Entering another classroom, the easy joyfulness strikes me just as quickly— students talking, sharing, heads bent together over a shared project, the teacher talking, laughing, smiling, joking, the atmosphere light and alive with energy. How does one make sense of this contrast? Luck of the draw? Did one teacher just get all the "bad students" and another teacher the "good ones"? Explanations that center around "What can you expect from students who come from backgrounds like these?" or "When you teach in the city you have to yell to establish and maintain discipline" ring false when the two classrooms described above are in the same building, at the same grade level, drawing from the same population of students.

Teaching involves making an immense number of decisions, and all these decisions have an impact on how students will learn, how they will treat one another, and what the classroom atmosphere will feel like:

Mr. Rimaldi passes back the math exams—in descending order of grades. By the time he gets to the bottom of the pile,

99

many of the students are snickering. Jason, who receives his last, is trying to act casual, but he shifts in his chair and his discomfort is clear. Another student calls out, "Way to go, Jason."

Ms. Herbert takes roll in the morning. After each absent child's name is noted, she comments that he or she will be missed and asks for volunteers to copy assignments, take handouts, and call the student that evening. She points out that the classroom community is not complete and expresses her hope that it will be restored soon.

Ms. Boyle talks excitedly about the upcoming Christmas holiday. She describes, at length, her own plans and the Christmas activities that will take place in class—a play, a party, decorations, singing, and an assembly. Almost as an aside, she remembers and adds, "Of course, not everyone celebrates this holiday," and then continues detailing the schedule.

When Mr. Danvers returns to his class after recess, he finds that one of the students has called the class to the rug for an emergency meeting. There has been an incident of racial name calling on the playground and the students want to discuss it. Students share what happened and generate a plan for addressing the problem with the students involved. As a group, they agree to meet again in a week to follow up on what has happened.

Each of the scenarios described above reflects something about classroom community. The kinds of decisions these teachers have made—often decisions within other decisions—have implications for the ways in which students will interact within the classroom and beyond. Deciding to return papers by grade has an impact on how Jason sees himself and is seen by others. Ms. Herbert's style of roll taking and attention to absentees change the ways in which students will talk about and respond to returning students. Ms. Boyle's apparent disregard for cultural, economic, and religious differences in planning a Christmas curriculum will affect Marya's willingness to talk about Kwanzaa, Noah's comfort in talking about Chanukah, and Paul's openness in describing his family's hard times which will make Christmas difficult for them. Mr. Danvers's establishment of classroom meeting times and spaces and his comfort with student initiation and leadership provide opportunities for students to think together about important issues like racism.

Teacher education programs have courses called Math Methods and Curriculum Design, but rarely is there a course entitled Building Safe, Inclusive Classrooms or Creating Hospitable Communities. For the most part, little direct attention is paid to issues of classroom climate and student-student interaction; such concerns are sometimes subsumed under topics such as classroom management or curriculum planning, but rarely are teachers encouraged to explore and strategize about how community is created and nourished. And so I wish to share here some of my thinking about the importance of community building and the ways in which such concerns must assume primary rather than secondary status in thinking about teaching.

I begin all my classes and educational presentations with singing. I teach a song to the whole group, often one about community or connection, and encourage full participation. Hesitant voices and embarrassment generally abate as the collective of strong voices produces a powerful and pleasing sound. And then I ask, "Why did I begin with singing?" Generally, people answer, "Because it's fun"; "Because it is something we should be doing with children"; "Because it helps break the tension." And often, someone will comment, "Because it builds a sense of community—because we sound better together than we would individually." From that point of departure, we discuss what makes a community and explore times when the students or participants have experienced a sense of community. People share memories of hiking trips, school plays, church organizations, political rallies, and other times when they worked together toward a common goal. Words like "friendship," "trust," "respect," and "caring" become part of the discussion as people describe the ways in which the community transcended individual differences and difficulties.

My next question is harder: "Well, I just led the first song; which of you would feel comfortable coming up here to lead the next one?" A few brave hands are raised. "Well then," I continue, "which of you would rather die first?" There is always nervous laughter and a spate of hands. And then the final, most central question is posed: "For those of you who would rather die first, what would it take—what conditions would have to be met—for you to be comfortable coming up to lead a song?"

"I'd have to know a song." "I'd want someone to do it with me."

"I'd want to know that everyone else would be doing it too." And then, the bottom line: "I'd want to be promised that no one would laugh. That no one would make fun of me or embarrass me." They want *Safety*: the safety to learn and to fail; the safety to show oneself fully and be appreciated or at least supported; the safety to succeed and the safety to be imperfect; the safety from humiliation, isolation, stigmatization, alienation from the group. This is the essence of community. A community is a safe space to grow, a space that welcomes you fully, that sees you for who you are, that invites your participation, and that holds you gently while you explore.

Can classrooms be made safe? In a time when keeping children from physical harm seems difficult enough, can we create classrooms that also feel psychologically safe? Emotionally safe? Can we create classrooms that welcome children for who they are, give them opportunities to know one another in a deep way, and encourage their interaction? This, to me, is the most important challenge to any teacher: creating a space safe enough for students to be themselves, to stretch toward others, to learn, and to help one another.

In order to focus on community building as an essential component of teaching, one must accept the following premise: *Time spent building community is never wasted time*. Community building is not what you do if you have time, or only for the first 2 days of class. Building a solid, safe community must be a priority and an ongoing commitment. Many of the tasks that teachers wrestle with throughout the school year can be more easily negotiated if there is a good classroom community. Individualizing instruction is less likely to be met with complaints ("Why doesn't Michael have to do the same problems?") when students know and understand one another's individual differences. Cooperative group work, fast becoming an organizing principle in many classrooms, requires a firm foundation of positive interpersonal skills in order to be successful, and the everyday conflicts that occur in classroom settings can be resolved far more smoothly when students know and trust one another.

In a recent course called Cooperative Classrooms, Inclusive Communities, my coteacher, Sarah Pirtle, and I spent a full hour talking about class norms and agreements with the group. We discussed and agreed to norms of confidentiality so that people could share freely without fear that their words would come back to haunt them. The class agreed to work at implementing a standard of "no put-downs of self and others." The ensuing discussion—"What if I really am bad at something and want to say it?" and "What if someone else says something that I find offensive?"—led us to establish additional procedures for resolving conflicts in ways that felt honest and forthright. The time spent engaging in this discussion was not something we rushed through in order to get to the heart of the class—the "real content." Having this discussion together, modeling ways of speaking, asking questions and disagreeing respectfully, and acknowledging the importance of having such a discussion *was* the content of this class.

Later in the week, a discussion of racism in American schools produced considerable discomfort and even anger. One student's comment was difficult for the others to hear, and the temptation to marginalize that student was evident. But Sarah and I, as teachers, were able to remind the students of our agreements about "no side conversations" and "talking to people directly about what's bothering you" and to urge them, as they left for lunch, to remember that our class was committed to hanging together through adversity so that we all could learn and grow, to open and honest discussion, and to listening well to one another. What might have been a major disruption in the classroom and the occasion for the isolation of particular students became, instead, a real-life example of the importance of setting a tone, of making the goal of community explicit, of taking the time to notice and care how people are being treated by others.

Although we all might agree that having a community is important, how do we know when we have one? What are some of the markers of community, and how can teachers foster a genuine sense of connectedness and concern in the classroom? Student teachers returning from the field often share observations regarding the ways in which students interact, and these can be regarded as indications of the quality of the classroom community—a way of "taking the community's temperature" as an indication of its health:

> In one classroom, the students are assigned to read with a partner every day. They can go wherever they want in the classroom, and they take turns reading to each other. The teacher selects these partners by drawing two tongue depressors (with students' names on them) out of a can. It is noticeable that when the teacher announces the selection—Freda and Manolita, Jeremy and Shamira, Nicole and Danielle— there are no groans, no "Oh, yuck"s, or "I'm not reading with her." This is a healthy community.

> In the cafeteria, children are teasing one another about what is in their lunches. "You eat tofu—that's disgusting." "Why

doesn't your mother pack you a real lunch?" "How come you don't eat meat—that's weird." One child is reduced to tears and dumps her lunch in the wastebasket. This is a community that needs work.

In a school that includes students with disabilities as full members of regular classrooms, a boy is helping a classmate learn to navigate on a three-wheeler in the hallways. A visitor stops, addresses the boy, and asks, "What grade are you in?" "I'm in sixth grade," he replies, "and [indicating his friend] so is she." The message is clear: She may not talk, but she's part of our class. Don't leave her out, even in your question. This is an inclusive community.

What are the underlying values and priorities that support community building? How can classrooms be structured so that they move toward cohesion and support rather than toward fragmentation and distancing?

COMMUNITIES PROVIDE OPPORTUNITIES TO SHOW OURSELVES FULLY

A safe classroom community is one in which students are comfortable showing themselves, being themselves, and being honest about who and what they are. Think about your friends. Who are the friends who know you really well—and still like you? Aren't they the ones who have seen you at your best, but also at your worst? The ones to whom you respond with the truth when they ask how you are, and you're not doing well? The ones who listen well? How does one create that kind of safety in the classroom?

I often begin class with "News and Goods." We take turns going around the room with each student offering something good that has happened in his or her life recently. In the beginning, the offerings are often limited: "I saw a good movie last night"; "I got a new sweater yesterday." As the group members begin to know and trust one another, they share more fully: "I had a wonderful talk with my best friend last night and I feel really good about our relationship"; "I found out that my sister is pregnant and I'm going to be an aunt." And sometimes, "I have nothing good to share—my whole life is a mess," to which others may respond with sympathy and support; often a touch on the hand is offered by the person in the next seat.

Students are allowed to "pass" if they wish, and no one is forced to share. But there are also firm guidelines about how the group listens—no interruptions, no laughing, no snickering, no remarks. Each person's turn is sacred—his or her time for personal sharing— and the structure is not competitive. I explain repeatedly that we can figure out ways to be supportive of one another. One person's triumph in no way diminishes another's. Patty's delight at passing her math test is in no way minimized by the fact that Larry got a perfect score on his. We are, each of us, working on different things, struggling with different issues. We can support one another. It is possible for us to be proud of ourselves and of one another when the competitive element is removed.

Teachers working in classroom settings that include students with disabilities are especially conscious of the need to establish an atmosphere in which every person's accomplishments can be noted and appreciated. Karen's learning to tie her shoelaces is a major triumph for her, even though her classmate Morgan has been tying hers for years. Annabel's struggle (and victory) over spelling is worthy of celebration because she has worked hard and improved. It is not celebrated only if it is the "best" spelling paper or a "perfect" paper.

It is difficult for many people to accept compliments. They hem and haw and look the other way. "Thanks for saying I'm pretty, but actually I've gained weight and I'm fat"; "The report wasn't really as great as you think—I left out an important part and it should have been better." Accepting appreciation from others is problematic, particularly for women, because often we have not experienced the safety to be proud of ourselves. Feeling "too good" about yourself can feel dangerous, like looking for criticism. So we have learned to diminish our own accomplishments, to put ourselves down before someone else does. Creating a space in which people can be proud of themselves should be a central organizing principle of classrooms. Delighting in and sharing genuine accomplishments is distinguishable from "bragging" or "showing off" when it occurs within the context of community; arrogance, egotism, and self-absorption are fueled by competition, insensitivity, and real or perceived scarcity of success, all of which are antithetical to true community. Teachers must ask themselves: How can I create multiple opportunities for people to share and celebrate their triumphs and ensure that all people in the class are acknowledged? How can I make that opportunity safe for all class members? How can I remove the competitive orientation that often surrounds feeling good about oneself?

A classroom that feels safe to students allows them to be proud of their accomplishments, but it also allows opportunities to be honest about their needs and to ask for support. In a seventh-grade classroom, I heard a boy proclaim loudly, "I don't understand the math." Immediately, three students rushed over to help him. This student had the safety to share his frustration and to ask for help. The teacher in that classroom had provided a space in which such a request could be issued and had established classroom norms that allowed other students to offer support and assistance.

I was stunned when my older daughter came home from seventh grade one day and announced, "Today at lunch, I learned to tell time."

"What do you mean?" I asked. "You already knew how to tell time, didn't you?"

"No," she explained, "actually, I never understood it. I always had a digital watch so I never really learned the other way. But I told some kids at lunch and they showed me how it worked and now I understand."

I was awed that she had felt enough safety with her peers—other 12- and 13-year-olds—to let them in on what had been a well-maintained (even from her mother) secret. And I was further touched by the fact that they had responded to her not with scorn or derision but with support and teaching. This experience speaks volumes to children's abilities to learn quickly and painlessly when they feel supported and safe.

COMMUNITIES PROVIDE OPPORTUNITIES
TO KNOW OTHERS WELL

Opportunities to show ourselves fully provide the possibility of knowing others well. When a safe community has been created and maintained, we can notice Rena's physical characteristics and the fact that she reads well, but we can also learn that she is struggling with her fear of the dark and her worry about nuclear war, that she is having a hard time with her older sister at home and is hoping to be a carpenter when she grows up. We can learn enough about Rena, in her many facets, to enable us to find similarities and differences, spaces and ways to connect.

Many years ago, I gave workshops for teachers on how to teach students about differences and disabilities. One teacher approached me after such a workshop and said something that profoundly changed my orientation to the issue. "You know," she said, "my special education students are painfully aware of the ways in which they are different from other students. What they don't see are the ways in which they are similar."

Since that time, it has become even clearer to me that we must help students see both the ways in which they are different and the characteristics, needs, fears, and skills they share. Focusing exclusively on differences can result in the ultimate alienation: There is no one here like me, so I must be all alone. Focusing exclusively on similarities can result in making children's unique characteristics invisible, for example, not noting that Shamika is African American or that Nicole uses facilitated communication to talk. One teacher put up a grid in her classroom, with each child's name written across the top and down the side. During the course of the year, they were responsible for finding one similarity with every other person in the class. In the square that was the intersection of their own name, they were asked to share one thing that was unique about themselves.

I have my students engage in a diversity treasure hunt during class. They circulate with papers and pencils and are asked to find people who fit into different categories:

> Find someone who grew up with an older relative.
> Write his or her name here _____.
> What's one thing that person learned from the older relative?

> Find someone whose parents come from another country.
> Write his or her name here _____.
> What's one tradition or custom that person has learned from his or her parents?

> Find someone who has a family member with a disability.
> Write his or her name here _____.
> What's something that person has learned by interacting with the person with a disability?

The rules are that you can write someone's name down only once, that is, you must talk to 10 different people if there are 10 items on the list. Students are encouraged to seek out people they don't know. The room typically buzzes with stories, laughter, delight in finding someone who fits into a category. People often find themselves sharing and listening to stories that they don't typically tell: about a younger brother with cerebral palsy and how hard it is when people stare or make fun of him; about a grandmother from Italy who makes wonderful cakes. After people are finished, they are asked to share what they have learned. People listen attentively as Michael shares what he learned from Janet, as Carmen shares the funny story she heard from Dwayne. Students begin to realize connections that they can build on: Discovering a shared interest in turtles leads to an exchange of books; hearing about someone else's triumph in learning to swim after many years leads to an offer to go to the pool together.

The classroom conversation and interaction after this exercise are always deeper, richer. The safety of the community and the structure for sharing allow people to see one another and to be seen as well. Teachers have also used this activity to alter students' perceptions in specific ways. Juan, who has just moved from Mexico, has been isolated because of his language difference. The question that says "Find someone who was born in another country and can teach you a phrase in his or her language" makes Juan a necessary and valued part of the group activity; his differences are honored, not hidden, acknowledged, not ignored.

Just as learning to say nice things about oneself is challenging, learning to notice and appreciate others (and accept that appreciation) can be equally difficult. One teacher designates a "Child of the Week" (with each student getting a turn). That child brings in things to share (family artifacts and photographs, if they are available) and is interviewed by classroom reporters (with the right to pass on any question). The week ends for Tyler, the child in the spotlight this week, with every student contributing a page to a book whose theme is "what we like about Tyler." The teacher reports that she has had to do very little coaching about how to write "nice things" and that the students notice and appreciate many different qualities and characteristics of the child: "Tyler has a good sense of humor. He makes me laugh." "Tyler let me share his sandwich when I forgot my lunch money last week." "Tyler is really good at drawing pictures of dinosaurs."

Other opportunities abound for noticing others and appreciating them. My daughter Dalia developed a Thanksgiving ritual that I have translated for the classroom. She gives each person at the table enough little slips of paper for every other person and asks them to write one thing they like or appreciate about each person. Little people who cannot write are encouraged to draw or dictate their messages. All the slips of paper are put in a box, and the box is then passed around the table. Each person takes a turn drawing out a slip of paper and reading it: "I like Annegret's warmth and the way she reaches out to people"; "I like the way Lucy giggles when something is funny and makes everyone else giggle too." The slip of paper is then given to the person it is about. Although receiving compliments graciously is difficult for some people, I have never yet seen a person who did not take these little slips of paper home, tucked in a purse or a shirt pocket. Many people have reported, years later, that they still have these pasted on their mirrors or on their desks.

At the end of a class that had used cooperative learning family groups all semester, I gave each member a piece of paper that said:

My name:
My group says that I'm . . .

I want to remember that . . .

Each group member wrote affirmations and appreciations for every other group member: "I love the way you kept us going when we got discouraged"; "I appreciate how much you know about different topics and your willingness to share." Each person completed the last section individually. "I want to remember that I have friends in this class"; "I want to remember that other people think I'm smart and worth having around."

As the level of safety increases, we can encourage students to see and know one another at deeper levels. In Australia recently, I asked teachers to bring in and share objects that were important to them. People brought seashells, old photographs, a precious ring, a treasured poem, and an old doll. After they had shared these objects with the group, I asked not "What did Sharon share?" but "What did you learn *about* Sharon from what she shared?" People's responses were profound: "I learned that relationships are very important to Susan—she cares deeply about her friends." "I learned that Keith loves nature and that he really notices the beauty around him." And, perhaps most touchingly, about a woman whose outward reserve could have been perceived as standoffishness, "I learned that there's a lot more to Mary than meets the eye. She really has a deep, spiritual side to her." Several were quite moved during the sharing experience. The joy of being seen so clearly and so fully by relative strangers was overwhelmingly affirming.

COMMUNITIES PROVIDE OPPORTUNITIES
TO REACH OUT, CONNECT, AND HELP

The third component of community building is the chance for students to interact with one another positively, helping and supporting one another, teaching and sharing their skills and strengths. When an atmosphere has been created in which people freely share who they are and learn about others, the possibilities for connection are boundless. For example, I have students complete a classroom yellow pages in which they designate those areas in which they can give help or support:

> HELP OFFERED:
> Able to teach double Dutch jump roping
> Know how to make friendship bracelets
> Am good at remembering my assignments

Students can also ask for help or support in a range of areas:

> HELP WANTED:
> Want to learn to play four-square on the playground
> Need help figuring out what to do with someone on the play-
> ground who is bugging me
> Want support for not wasting time and getting my work done
> so I don't have to miss recess

Students are encouraged to find and support one another. The class is not divided into "those who need help" and "those who give help." Every child is both a teacher and a learner, a person who gives support and receives it.

In another classroom that included a child with challenging disabilities, the classroom teacher was eager to encourage support for her without stigmatizing her further. Rather than listing only Arden's goals on the board for the class to see, she invited each student to write a weekly goal and paste it on his or her desk. Students were invited to set their own goals (finishing my math, not getting into fights at lunch, reading more) and to figure out ways of supporting one another. Rather than marginalizing Arden as the only one with an educational goal in the classroom, the only person who needed help, the structure encouraged all students to see themselves as having goals and as being capable of giving support (including Arden).

The opportunities to promote positive social interactions and support emerge constantly during any school day. Classroom jobs can be completed by pairs of students rather than by individuals, students requesting help can be directed to other students for that support, and students can be explicitly taught how to help others. ("Don't give people the answer—help them figure it out themselves. Here are some ways to teach that.")

Learning to give help and solve problems can even be an explicit part of the curriculum. In one school, teachers have taught students to implement a collaborative problem-solving method in which they learn to use brainstorming and problem-solving skills that stress flexible thinking and creativity. Because the school district is committed to full inclusion (students with disabilities are full members of regular classrooms), the teachers and students have used these problem-solving skills to figure out how to ensure that students with disabilities are fully integrated. Students have brainstormed, for example, how to involve a young girl with cerebral palsy in a puppet show activity, how to allow a boy with limited body movement to play a dart game, and how to support a little girl on the playground so that she could use the equipment like other students. Learning to support others and include them is operationalized in the school's curriculum.

Other schools have implemented conflict-resolution training for students so that they can acquire the skills necessary to resolve fights on the playground and in the classroom. One teacher has a conflict-resolution corner set up as one of the learning centers in the room. Students who are experiencing difficulties can select another student to serve as a mediator, and the three students follow a step-by-step model for resolving differences. Teachers can model for students a commitment to working things out together, to developing the skills necessary for the classroom to function as a community.

CONCLUSION

Communities don't just happen. No teacher, no matter how skilled or well intentioned, can enter a new classroom and announce, "We are a community." Communities are built over time, through shared experience, and by providing multiple opportunities for students to be themselves, know one another, and interact in positive and supportive ways. Community building must be seen and felt as a process that we're all in together rather than as a task that is important only to the teacher.

Although the teacher is but one person in the community, the teacher's behavior must provide a model of acceptance, support, and honesty for the entire class. It is unreasonable to expect students to be loving and supportive of one another if the teacher puts down individual students or uses labeling or name calling. If teachers are working in settings in which they do not feel valued and supported, it can be difficult for them to provide that kind of support for students. If, as a teacher, you perceive a lack of community within the school or feel that teachers are not thought about or cared for, part of the task of community building for your *students* must include building a community for *yourself*.

It is essential to honor the fact that community building is neither automatic nor easy. Teachers must demonstrate a willingness to be honest with students about the conflicts that arise in forming and maintaining a community. Students may ask questions about issues related to other students: "Why does Michael go to the gifted program and not me?" or "Why doesn't Donnel talk?" Concerns and problems about working with others will be voiced as well: "Carolyn smells and I don't like to be around her"; "Shannon isn't doing her part when we work together." Some teachers feel that responding to such questions will make trouble or raise difficult issues. In reality, however, students are already aware of classmates' differences and differing needs, and failing to address such questions does not eliminate the concern; it simply drives it underground. The teacher must be willing to answer questions honestly and with integrity. The mystery of unexplained differences and the establishment of certain topics as classroom conversational taboos seriously impede the formation of a classroom community that feels safe for all students. In working toward the goal of an inclusive classroom community in which all children—regardless of race, disability, cultural or family background, or skill—are able to function as a cohesive group, teachers must engage students in forthright discussions of the joys and difficulties of building and maintaining a community. Such discussions may be hard and even painful, but the willingness to open up issues of exclusion, fairness, difference, prejudice, and discrimination, as well as the challenges of learning to work together can enrich the community as a whole and deepen teacher and student understanding of the many forces that keep people separate and isolated.

Taking on the task of building and maintaining a supportive classroom community can become a central organizing value. Teachers can examine every decision they make—about curriculum, about teaching, about grading, about management—and ask: How will this decision affect the classroom community? Will it bring students closer together, or will it push them further apart? Asking these questions and being willing to change our behavior can bring us closer to creating classroom communities in which all members—teachers and students—are nurtured.

CHAPTER 10

Harout and I: A Short Story for the Becoming Teacher

Artin Göncü

To Joe Becker with appreciation.

Harout was going to go back to "his" country after receiving his doctoral degree and become a proud leader in child development and education. That's what his people expected from him, what his country needed. Unfortunately, nothing happened as planned. When he graduated, going back was no longer an option. The political turmoil in his country had reached its peak. The government held the university responsible for the unrest; his most beloved friends and professors had been fired, jailed, tortured, or killed in "accidents." The government censored lecture notes and required permission to do research. There was no longer "free" teaching or learning. The surviving professors were leaving the university one by one.

The world of Harout shattered when he realized that he now had to live in a land where people made fun of his accented English, criticized him for his lengthy sentences, and shamed him for being too philosophical in his writings without any "empirical data."

He now felt the need to answer a host of overwhelming questions that he tried to avoid all along: Are there movie theaters in your country? Do people use silverware when they eat where you come from? Why do women cover themselves in your country? Which country is better, yours or ours? Where is your country? Come on, don't be such a "turkey," why don't you answer the questions?

He now had to get a job. Without any publications, he felt unprepared and inept in the face of fierce competition for academic jobs. "I just don't know what to do," he sighed to his wise man while his desperation found its way out of his eyes.

"Stop this anguish, forget the academic jobs for a while, go do something that you would enjoy," said the wise man in his emphatic foreign voice.

"Like what? For what did I do all these studies?" Harout queried in irritation.

"Oh, you are more creative than that. There are many interesting things related to your academic work," the wise man said, as he stared into Harout's eyes with affection.

Harout was energized. He washed, starched and ironed his white shirt by himself; he made sure that the crease of his pants was flawless, his shoes were polished, and the curls of his hair were all in order. He filled his fountain pen and borrowed his best friend's briefcase. He asked for a ride, for the sun was hot and he didn't want to sweat. He was going to a job interview.

The director of the human development laboratory was welcoming. "How nice that you want to teach preschoolers. We don't often get men or Ph.D.s for these jobs," she said with curiosity in her voice.

"I love children and I am not sure if I am ready for a faculty job yet," Harout responded.

"Do you have any experience in teaching young children?" she asked.

"Yes, I taught dance to preschoolers and juvenile delinquents in Turkey," he responded confidently.

"But you never worked in the classroom as a teacher, right?" she asked directly.

"No, but I really want to work with children," Harout said bashfully.

They came to a shared understanding quickly. Harout agreed to take an undergraduate curriculum course in early education, do a research project with the director, and be employed as an aide to one of the lead teachers. He was so happy! "I've got degrees, I've got a career, I've got my children. How could I ask for anything more!" Harout sang, tapping his way back home.

In the preschool, I came to be aware of a new professional identity. Being a teacher was different from being a scientist. As a scientist, I interacted with children only to the limited extent necessary for the completion of experiments and saw the children narrowly in terms of my research questions. I took children's behaviors at face value while inquiring into (presumed) universals about children. Finally, I learned to pack my work in a formal language of observation that was totally consistent with this rendition of science.

In contrast, as a teacher, I got to know every child as a whole and unique person in the classroom. This knowledge enabled me to understand how each child's history and personality played a role in his or her learning. To decide whether children were ready to venture into "new" areas of life required interpreting their current lives for and with them. Thus, I learned how to be intimate, interacting with children on personal grounds, and intersubjective, interpreting the meaning beyond children's actions, feelings, and thoughts.

For example, in my effort to understand James, I had to consider that he attended two different schools as a result of his divorced parent's conflicting educational philosophies. When James destroyed a bird nest, I knew that this was not due to hatred of birds, for he regularly looked after them. Rather, the timing of his action led me to believe that it was a protest against having to change residences, schools, and parents for the summer. James's father and I had to engage in a series of talks to make sure that we had a shared understanding about how we could help James move on.

Thus, my new professional role as a teacher constrained me in a way that was different from how I was constrained by my role as a scientist. It forced me to limit my arguments to my own unique experience and to adopt a new language that goes with it, pushing me to tell this story from my own subjective "I" rather than from his "objective" eye.

Soon after I walked into preschool, it became clear that no other experience with children can be equated with classroom teaching. Looking after my younger sister when she was a baby, dancing with the preschoolers in Turkey, and playing with my friends' children were not at all the same as teaching preschoolers in the classrooms. Teaching preschoolers required learning the culture of the classroom, a culture that was different from anything else I knew.

(Although I didn't realize it then, the struggle to enter this culture provided me with an opportunity to see in a deeper way the questions of cultural difference that disturbed me in my adult life.)

There were about eighteen 4- to 5-year-old students in the classroom. They were mostly the children of university employees—from professors to maintenance staff—although some of the children were from nearby neighborhoods. The children varied along many dimensions, such as ethnicity (African, European, and Asian American; Latino; and international), parents' marital status (from single to married in an extended family), and income (from rich to welfare recipients). Some children were adopted. Some were "only" children. Some were part time, and some went to more than one school. Some had emotional problems.

Despite their diversity, however, they had a shared culture in the classroom. The most striking feature of this culture was the children's tacit understanding about what was appropriate communication. Depending on their partners and the context of their interaction, children accepted only certain types of communication as appropriate. Efforts that did not fit the hidden rules of appropriate communication were rejected. Learning about the features of children's communication was important for me both professionally and personally. So let me tell you what I learned from children about their communication (and about myself). The focus is on their communication with me as well as that with their peers in the areas of etiquette, pretend play, and problem solving.

Children were explicit and direct with me, especially in their efforts to get to know me. They first wanted to know whose father I was. After finding that I was a teacher, they moved closer. They wanted to learn my name, but it gave them trouble. One day, "Hey, hey," Jeff exclaimed to get my attention, interrupting his block construction with Aaron.

"Yes, Jeff," I acknowledged him.

"What's your name?" he asked.

"Harout."

"What?" Jeff replied.

"Harout."

Jeff then asked Aaron whisperingly, "What did he say?"

"Art," said Aaron.

Not satisfied with Aaron's answer, Jeff responded to him playfully, "He sure talks funny."

There is no escape, I thought to myself in fear.

"He said that you talk funny," Aaron told me, trying very hard not to burst into laughter.

I asked Jeff pleadingly, "But you understand me, don't you?"

Jeff's response was honest and assuring, "Sure, but you sure talk funny."

Inadvertently, I said "talk funny" in amusement, and they followed me in tandem saying "talk funny" as we began to laugh together at talking funny.

(This experience brought a solution to an age-old problem of mine. I really didn't care how I sounded so long as I was understood and accepted. Once that was assured, I could even laugh at myself. Since then, talking funny has become my elegance rather than my embarrassment.)

Children could be as direct and explicit with one another as they were with me. For example, if a newcomer was disruptive or direct in expressing the desire to participate, children often explicitly denied him or her membership in their group. John and Josh simply turned their back on Walter, who tried to persuade them to ride bikes instead of playing hide-and-seek. None of Kelly's "I wanna play too, I wanna play" received acceptance from the group of girls who were jumping rope. To the contrary, the other girls mercilessly screeched in a choir "Nooo," protesting the disruption caused by Kelly's direct efforts to join.

However, if the newcomers were implicit and not disruptive in their requests and complied with the group's agenda, children often welcomed them into the group. Tricia did not have trouble gaining access to the group, since her moves to join were not disruptive. She would watch what the group was doing and then slip into their activity. Similarly, Fernando often did something that was consistent with the group's activity, such as talking to the group about the game in question, leading to his membership in the group. After hovering about a group of boys for some time, Jason exemplified this strategy at its most effective by telling them how to proceed when they were stuck in digging a "secret" tunnel to escape from school.

(Observing children's rejections and acceptances helped me personally. I finally understood why my attempts to join in the conversations at parties or to meet people in bars had been rejected. I had to learn that in the bar culture, unlike the other cultures I knew, people did not gain acceptance into the group by introducing themselves, shaking hands, and exchanging names. They watched the group and did what the group was doing if they wanted to join in. If you wanted to be part of the group, you had to join them in singing along with Judy [Garland] in front of the big screen. You could then talk about her red shoes, and the conversation would branch into other subjects. Exchanging names and shaking hands could occur, but they almost always came at the end of the conversation. You said, "By the way, I am Harout," and extended your hand while you were getting ready to say good-bye.)

Harout was struck by the similarities he observed between adults and children in their etiquette: Both commented on his language and had a shared understanding of how to go about joining an ongoing group. He had thought that children were socialized into a world that had been established by others long before them and that this happened through specific strategies of etiquette.

Children's understanding of what was appropriate communication became even more evident when I began to observe children in pretend play. On some occasions when they pretended with me, they were quite explicit in telling me with their words if I was doing the right things in the right ways. One day they hastened to tell me that my blond wig looked silly with my black mustache, although they were terribly amused upon my appearance as a blond lady in a purple kimono.

When children pretended with one another, they hardly ever accepted or rejected one another's ideas so explicitly. If they liked their partners' ideas, they built on them with their "and thens." If they disagreed with their partners, they tried to change the topic with their "yes buts." Or they remained silent. Saying no at any time could bring the pretend play to an end and thus was not effective unless that is what they wanted to do. Sara demonstrated this understanding by not explicitly objecting to doctor Evan's apparently hurtful "shots" but by changing her role from a patient to another doctor.

Children's pretend play with their peers had a striking quality, a quality not easily seen in their play with adults. In pretending with their peers, children sometimes conveyed their play meanings in terms of the emotions they represented without relying on words all that much. So long as Maya responded to John's pretend fright with fright, they were in communication and in agreement. What mattered most was having that expression on the face and that pitch in the voice. With the representation of emotion established, what they said did not always matter. The essence of pretending with peers resided in the understanding that relevance in communication can be established at varying degrees of explicitness through many means such as words, vocalizations, gestures, timing, and distance.

(In the comfort of trustworthy company or on stage, we are just like children in our "play." We get in and out of many roles and communicate with others through many means. The flexibility in the choice of the means of communication allows us to leave a lot of room for interpretations, reinterpretations, and even misinterpretations. It is this flexibility that makes the pleasure flourish in our play interactions. I will never forget the day when the city councilman became Cleopatra at his birthday party, communicating "his" or "her" meanings through verbal insults, sharp stares, mischievous smiles, makeup, and a snake, among other things! As for us, we stood transfixed, taking pleasure in our effort to make sense of the "character.")

Harout's insights about how children communicate with one another began to develop further: We could learn something about how children are socialized into a world already established by others by studying their pretend play.

My communication with children in the context of problem solving had a very specific character. The experiences I remember most vividly are marked by the questions we asked each other. One day when we were playing a board game, Nick wanted to take a second turn in rolling the dice in his effort to get a higher number than he had gotten the first time. I asked, "Whose turn is it?" Upon realizing that Nick was ignoring my question, I asked again, "Children, don't you think everybody should take a turn before Nick rolls the dice again?" Nick's response was the beginning of a long discussion on ethics. "Why?"

On another occasion, we were experimenting at the water table. Aisha asked me, "Why your boat is swimming?" as she looked disappointedly at her sunken boat. I responded, "Do you want to try again with another boat and then we'll talk about it?" She responded, "Do I?" before she enthusiastically moved on.

Children did not talk in terms of questions in their own efforts to solve problems. They spoke in terms of directives or declaratives. They simply told their peers what was right or what to do. "Tutors" did not give their "pupils" much time or much space to think about the problem. Those who "could" count would simply count for those who couldn't. My memory is full of children's utterances such as, "No, that's not how it goes," "Lemme do it, Lemme do it," "Here you go," which accompanied children's actions with their peers.

Children tended to adopt the same strategy in their approach to solve interpersonal problems. At times of conflict, they labeled each other's behaviors as "no fair," without much inquiry about motives. For example, James thought that it was unfair when another boy pulled James's bike away from him before he was finished with his ride. He appeared to assume that "no fair" conveyed his feelings and reasoning about the matter sufficiently clearly.

So Harout pondered the difference between children's problem solving with him and with their peers, how they questioned him and were directive with one another. Harout formalized his questions in terms of the differing roles of adults and other children in children's learning about different aspects of their world.

I have come to feel that my year in the preschool was a time of integration—integration of the personal me, the scientist me, and the teacher me. What I learned as a teacher helped me understand things that troubled me personally. My knowledge of developmental theory and my experience in the classroom met and made each other more meaningful. I enjoyed the legitimacy this meeting gave to my research interests. And finally, I came to see that what I learned in graduate school as scientific research was one of many potentially legitimate ways of getting to know children.

In my life, I have experienced such integrations a few times. I have always felt them as transformations. These transformations were about realizing that I could be both Turkish and Armenian, both gay and unashamed. The summit of these transformations was marked by a freedom to announce my "new" self. Now, in my professional life, I no longer seek to exclude either my personal intuitions and style or the experience of teaching from my research. Indeed, Harout and I now feel fairly comfortable in one integrated world of scholarship and experience.

The meaning that I especially wish to convey in this story is that we are often encouraged to consider our professional and private lives as isolated from each other. We are tempted to engage in a struggle to maintain this isolation. There are good and bad reasons for this. Nevertheless, both we, as teachers, and our students stand to gain from an emphasis on the whole person. For us as teachers, this means exploring the unique self underlying our personal and professional lives as well as celebrating, elaborating, and developing this self.

PART III

REINVENTING SCHOOLS

William Ayers

At some point, parents and educators need to stop talking about school reform and begin the difficult task of reinventing schools, top to bottom, completely new. We need to move beyond tinkering in the name of reform with this or that piece of the school curriculum or instructional program and do something dramatically different. We need to reject the conventional language of reform—cliché ridden and corrupted—and the educational gurus who promise painless change and easy solutions. We need to break cleanly with the habit of failure and with a system that has defeated the hopes and dreams of generations of our young. We need to create something fresh, from the bottom up.

The place to begin, I believe, is to rethink the large purposes of education and of schooling, to consider questions like these:

- What are the core values of our school community?
- What knowledge and experiences are most important for our kids?
- What kind of person do we hope will graduate from our school?
- What human qualities and habits of mind are embodied in our work here?

A serious encounter with these kinds of questions can be illuminating. Members of one local school council in Chicago recently took up the question of what core values they hoped would power their particular improvement project. After a lot of work, they reached consensus on several, including compassion, respect for self and others, creativity, and intelligence. They then took the next step: They did a thorough search for these values in the school environment, routine, and program. This was part ethnographic inquiry and part archeological dig. They were startled to find so few examples alive and well in the school. In fact, these values were all but invisible in school practice, and they found instead a lot of contrary evidence: disrespect in the lunch-room, dullness and conformity in the curriculum, bitterness in the hallways. They discovered that all the machinery of schooling—the bells, the intercom, the rows of desks, the mass migrations to the toilets, the obsession with quiet and order, the endless testing of discrete skills, and on and on—had become a context that resists intelligence. They concluded that any normal kid, wondering what kind of intelligence is needed to succeed in this school, could sensibly decide that being quiet and dull is the only reasonable way.

Recovering and exploring large purposes is a necessary first step, but it is only a start. A collective commitment must lead to the construction of a framework for change. And this framework for change, at once idealistic and practical, must allow for the achievement of these large educational purposes for *all* children. It is not enough to have high expectations for some learners, with the majority tracked off into the educational wastelands until they are old enough to drop out. Reinvented schools must be based on a belief in the educability of all youngsters. They must hold ambitious goals for everybody's children.

A school structured around high expectations for learners will have to rethink much of the received wisdom and common sense of schooling. Typically, schools are little factories, with everything neat, ordered, and on schedule, or at least those are the goals. Children are the products, moving along the assembly line, being filled up with bits of subject matter and curriculum until they are inspected and certified to graduate to the next level. Never mind that in our largest cities half the kids fall off the line altogether, and for those who keep moving, the end of the line rarely represents an opening of possibilities. The line itself has become the important thing—the line and the stuff being poured into the youngsters.

In reinvented schools, the factory model will be rejected in its entirety. Reinvented schools need to be based on what is known about learning: People learn best when they are actively exploring, thinking, and asking their own questions; people learn constantly and in a variety of styles and at a range of paces; people learn when their emotional, physical, cultural, and cognitive needs are met. Lillian Weber, founder of New York's Workshop Center, argues that we should consider building school practice on the model of learning in a family, where children learn by "following along" in the real work of shopping, cooking, cleaning, repairing, singing, whatever.

In reinvented schools, children will be active, engaged with a variety of concrete materials and primary sources. Youngsters need to be involved in purposeful work appropriate for their ages. Teachers need to reject the role of clerks delivering a set of prede-termined curriculum packages to passive consumers and become instead coaches, guides, and colearners. The first responsibility of teachers, then, will be to see each student in as full and dynamic a way as possible, to discover the experiences, knowledge, prefer-ences, aspirations, and know-how the children themselves bring to school. This is a complicated and difficult proposition, but neces-sary if teaching is to be constructed on strengths rather than deficits.

Teachers will create environments for learning, transforming the little lecture halls that now exist into laboratories for discovery and surprise. In an early childhood classroom, this might mean having a large block area, a comfortable reading corner, and an easel with red, yellow, and blue paints available. Working at the easel, a child might encounter purple and construct knowledge about primary and secondary colors upon this dazzling discovery. Along with the color purple comes confidence, self-esteem, curios-ity, and a sense that knowledge is open-ended and that knowing is active. Worksheets are rather tame and anemic alternatives, with lateral lessons about knowledge as finite and about knowing as passive.

Essentially, teachers will struggle to build bridges from the knowledge and experiences of youngsters to deeper and wider ways of knowing. Older children might connect issues in their own lives concerning society and the crowd, group identity, jealousy, and revenge to a deep encounter with *Romeo and Juliet*. It is all there after all—in their lives and in Shakespeare. Teachers will find themselves covering less stuff but teaching everything more deeply.

In reinvented schools, assessment will reflect the whole child and will illuminate strengths and interests as much as areas of need. Assessment will always be in the service of the next teaching question and will be broad and adaptive rather than narrow and fixed. Reinvented schools will reject the obsession with a single, narrow assessment tool as inadequate to capture the complexity of human growth. It is well known that if the only tool you have is a hammer, you tend to treat everything like a nail. Reinvented schools will develop a range of tools in order to achieve a rich contextual portrait of learning.

Reinvented schools will treat youngsters and adults as if we live in a democracy. There will be an abiding concern for justice, equity, and respect in the school as well as in society. Teachers will work to create classrooms that are places where people can think, question, speak, write, read critically, critique freely, work cooperatively, consider the common good, and link consciousness to conduct. In other words, classrooms will be places where democracy is practiced, not ritualized.

We live in a time of radical reform rhetoric and conventional classroom practice. Transformative ideas are turned into slogans and reduced to meaninglessness as they are worked into the existing regularities of school practice. I was in a school where the principal said, "We do 'whole language' from 9:00 to 9:30 in ability groups." In the same school they had instituted a program of "critical thinking" after lunch, and the morning was presumably all about habit and stock reactions. "Character education," "cooperative learning," and all the rest are useless as add-ons and predigested packages. It is time to move beyond rhetoric and beyond petty skirmishes about change. Nothing short of radical change will make a dent in the downward spiral of our schools. It is time to reinvent schools.

CHAPTER 11

Reexaminations: What Is the Teacher and What Is Teaching?

Lillian Weber

GIVING PRECEDENCE TO WHAT THE TEACHER IS AND WHAT THE TEACHER COMMITMENTS ARE

As I look back over 25 years of my articles, speeches, letters, and other statements about the changes we've made in the schools, I find that I have concentrated on constant reexamination of issues of teaching and teachers, questioning their pertinence to what I have come to see in more expanded fashion as the reality of children's learning. In my first formulations about school change in the late 1960s, I concentrated on creating a context in schools of relationships of teacher to child and child to teacher that would facilitate the child's use of context and enhance the child's possibilities for building, for questioning, for rearranging in new forms. My comments were a critique of the barrenness and sterility of context in schools. I was full of wonder at what I had seen of children's learning, for example, in English infant schools, where there was a rich surround of environment and easy relationships that joined them in what was focusing their attention and responded to their attention with recognition of the importance of this focus for them.

Teachers interested in creating new contexts supportive of children's growth and development were interested in these relationships stressing observation and appreciation of children's functioning. But the teaching was always in a school, and soon after our initial school changes, teachers began to express the need to cope with the institution, to confront institutional obstacles to newer relationships and context. My writing on teaching became descriptions of successful arrangements and suggestions for how to move toward such arrangements. Teachers, too, have written about their own struggles to recreate context and relationships, and about the discoveries they have made about what worked or did not work in their practice.

But as time went on, it seemed to me that the emphasis on teaching became an overloaded one. The teachers' focus was strongly on *their* own struggles to unblock the institution and to free themselves; one reads again and again about teachers' efforts to share in decision making, for example, to participate in curriculum building. What the teacher had built, had found it possible to change, was important to his or her development of self and sense of empowerment.

Meanwhile, however, many things that had been important in the first efforts to change—for example, the building of community with other teachers, parents, and the community around the school—although not lost as worthy goals, were certainly muted. The observation of children, although remaining important, was given importance to some extent in terms of how the teacher could manage to have *this* child focus on the goals the teacher felt were necessary for the classroom, for the control of so many different children, and for certain curricular goals.

The teachers' struggle for self-definition has taken place increasingly in a context of severe criticism of the schools, often focused on the old schools, not on the modified schools that had become more exemplary of teachers' decision making. In such an atmosphere of criticism, parents worried and organizations were founded that concentrated their criticism on teachers and teaching and failed to fully criticize the emptiness of context in schools and of relationships within the school of child to child, child to teacher, teacher to teacher, parents to parents, and so on.

The teacher education institutions have been analyzed and re-analyzed as cause and source of teacher and school deficiency. The word that seems to express what is found wanting (and what many think should be a central focus) has been "professionalism." This led to the proposition that the universities ought to offer material that would bring out and focus teacher education on strengthening the teacher as a professional. University focus settled on teachers' formal knowledge of their content fields and on research that would indicate the best mode of teaching. The focus of this critique (and on a "best" mode of teaching) was narrow rather than broad, and neither the child as learner nor the school as institution was being examined under this magnifying glass. The questions about "professionalism" seemed shallow, and they bypassed what it is that defines the teacher. This then became important to me.

The analysis of the school as an institution that *blocked* the teacher from functioning in ways that I thought were related to this definition and to the teacher's commitment raised the need for rethinking, for "deconstructing," "deschooling," and "deteachering," in order for those first goals to emerge again with some strength and clarity. It was important to take the discussion of limitations away from limits in children's capacities to learn and toward the pervasive limits all around us—the structures that both facilitate and limit our family and social life. How much and what in a school can be "deschooled"? How much can we move away from the existing view of the teacher as mechanic carrying out already set plans? How much of this view can be revised toward a new view of the teacher as creative constructor? What could allow some refocusing on the commitment of teachers, on the definition of teachers' roles, on the teacher as supporting the child's learning rather than as *teaching*?

The preparation of candidates for teaching follows from the analyses we make clarifying the definition of teacher and the analyses we make about teaching. The teacher's commitment must include the context supportive of learning and of the child's further development or education.

For every aspect of teaching that has been discussed as professionalism, in my view the definition of what the teacher is and what the teacher's commitments are must take precedence. These are the questions I've explored for the past 5 or 6 years and hope to pull apart in the following remarks.

I take from the North Dakota Study Group's 1993 planning document the oft-reiterated phrase "the schools at their best" as my starting point. What is the "best?" I think of the best as the *conditions* that I see as necessary accompaniments to human growth and development. These conditions are not limited to schools but are present in many contexts.

One constant accompaniment to human growth is the presence of people of many generations, some of whom are further along in growth and others of whom have not even approached this growth. There is inherently and usefully a kind of positive unevenness in the child's human and material surround that is multifaceted from the first moment of growth. The numerous facets increase as we live. We can increase the impact of one condition over another in a conscious kind of way, but only rarely and questionably do we do this in planned fashion, like in a laboratory. Human growth doesn't seem to take place in a laboratory way. Thus, the study of that *context*, in all its specificity and dynamism, where human growth does take place is obligatory if we are to impact supportively on the child's growth in school.

What is the context within the school? We have to examine whether the context is multifaceted enough. Certainly the "context" has often been a single strand, one whose conscious purpose was to sequence one lesson after the other and to have everything else either removed or at least controlled—controlled meaning quiet, for example, and with all attention on the teacher's presentation. But in my view, school "at its best" would take some of the multifaceted context of the world that exists outside of school and have it within the school. In such a context, the stimulus of past experiences, the memory of them, can still impinge and weave its way around again for focus that may be individually determined or group determined.

Another constant accompaniment to human growth is continuity of context, which can help weave the sense of personal continuity. Continuity is far from existing evenly in the various contexts in which human growth takes place. There can be great unevenness and interruption in the continuity of the child's, the human's, history, at the most intimate level of one's remembrances. But discontinuities in growth and relationship do not obviate the simultaneous continuities, the importance of which becomes evident when they are lost. The continuity represented by our remembrances of who we are and of our surround is supported by the continuities in the surround of others. The family from which we emerge has a major function in carrying the memory of who we are. Before we could remember and when we can't remember, the family reminiscences keep us whole. Among new people a group memory exists. New people estimate how old we are and where we came from, and acquaintances carry at least a generalized memory. Without these different memories that give us continuity with ourselves, we would be seriously handicapped.

Schools, even at their best, are impediments to this continuous memory. They have perhaps the longest contact with the child outside the family, but in most schools, 9 months is the maximum time of continuous memory carried in any adult's mind. Say that it is even 2 years or a little more. It is still without the genuine continuity that exists elsewhere. Continuity in school is mediated through organization of progression and records. It is focused around a selective memory of performance and engagement with current tasks. Assistance to children who do not fit this narrow kind of memory requires the revival of a broader memory and an assertion of who they are in a more whole fashion than school accommodates.

Thus we come to an even larger condition that supports human growth and development. This is simply the acceptance of the child's own identity, the acceptance of who the child is as a person. And that is not bargained for in most schools. It is not weighed as important. I am not talking about acceptance if the child does certain things the school requires. I am talking about unconditional acceptance of the child's "is-ness."

All humans are born into a multigenerational context. The child is born to somebody, a somebody who is within a network of other relationships, within a set of mores and culture and historical moment. The child absorbs the particularities of relationships one way or another, but the fact of his or her belonging and relatedness is without question. Obviously, such unconditional acceptance is not part of schools, even at their best. On the contrary, discussion of assessment, equality, excellence, and standards bears with it the condition of performance as the price of a child's acceptance.

The question is, *can* schools accept the child unconditionally? If we talk about schools "at their best," would they, at least, be moving determinedly toward unconditionality? And what could this mean for schools, not only with respect to assessment and performance but also with respect to race, ethnicity, difference, and the right of children not to divest themselves, on school entrance, of their culture and language?

On this question I have to go to, What exactly is the teacher's commitment? Obviously, this is extremely complex. If the teacher is defined by a commitment to every child within the group, if every child is accepted as part of the teacher's commitment to further growth and development, then there is an unconditionality. But mostly what we have is unconditionality in absentia or very much qualified with, "Well, I certainly do the best that I can, but after all, he has to perform a certain kind of way." I realize the hedging and the problems around conditionality, but I think that it is central to our discussion of schools at their best to face what follows from the commitment of the teacher and to decide that, yes, the commitment does indicate necessary revisions of school context that can stretch existent modes into the utmost unconditionality possible.

Rethinking the conditions accompanying human growth and development has led me to ask anew, What is it possible to demand of the school? Another point of rethinking has been prompted by recent articles by a number of writers in counterbalance to a search for professionalism relying on university research. This has been the question of the meanings attached to the teacher's commitment to the profession. What is professionalism, and what is central to it? This question highlights a difference between those concentrating on professionalism in a limited way and those related to it in terms of human caring and human compassion.

FIRST CHANGES AND REASSESSMENTS

When I first looked for aspects of public school context that could be modified, I did not have a list of the conditions necessary in any learning context to assist my analysis. My focus was first on the life of the classroom and the quality of life in the classroom. I looked at the classroom and at the child, at the possibilities of meshing with where the child was, and how I, as an enabler, would help the child go forward. What I saw in England in 1965 reinforced the feelings I had previously developed in working with small children and focused my observation in New York schools when I returned. I thought of the teacher as being engaged with where the child was going *anyway* and enabling the child to fulfill what was already existent and pushing forward in the child.

The question of difference and unevenness in children's growth was interesting and enormously important to me. The teacher had to understand that what was set up to foster the child's development had to be responsive to this difference and unevenness without predictive conclusions. The need to take a long view of the growth of a child was important to me. It could not be assumed that the unevenness was a stable thing or that differential development within the child was forever. That is, if the child was not yet speaking, it could not be predicted that the child would never speak. Making an educational situation supportive of the child's further education and development meant taking a "let's wait and see" stance and creating an enabling environment in which whatever you were *not* seeing in the child was encouraged to emerge. The setting could not be one in which an existent state of the child or any observation of that moment would lead to conclusions about the permanence of what was seen.

I considered the possibilities for change in institutional structures. How could these structures be at least partially bent to become less intrusive, less interruptive of any efforts to change? The administrative structures were so detailed, the judgments were so external to the particular children. They were not in relationship with where the child was and where he or she was going. One had to look and see where there were cracks or entry points where one could make some trial efforts at bringing the school structures into another relationship, or where one could interlace with them and so turn their operation away from blocking development.

In this early period of my thinking on change in the public schools, there was no template for how the teacher should act. Rather there was an idea that what was true about the child was the capacity for growth and interest in the world, and that ways had to be found to bring at least some of the child's earlier interactions with the world into the school. There was not really a questioning of the fact that school existed and was compulsory, or of the idea that school was valued for many different reasons by parents, perhaps even eventually by the child, or that this was the teacher's work and that training had gone into the teacher functioning in the school.

Initially, my question was how to evade the structure of the school and thereby release some of the interaction and reinitiate some of the things that had supported the child's learning and education *before* the child got into school. That was the meaning of what was called in England "informal education." I sought for what would free the teacher to be supportive of the child at a more fundamental and general level, supportive in a context of awareness that outside of school children did not learn in an empty set or with an exclusive, constant focus on the adult. Instead, they reached out tremendously from the first day of birth, making use of whatever they could in the environment to continue their growth. The child was not an empty container being filled by the teacher.

The Open Corridor program, started in existing public schools in 1967, was an effort to create a space where people could see and interact with one another and to create a broader diversity of children (in age, for example) and of activities that could be chosen, where engagement would be in and out so that there would be relaxed control and diversity in modes of teaching. It involved grouping four to five classrooms of volunteering teachers in a single corridor, which could then be used for overflow and different activities. Children could go in and out of the classroom and into the corridor. Classroom doors were open so that children's inquiry activities could be visible and joined with. A teacher might be reading a story, a child might be drawing a character of his or her choice, and so on. The open corridor presumed that the teacher had created a context, was moving around to catch the thread of the child's engagement with the context, and was adding to the context. The open corridor also presumed that the child was adding to the context and that the group would sometimes draw together to share their perspectives and be stimulated to additional possibilities, to new thrusts. Teachers could help one another by being visible to and thereby stimulating solutions in one another. A teacher would have an idea for getting through some of the institutional blocking points and then another teacher, seeing the implementation, could say, "That's good. Let's try that." The whole enterprise would then gain in flexibility.

To assist the teacher in relating to the child and in making use of whatever pliability of context was possible, I also came up with a notion of the "advisor," drawing on the role of the English headmistress. The advisor was somebody who would help the teacher with what followed from an awareness of the child's own pushing forward. The advisor could observe what was going on, see what the teacher was trying to do, and share what he or she had observed of the other teacher's efforts. The advisor could point out and assist the teacher in finding some of the flexibilities and stretch within what sometimes seemed like a granite structure that had no entrance points.

The advisor had to have a role that would be allowed in the school but would foster the strength of the teacher in finding flexibilities for growth. The advisor role should not be grafted onto the old supervisory role of making judgments and evaluations of the teacher's performance in relation to mandated standards. The advisor had to be helpful to the teacher, recognizing in the teacher the same differences and unevenness that I hoped the teachers would recognize in the children's development. She or he had to appreciate some aspect of the teacher's strength, the teacher's courage to try to explore the possible. In our own continuous evaluation of the advisor role, we fine-tuned the ways the advisor could relate to the structures of the school to give the teacher more space.

It became clear that we did not totally control the advisor's function. The institution allowed the advisory but also often reinforced its own limitation and control on what could be done by claiming that the advisor was essential. Without the advisor, it was said, teachers could not develop new ways of working through their own reflection, conviction, fascination with children's growth and of sharing with one another and estimating Where are we now? What has happened with the children's growth? Trust in teachers' capacities was not a quality many administrators had. By saying that the advisors were essential, administrators put blockages in the way of teachers who were individually and personally assuming responsibility for searching out the ways and paths of their own development. Mandated paths for teacher performance had to be followed unless someone graced by further education guaranteed that no terrible disaster would occur.

It was my conviction that what I believed was true for children—that learning occurs in context and through interaction—was also imperative for teachers. That is what gave meaning to the teacher's role. But I did not believe that this *required* a prior preparation of teachers by advisors. After all, as attempted actualizations and descriptions of practice in the modified settings grew in number, more and more teachers—experienced, beginning, or students—felt hope in possibility and reinforced in the meaning of their commitment. I felt that one had to think of moving in the direction of teacher autonomy in making decisions and of respect for the teacher's own observations, believing that teachers *could* learn and reflect. And that was also an essential piece of their belief in the children.

Nevertheless, it was the children who came first in my mind. In talking with teachers about joining a group that wanted to begin a process of change and to work with us in looking at context, interaction, and primarily children, I felt that the teachers' belief that it was possible to do so, and their unhappiness with being cogs in a mandated situation that did not respect their roles in interaction, were more important than anything else. What was necessary for the growth of change was that the teachers *wanted* to change and sought out supports for that process. Change could not be a designation from the principal, as if teachers were interchangeable cogs—"You can have any two teachers for your project." Those two teachers had to be *interested* and *critical* of what the current situation was. Did they fully understand the critique? None of us did. Did they fully understand how to go forward? None of us understood that. But that they felt that it was *possible* to go forward—that was the essential, the sole condition, not intelligence or talent. Those were assumed.

For me, the complexity of a projected direction is possible to understand only as the direction is pursued in a *lived* situation, wherever it is located and with many people participating. My idea for maximizing what could be learned from trials was to release the teacher from the bondage of isolation in the classroom, to find ways to break the barrier of the closed doors. Then teachers could see the trials and the small efforts of their colleagues; they could also see the children in a larger setting than just in response to what that teacher had prepared. This would give them new material to think about. The idea was also to open the classroom to visits by and interactions with parents who had, like the teachers, made a voluntary choice to explore the modification of the institution to which they had entrusted their children.

The deprivations to the teacher's autonomy in the administrative structures of the formal school had been so marked that even small releases—for example, being able to make small decisions about what to put into the classroom to build up a denser and richer setting for exploration and interaction—were intoxicating to the teachers. The settings we created, which allowed social interaction with other teachers and widened the classroom environment to include several other classrooms where changes were also being tried, were experienced as pleasant by many teachers. But complexities about identification, ownership, and domains became apparent, not only in the original Open Corridor communities but generally as part of the process of change of any teacher attempting to work in a new way.

A strong push from the teachers themselves began, to reassert teacher territoriality. This was *their* classroom, where even the advisor was present on sufferance. The *teacher* was making the major decisions in the classroom. That door was important and was open only a little bit, but even that little bit was a big change from the previous total closure. Even though the teachers wanted something different from the past, their vision of community was weak. The structure of the school was much stronger, and the teacher's only domain that was reliably hers or his was that classroom, even though in a freer way.

How did this reassertion of the teacher's authority in the classroom operate with respect to the original focus on children? That focus remained, but the teacher's creation of context became an expression of the teacher's creativity, which was terribly important to the teacher, and understandably so. Still, a question was left floating in the air. Was this context various enough, dense enough, to be responsive to and supportive of all the particular children and groups of children? Was there a sufficient mesh with the children's interests? Were the children's contributions to context encouraged? Were the children's interests even understood? Questions of children's interests were not really discussed at length until we had been doing this kind of work for quite a while. The teacher as a person had become an enormously important focus for the teacher and for what was developed, at that point anyway. The sense of the teacher as continuing to control and direct the children's focus came to the fore in the notion of the need for a corridor teacher. There was a sense that the children needed to have the control and supervision of a teacher at all times. A loose piece, not clearly preenvisaged by a teacher in its use, was found to be uncomfortable.

Conflicts in the understanding of community within the school and of supportive interaction between children, classrooms, and teachers emerged as the Open Corridor program continued in the early and mid-1970s. The effort toward community took second place to the teachers' sense of territoriality and control of their classrooms as they experienced a positive growth in their sense of themselves as persons with interests, fresh experiences of their own learning, creativity, and possibilities for further development. In schools where a process of change was initiated, it was usual to feel an atmosphere of friendliness in all the connecting structures of the school: in the office, in the playground, in the corridor. The children could walk to the office without being challenged as to why they had left the classroom. There was an assumption that they were part of the whole. The children benefited from the increased richness of the teachers' presentation. But it was a question of degree, and retreat from the community and the Open Corridor development itself as supporting community and place was real. (Of course, the retreat was not total. Use of the whole school, of the corridor not just as a passage but as an additional place to explore and to develop communication and collaboration between children and classrooms, and, of course, the small alternative school development, represented instances of continuation of the efforts to build community.)

The further development of the teacher's own resources, experiences, and awareness of the role of context and interest in learning facilitated the teacher's growth in ability to work in a modified way. It was reflected in greater support for children, in greater conviction about children's capacities, and in greater awareness of these forces in children. It was visible in the greater richness and density of environmental context. The Workshop Center at City College was founded in 1972 as an educative force supporting these developments in teachers and became a major factor in our analysis of appropriate teacher preparation. Investigation at the Workshop Center made teachers more aware of their own learning process and what supported *their* continuation of investigations.

Teachers with confidence in children's capacity for growth could seek to develop a situation that was more supportive of children's growth. They sought to examine the context that would further the children's focus and reaching out to understand the world, one another, and themselves. What was an educative context? What were the contexts that would be supportive? Was school such a context? What would it take to make school more so? For this child, or that one? Raising these and related questions began to shape what made sense in teacher education because, in raising them, you were expecting the teachers to look at what would be supportive. Your responsibility was to enable them to go further in assisting the child to go further.

Expanding the view of the educative context that supports learning and development in teachers was one factor in an increasing emphasis on observation of how children used context. What in the context of home and home relationships had fostered growth and unfolding in power to understand and to use? What in the street? In the neighborhood? In the stores? In the community? In the world? Journals became tools of reflection. A reflective attitude that encouraged self-observation, observation of one's own doings and the doings of others, became a way of developing sensitivity to the impact of even small changes in setting and interaction on their scene of action. Reminiscences about what had been educative to the teachers when they were children became strong in the analysis of their own learning. Also raised was how other people seeking to understand the interdependent roles of teaching and learning had considered these questions.

All these aspects of change, at least in awareness, began to appear in discussions of teacher preparation, but it was also clear that the already existing and mandatory modes were strong as countervailing forces, and that what we were really pointing toward had been actualized only minimally. We did not have sufficient examples of other ways.

One way that had moved me to much thought was the requirement in Norway's early childhood teacher preparation programs for prospective teachers to spend a year living in a family to experience the variety and complexity of children's reactions and the relationships in a home. In our U.S. teacher education context, where this was not a requirement, reminiscence about one's own growth, the evocation of one's own childhood, and descriptions of childhood in literature could help but could not obviate the need for study of this major educative setting for the child. Home observation certainly was an absent aspect of teacher preparation. Another missing element was exploration and thought about the community where the child lived as educative context. The school had to think of the community differently, as full of things that contributed to the child's understanding of how things work, as full of relationships of positive complexity.

Throughout the 1970s and 1980s, in the context of continuing and widespread failure in the accomplishment of mandated goals, just about all aspects of schooling were criticized as inadequate: The parents were inadequate; the children were inadequate and ineducable; the teachers were inadequate and ignorant.

In view of such an overwhelming and all-inclusive critique, where and how could change begin? What in the situation seemed more manipulable? It was difficult to critique the parents, because at least to some extent they held political power over the school. It was difficult to critique the children, although they could certainly be ignored and devalued. After all, if they *were* ineducable, then what was the point of the teacher's efforts? Criticism was more easily narrowed to focus on the teachers, who were wage earners within the school system and dependent on the salary and therefore on approval and acceptance. And so, by default and by accessibility to critique, it seemed possible to center all criticism on the teacher. But the teacher who was critiqued was not the teacher we saw in the Open Corridor, the enormously hardworking teacher thrilled with new possibilities, new responsibilities, and creativity. She was the teacher in the context of the old sterility—without significant indictment of the institution as a source of deficiency. Displacement, it seems to me, had occurred in clarity of vision and in focus about change.

The university school of education was also faulted, accused of pandering to subject ignorance with a thin gruel of methodology. It was not fostering in the teacher a knowledge of the research in the field of teaching and certainly not, as we urged, raising the teacher's thinking capacity to enable a multifaceted kind of response and support for the child. Teach for America, for example, the program for raising teacher performance by recruiting "the best and the brightest" from Radcliffe or Swarthmore, illustrates the limitations of any program based almost totally on critique of teacher ignorance. The new recruits' knowledge of subject was supposed to remedy everything. Unfortunately, this was not accompanied by any depth of question raising about children or the teacher's commitment. It was not focused on observation of children that could lead to new flexibilities or responsiveness to how the perspectives of children as they relate to content can affect teaching.

The Holmes Group efforts (1990) to improve teacher education and preparation magnified the role of university subject expertise and the importance of the teacher knowing about "research." The research was seldom judged on whether it was based on careful observation of the impact of small changes to the environment, or the impact of what the teacher modified or adapted in an effort to mesh with where this or that child was. There has been some progress in reestablishing this priority and encouragement of what are called professional development schools, where the school context can be controlled enough to guarantee teacher education students such new experiences. But I have not yet seen persistent, clear questioning of the institution itself—of its retrograde mode of lockstep influence; its continuing power to restate and shift priorities about change; its impact on the teacher's commitment to the primacy of the child's possibilities and to the support of the child's development of such possibilities. That kind of questioning, in my opinion, has lost—it constantly loses—focus and must be constantly revived.

FURTHER REEXAMINATIONS:
CONTINUING OBSTACLES TO CHANGE

My review of my previous writings has prompted not only reassessments of earlier work but also recognition of limitations on change and further thoughts on the obstacles to—and the imperatives for—change, which I share now.

The *facts* of the institution—that the class is a *group*, that the teacher is presented with a *group*, its group-ness including predeterminations of age and of likeness or unlikeness—make it difficult to concentrate on how individual children develop. This results in enormous institutional determination, definition, and focus and modes of carrying through focus. The *fact* of the numbers of children and of a space that has inherent limits, and the fact that the teacher is responsible for these numbers in this space, means that there is immediately some definition of the teacher as responsible for this group and therefore required to be in control. In this description of teaching, the teacher is defined first by the school's being a holding institution for groups, not by her role as an agent of the child's further development and stretch into the world. What is happening in the growth of any child and how the teacher can support and enrich the child's path are not the first questions that the teacher has to contend with. On the first day, she has to contend with the fact— here they are. There is *this group*. The importance of the group in the child's learning is secondary to the simple fact of a group. It takes the teacher quite a bit of learning about her relationship to the group before she can feel confident and relaxed about individual as well as common uses of the terrain known as the classroom. The critique of the school that I started with in 1967 is incomplete because this major definition of the school's function largely remains as it was at the time of my first formulation. The allocation to the teacher of responsibility first for the group is still there. Even as the teacher critiques the school as institution in its most controlling forms and in its control of what she is doing about understanding the children, she must still adapt to the facts of limited and specific space and to the numbers of children for whom she is responsible.

The possibility of separation between what happens educatively and what happens because of what seem to be the institutional necessities requires the constant confrontation of issues of responsibility and accountability, for example, about the curricular material that children are expected to take in. There is little analysis of the origin in real life of what children take in and how to make the school a place that can hold experience so that, for instance, rainwater is not just something the child passes through quickly, holding on to mother's hand, so as not to get wet, but something that can be held in the classroom for examination in a more detailed fashion, relating to the various perspectives of different children.

The kind of accountability reflected in tests based on a determined lesson format might result in learning experiences not too different from the quick passage through rain, a momentary drenching as one passes through. The sequential curriculum of the old patterns sets a restrictive tone: Now it's finished; now we go on to the next thing. But its shrinking of the experience of the surround to a quick passing-through nevertheless still allowed thoughts about, and return to, the experience if the classroom retained any traces of it, however inadvertently. Such returning, allowed "on the side," may indeed enrich greatly. Of course an actively negative stance toward the classroom surround as a place of experience can even further restrict the surround and equates with the curricular barrenness we all know.

In the kind of accountability represented by the teacher looking at how the teacher functions with response to the child in a particular institution, the critique of the institution involves a break in the sequential, lockstep curriculum. It involves the building of a surround that can be available to the children, where things can be a focus at one time and a passing-by, peripheral observation at another. This enables the stirring of memories of how it was: "Oh, it's a little different than it was yesterday," or "Last week this wasn't there." Acceptance by the teacher of responsibility in critiquing the existing institution and of creating a different kind of context involves reviving the teacher's own self-awareness as learner. The teacher has to reconfront many experiences and get excited about the world again.

In examination of the teacher's situation, often a double strand was clear. A context had been created that was sometimes rich and intensely used, but the primacy was, and is still, around what the institution mandates for curriculum and progression. This mandate may be modified by the teacher enriching the curriculum with her own understanding and interest. The mandated focus is retained. Perhaps a few additional perspectives are added in, but still "we have to move on." In this situation, the centrality of the teacher continues, without the teacher assuming the additional roles that come from seeing the child's centrality as definitive. These additional roles involve sharing with children the teacher's lifetime of interests, joining with the children's interests, and then weaving the thread openly and obviously at a pace that doesn't cut out and leave stranded those interests. The new perspective not only is a brief nod of acknowledgment at the child's different focus and perspective but also is at least an attempt to make the joining of the teacher with the child's perspective and the child with the teacher's perspective a true one. Within the new frame there may be a need for direct presentation of things unknown to the child, that the school as institution may demand and the parents may worry about ("When will they learn about this?"). What results is a mixed situation with various degrees of presence of one mode over another.

I think it's important to unpackage the complexity of these stances because, in our changed situations, teachers' entrancement with their own creativity is so great—inevitably and understandably, considering that such response has been suppressed for ages—that one must step back and get reentranced with this or that child's way of entering this world. One must do that as part of one's commitment as a teacher, not as something lesser but as something wonderful: "Isn't it amazing that the kid saw that? I remember something I once saw—ages ago."

In the building of context and relationships that are stimulating and responsive to the child's thrusts toward understanding, observation that notes the impact of small change, the direction of interchange, and how the child latched onto something that the child finds of value and interest is enormously important. Without that, and without the teacher's entrancement with her own commitment, the job becomes intolerable. It is clear that there is no education without the child having latched onto something that helps the child endure, live through, and continue growing in spite of all the errors of control and interruption that are inevitable as numerous people—parents, teachers, others—interpret and come in and out of the mandated structure that surrounds the child's living in school. The teacher's identification with the commitment to build an educative context that supports the child's efforts to understand is or can be the engine forcing change.

I saw the importance of the Workshop Center through teachers' engagement with their own learning and their total enjoyment of the chance they had there to shape the focus and path of their explorations. I saw also how the difficulties of direct translation to the classroom were a constant overwhelming reality for them. I remember one instance when a few of the teachers were looking at plants that had tubelike structures carrying fluids to the far reaches of the plant. Comparisons with aqueducts and pipes came up during interchanges over the exploration. One of the teachers worked out a system of tubes carrying fluids quite a distance around the Workshop Center and then worked out how to do this in the classroom. None of his concerns dealt with the need for connection with the interests of the children. His report on the project illustrated the difficulty. "You know," he said, "I spent all day Saturday working this out at the Workshop Center, but when I tried it with the kids, they were bored stiff, the little bastards." Well, it's amusing. Who hasn't seen that? One's choice of a story falls flat and accommodations are made along the way. But it is important to pull this phenomenon out and look at it. It may well be a necessary first step for the teacher to accept certain boundaries and demands of the institution, but certainly he must work toward a situation where he will determine the specificities of the work in relationship to his commitment to the children.

Sometimes the teacher's fascination with what's been happening in her own head, and the examination of the content more abstractly, leads to a change in profession. The analysis of the process becomes all-fulfilling. The engagement with the trials of understanding and close interaction with *this* child become of less interest. The daily interaction with the wonders of the ordinary for this or that child—in which there's an element of interest in how you yourself have understood or modified your understanding as well as in what it is you're understanding in that child—wanes in interest. It has certainly happened that teachers have become researchers, let us say, or professional students of the interaction of teachers.

My reexamination also unpackaged the intense desire of the early period of change to deal with the teacher's isolation, the fact of being alone with the children and all that implies of helplessness and the need to control. There was an intense desire to open up—for that one teacher alone in the closed-door arrangement of a group in a limited space and with a limited definition of difference—as the first overture to change. This was at the root of the concept of the Open Corridor program. The corridor could be a mechanism for each teacher to see what other teachers were doing and to converse with them as adults. The children could see some of the teacher's planning, hear conversations about the whole, and thus see the teacher in this working enterprise, not entirely focused on them but focused on trying to create an atmosphere in which they, the children, had a stake and could cooperate in defining and shaping this whole. The children could see a wider range of other children's interactions— "Look, there are some older kids doing something we may be able to join now, or see what it's about before we take over next year"—and not just have it reported to them.

In an interesting way, the wider interactions actualized by the Open Corridor had complications of their own that affected the development or nondevelopment of children and teachers. As teachers saw the possibility of creative engagement with the shaping of curriculum, with some interaction with children's interests, the limitation of the classroom, defined as the *teacher's space*, became clear. This limitation really took precedence for many teachers over the struggle against isolation and the idea of community.

The parallel development of what I consider positive directions in the modification of the school and inertness about modification is what currently focuses my thought. I am looking at the limitations of the changes that have been made, not because I think it's the end; I think of all modifications as being incomplete. But there must be clarity about whether one wants change to go in that direction, and there must be continuity in edging around these desired directions. Several other aspects of development in the Open Corridor situations illustrate this.

Sometimes it was difficult for teachers to have confidence that children could learn, by direct engagement, that each thing didn't need to be controlled for its possible outcome. Some teachers found the open door to the corridor threatening, formulating this in the question, Who is in control? The structure of an open corridor demanded ease in including children's inquiry that perhaps had not been planned for by the teacher. Teachers did not necessarily appreciate this or that activity in the corridor, or in their classrooms, that was now visible.

Moreover, once teachers began to see in the corridor work the possibilities in children's activities, and began also to enjoy their new freedom to exercise decision making about curriculum, there seemed to be a growth in the teacher's desire for ownership of classroom and curriculum, for acknowledgment, for resumption of control. Children were often called back from the corridor. For all these reasons, some teachers, and usually the principal, saw the corridor as needing its own *special* teacher.

An obvious limitation in reorganizing a school is that the budget isn't open-ended. At the outset, it seemed to me that if you wanted change to be espoused by teachers who wanted to try but who were not in direct relationship with an Open Corridor advisory, you had to focus on the minimum of personnel or special arrangements with which change could be initiated and continued. That, after all, was the sense of working small, using existing facilities and personnel, and doing something as minimal as moving teachers to the same corridor so they could use it to expand the possibilities for children's engagement and to break into their own isolation. But once the idea took hold that you couldn't have a program in the corridor without a special teacher assigned to it, the in-and-outness and interaction between what was happening in the classroom and in the corridor at least partially ended.

Rereading what I wrote about the corridor development in the 1970s, and the questions that arose about the corridor needing its own teacher and observations of how the privacy of the classroom came to be reestablished, I am confirmed in my thinking that these factors in the decline of community must again be confronted. Although there remains a friendliness in schools where a number of teachers are working openly and responsively to interaction from children—a friendliness not often seen before the period of change— the definition is still "class" and "classroom," with control and accountability also so defined, even though in different ways from the past way of punitive control, which is to be applauded.

"Community" on the part of the school's inhabitants could include the sense of responsibility for the school, of identification with the school, but it was certainly something wider than the classroom. The sense of the school as a community could help a school function in a way that recognized its relationship to the context of home, neighborhood, stores. But this local world is in fact far less recognized as important to school definition. Only very slightly is the school seen as a positive force in the local community, and the local community as a positive force in the development of the school. There are all too many schools that regard themselves as saviors of the children, as a bulwark or barricade against the community. But communities are where the children live and where positive forces also exist that can regenerate community and contribute to the development of the possibilities. The school has not yet really emerged as a force in this regard, even within the school, even within the relationships within the school, where the *classroom* still defines the teacher.

Reconsidering the residual effects of the teacher's retention of control on children's inquiry and the persistence of teacher "telling" as the source of knowledge, I reconsider the many forms of intake that in fact exist, additional to the child's own independently propelled question asking. I see important roles for the adult *beyond* "telling" and even beyond support for the child's independent learning. "Telling" is only one aspect of teaching. Teaching is also present in the *context* that allows or fosters noticing, following after, and joining with, as well as providing support for the child's independent inquiries. The adult carries the context of life into the classroom or into the school, thus making important contributions to the functioning of the whole educative context. The adult functioning in this way can include the cooperation of the child. The teacher is not *just* assisting the child. The teacher is present as adult and adds to the educative context of the school by that presence. The work of the teacher has to be visible so that—very much as the child considers everything he or she observes about the adults at home or about the adults working in the world—the child is able to consider what it is the teacher does.

In the traditional school and sometimes—too many times—in the school as revised to be more responsive, adult functioning is difficult for the child to see. The process of building context, of collegial sharing and discussion—little of that is observable by the child. Many teachers, propelled by their commitment to the child, want very much not to take anything away from the time the child has to do his or her own thing or from the path of the child's own grappling for understanding. The inclusion of the child in the adultness of the classroom or the school—something one takes for granted in the child's home—is left out, as if that isn't also part of what the child wants and needs to make sense of.

Questions about grouping and assessment and judgments about whether the child can go on or not remain big issues in schools. Ideas of capacity and unconditionality are certainly not the ruling convictions. The judgments the school makes as gatekeeper are still central to administering the school, even though modified a certain amount. The way in which the child is held back may be modified by mixed-age grouping, for example, but it still exists.

Changes in school proceeded in limited kinds of ways, not as a big sweep that could then have support from the larger social setting. They were insufficient to really impact on the sweeping critique of the schools (others would say of education) as well as of the children and parents mentioned earlier. It remains easiest to lay the cause of failure on teachers.

I cannot say strongly enough that the focus of the widespread societal critique is not what I've been critiquing. Everyone was unhappy with the old, empty, lockstep teaching, with sterility of context. We focused differently on causes. I have been critiquing the limitations of change, the loss of focus on institutional change and on community.

THE IMPERATIVES OF CONTINUING ACTION AND REFLECTION

The questions I've been asking, in the presence of both old critique and formulations and more recent ones, are questions about the changes we were trying to make. How much has been actualized? How much of the old is still present in current efforts? What are the limitations and possibilities today? Each reexamination summed up what accomplishments had been found serviceable in practice but also pinpointed their limited relationship to what had been aimed for. The restatement of goals was clarifying, gave sharpened focus to our efforts, but also raised questions about limitations. The questions raised stemmed from what I think was a deeper and broader understanding of what the goals implied, a view not accessible before the modifications made more visible the possibilities and the difficulties.

The current critique of the schools seems to me still largely related to the unmodified school, not even attempting to build critique that took account of any changes attempted in the last 2½ decades. My own efforts are to take account of the impact of these attempted changes. What I have written here is all a reevocation of what it was we were trying to do to start and a reassessment of where we were at any given point and whether what we had done was consistent with our first commitment.

Doing what is moral is the first commitment. If you're support-ing the child's development and capacity and you know that the test-ing structure in no way does this, you may decide that—since no option exists that allows you not to administer the mandatory tests—you have to go along obediently. But if so, then your "going along" is not one of your moral acts. You know it's wrong, and it's hurting the child. You may not be able to help it, or you may make a judgment that "at least I can continue working against this." The moral effort for teachers always has to go back to the search for what is better and to support what is possible for that child, in that situation.

Then there is the question of why one struggles anyway, given that here is the institution? In spite of clear insight about limitations, the struggle is carried on because the goal is too important to dis-miss and a way must be found. The conclusion arrived at is that even small accomplishments were worthwhile because they created some easement and space for the child's development. Thus, movement toward *continuity* of experience and connection with past experience continued, even though it was plain that accomplishments were lim-ited. Some schools created a better experience for children than oth-ers, and this phenomenon was examined for the factors of continu-ity that had produced differential success. But here, too, a barrier to fuller accomplishment was evident. My understanding of settings where the context of educative support was not so limited became deeper through reexamination of what happened and didn't happen within the school setting. Other settings besides school—certainly the home, and also the neighborhood and the community, with sustained occupation of the site by the same people—might offer more conti-nuity of experience and more simultaneity of multifaceted experience. The obligation to learn from these nonschool settings and take into the school whatever could be taken from them, even though it would be limited by the nature of the school, became clearer and clearer.

The simple fact of the numbers of children within the institu-tion created its own imperatives. The attempt to modify and ease the impact of the numbers and groups had partially succeeded, but very partially. The imperatives of the fact of the group meant a responsi-bility for the teacher that partially equated with custodial functions, with control rather than with seeking how to rethink and redefine the institution. Yet on examination, the multiplicity of learning drives present in any group and even in any person could also be consid-ered positive aspects of the group: What does a group *give* to a child in his or her learning efforts? What does the child draw from that presence and interaction with a group that doesn't equate with control and all doing the same thing? What is the nature of cooperative learning? The accountability to parents who demanded specificity and individual focus, which for teachers meant that at some point there had to be a story of where *that* child was, certainly tended to continue the isolation, competitiveness, and stratification of the school setting.

The modes of teaching that we conceived in our first attempts to change—from more direct to more indirect support and stimulation of the child's interest through the setting, and then facilitation of what it was that the child wanted to do with the setting—were not as complete an account of modes of teaching as we had first thought. Many reexaminations over a long period of practice time directed our attention to additional forms of learning that were not contradictory to active learning. At no point is the human being inert like a chair or a stool or a pot. But saying "active learning" deals insufficiently with the differences in the relationship of learning to setting and to teacher. *How* do human beings take in from the neighborhood, the street, the home, the community? In each educative setting, what are the modes of learning?

The major mode of learning in all the outside-school settings is *noticing*. Certainly noticing is an active process. But the mere fact of noticing, and of course of cogitating about what is noticed, is important to underline as a mode of learning and to underline also in thinking about what the teacher's role is. How did the teacher support this mode? How did the setting impact in a facilitating manner? Such questions stressed the teacher's responsibility for the setting and for modifications of the setting in light of how children used it.

Observations of other settings pointed to the obvious: The child at home followed after the adults and even other children. Studying that mode could lead to some greater insight into the attraction, the glue, within *any* group development. The patterns of leading and following after—not simply of obedience and following directions—are again more apparent in home settings. The adult carries on the adult work openly in front of the children, and there is either a conscious invitation for the child to "join with" or it happens anyway, even when "joining with" is rejected. I remember my son putting up a heavy outer door, over 200 pounds, and his not-quite 3 three-year-old running after him saying, "I help you, Daddy!" and my son roars, "Out of my way!" because of the danger. Nevertheless, the fact of the danger, the fact of being pushed aside, is part of "joining with," of seeing what is dangerous and what isn't dangerous. This happens in the kitchen and everywhere in the home.

What I came to see was that at least some insight into the teacher as adult person grappling in continuous ways for understanding, for how to shape, was important for the child. The work of the teacher, as an adult carrying out an adult occupation, is nowhere near as evident to the child in school as parent activity is at home. What the child sees in school is the teacher's focus on observation of the child, on facilitating the child's work, on controlling the child. But the teacher's prior-to-class work as an adult preparing the context is not evident. The thought of the adult in collaboration with other adults in this thing called a school, the reporting and thinking and developing, is not evident. So if a child is to play out what it is to be a teacher, the child enacts the stereotypes of control—"Sit down!"—even if, in that school or classroom, control may not be a major mode of teaching or a definition of what the teacher does and the child has thus had different experiences. The play shows no sense of understanding the complexity and multiple strandedness of the teacher's work and very little "joining with" such work of the teacher. Though the teacher may join with the child in the child's efforts, joining with the *teacher* in her work is virtually nonexistent. But perhaps at least bits of this *can* come into the boxed modes of teacher function—"Oh, I mustn't waste a minute of the teaching time"—and can ease the image of ideal teacher performance in the minds of parents, administrators, and teachers themselves. It seems to me that this limited and closed view must be opened up to at least a little wider view of teacher function. After all, the child's effort to uncover the path to the adult world requires that perception.

Joining with is partly dependent on an expansion of the view of ownership. What is understood at home—"This is your home and it can't function without your participation"—is not really understood about school. The school cannot function if it is a place solely for the child or even groups of children to produce to adult mandate or expectation. What enables the school to function is participation. A sense of identification and ownership of the place, an openness— "Well, we can't get *this* done without getting some of *that* done"— must be built into the daily functioning of the participants in the life of that place.

Discussing the participants' relationship to school as involving ownership and contribution of work that is valued gives body to the ideas of the school as community and of joining the community. The idea is community feeling not only in the sense of, for example, a cooperative group production ("Here's what the third graders could do to help") but also in the sense of contribution to the whole school.

That is where the teacher's possessiveness about the classroom and her closing off from the school as a whole, protectively for herself and, as she thinks of it, for the children, become a problem. Work for, contribution to, value for *our* place has some resonance in the classroom, but it has a larger resonance when there is identification with the larger context of the whole school.

Unfortunately, many teachers and administrators turn away from the community around the school as harmful to the children. The school is conceived of as a savior, a protector for the children. Even in this conception, however, an eased sense about work and contribution would help with the supposedly savior aspects of the school. I am proposing that there is no way to relate to children as though they must be protected from their homes and community context. There may be enormous negative factors in the community, but the elements that can rebuild the community are also situated within that community.

With all its limitations, there is the school. We have it. Without being the savior or the bulwark against the community, school exists as a place that children inhabit for a long time, and it exists in a way that, in the past and today, poisons children's feelings and causes teachers' feelings of despair and disappointment because it is not working as they imagine it might. Seeing this, we continued to make efforts to learn about other settings and to be more observant about the complexity of the process and more respectful of the complexity of each bundle of capacities that is the child. The school exists, and so one continues the efforts to make it better. The first principle of making it better must be to do no harm. This is an operant imperative within all the caring professions. First, do no harm. Second, continue your efforts to understand the thing enough to make it possible to continue trying to better the impact of one's efforts and to release the efforts of the child.

The path of constant reexamination, of grappling with, that assumes no final end or conclusion or perfection in any of the settings is a feature inherent in being a teacher and in being an educator of teachers. It is a process that can help sharpen our focus on any setting, since we are teachers, and on the school in particular as an educative context. The process includes examination of what isn't there and what is there. It includes the effect of certain processes that we didn't even notice before but that now emerge, perhaps because of something released by a small change, and how we can take advantage of it. And so on. This kind of reexamination is what I have tried to do, giving the history of what and how things became visible for me in many, many reexaminations and what they meant to me in terms of how children's learning process was affected by the teacher's commitment and clarity of commitment and the teaching process that resulted from that.

Teacher education and preparation, it seems to me, comes down to an intensified examination and reexamination of this type, to learning about the various educative contexts, to learning about what is inherent in a teacher's commitment, and to recognizing that what teachers do—teaching—cannot be defined as only direct telling. On the contrary, that is only a bit of the adult function. The ways of carrying out the teacher's commitment are various and complex. They expand and grow as we practice our profession and reflect on it.

REFERENCE

Holmes Group. (1990). *Tomorrow's schools. Principles for the design of professional development schools: A report of the Holmes Group*. East Lansing, MI: Author.

CHAPTER 12

Is There Room for Children's Inventive Capacity in the Curriculum?

Hubert Dyasi

In 1987, a group of teachers at the Washington School—an early childhood school for children aged 3 to 5 years in New York City—compiled a book of children's ideas about a variety of natural phenomena. The ideas had been expressed in response to questions such as: What was it like when the world began? What are clouds? Where does the rain come from? What made early people different from apes? Where does the sky start? What are thunder and lightning? I was fascinated by the book. I wanted to know what prompted the teachers to seek children's ideas about natural phenomena, and I wondered what I could learn about the children from their expressed ideas.

My question about the teachers' views of children was answered quickly and easily. In the preface, the teachers state that they believe that "children are curious creatures. They want to know why and how, and it's one of the best parts of teaching to listen to their questions. And answers." These statements express the educational foundation of the work of the Workshop Center at City College; that curiosity, as manifested through questions or inquiry, is a fundamental human trait.

As I continued to read the book, I also learned that the teachers believe that "children are story tellers. They daily invent and re-invent their world. We are fortunate enough," they went on, "to have children who trust us enough to share their secrets and visions." These words evoked in me countless expressions of the same notion by many scholars as it applies to all human beings in general.

More than a decade ago, Philip Morris, professor of physics at the Massachusetts Institute of Technology, presented illustrations of the inventiveness of the human species in contrast to the lack of inventiveness of nonprimates when he delivered the Second Bronowski Memorial Lecture. In that lecture he gave a detailed account of how termites build their "homes," complete with intricate channels. But wherever termite mounds or "hills" are found, he pointed out, they have the same architecture; they do not show any signs of inventiveness on the part of termites. Termites and many other animal species have a fixed adaptation. In his *Ascent of Man*, Jacob Bronowski (1974) uses many examples, such as the grunion fish and the horseshoe crab, to make that same point about nonprimates.

More important, however, Bronowski demonstrates that humans are not born with an exact adaptation to a specific physical or cultural environment. At the outset, humans are not specialized but are born with a generalized adaptation framework characterized by plasticity or flexibility. It is a framework with immense possibility for ingenuity and inventiveness.

Underlining this attribute of the human race, Peter Wilson (1980), in *Man, the Promising Primate*, points out that over time, the human is the one species that has been capable of transcending many limits imposed by physical environments. But a generalized adaptation framework by itself can be disadvantageous to an organism unless the organism can take advantage of its plasticity, for example, by adjusting or seeking out alternatives or by capitalizing on opportunities to experiment, engaging in trial and error, search and find. It has the capacity to invent, but it must also have the opportunity. At the heart of adaptive activities and giving energy to a person is curiosity. But curiosity is not a sufficient condition for inventiveness. In order to invent new ways of doing things, humans must also be able to abstract from experience. Experience is embedded in the trials of new ways of doing things (in the applications of inventions or products of imagination), and abstraction implies that the results of the trials must be turned into lessons, and the resultant knowledge and understandings must be organized and reorganized continually to create new meaning.

All these thoughts came to my mind through the examples provided by the children of the Washington School. Here are some of their answers to the question Why can't animals talk?

> Animals aren't as smart as people. They have their own
> language like giraffes have their own words, like every animal.
> A bunny rabbit can talk to a bunny rabbit.

My cat jumps on my mom when she wants to eat. She just doesn't talk like a person.

Bears talk to bears, but they can't talk to children.

The common theme is that animals communicate with their own kind in their own ways, and some animals, such as the cat, communicate with people in ways that cats and people have come to understand. These answers seem to represent children's own ideas arising out of their experiences.

Among answers to the question Why does it rain? are the following:

God was crying. [Then why did God cry?] God's girlfriend died and all the crying came into a cloud. He gets more and more girlfriends but they keep dying. When it's sunny is when he has a girlfriend.

Because birds told God to make rain and he pressed a button and the plants and grass grew up to trees and the trees grew up to the top of the air.

There was a big cloud and each time it bumped another cloud they both opened up because they are not too strong.

Note that the last answer is qualitatively different from the others. The answer does not give qualities that relate to people or other living things, and the given qualities do not distort the nature of the entities that bring about the observed effects. This point is also true of the following answers to the question What makes waves?

The current. Sometimes it's so strong that the waves are really high. Sometimes the current is very weak and don't do so high.

I think it's just the wind pushing the water.

Pressure from the wind makes the water go faster. When it's not so windy, the waves aren't so high.

But the answers below are quite different qualitatively. They portray a notion that it is only living things that are responsible for the observed events.

I know the real real real real real real way. I think waves are made by the creatures and the shells underneath the water.

The sand moves and when it moves quickly, it makes big big waves.

I think there's something in the ocean pushes up water from the bottom of the ocean where sand ends. It pushes water up so fast, it makes waves.

As children grow older, the source, content, and quality of their observations and intellectual understandings may change, but the invention of explanations remains an abiding characteristic. In his analysis of first graders' discussions of the sun's heat and the ways they had experienced it, Edward Chittenden (1990) of Educational Testing Service cited a situation in which one of the children posed the following problem: "If the sun makes it hot, how could it be hot at night, even though the sun has gone down?" Another child offered this explanation:

> The sun reflects off the moon so there's going to be some heat left in the moon . . . if there is a lot of heat in the moon then it will be warm at night . . . if a little heat then it will be cold. (p. 227)

Regardless of its flaws, this explanation is a child's way of re-solving an apparent discrepancy between a plausible explanation and observations. The explanation does not resort to attributing charac-teristics of living things to either the sun or the moon. In kind, it does not differ from what scientists and other adults do to make sense of the world.

To some adults, the children's responses to the questions might appear nonsensical, cute, or even ridiculous. But they say a great deal about human explanations: They do not arise de novo, and they are based on identifiable frames of reference. Some of the children's explanations use social interactions as a frame of reference (e.g., rain as God's tears as a result of being jilted), and others are based on poorly understood physical explanations. It appears that from the children's perspective, explanations do not necessarily have to be correct as long as they are believable. If the element of believability of a frame of reference is actually important in children's explana-tions of phenomena of nature, then that same element might be important in people's acceptance of, for example, scientific frames of reference.

The above examples are instances of children's intellectual in-ventions arising out of their experiences generally rather than from some preplanned instruction in school. In most cases, however, they are also responses to specific prompts from an adult. The human capacity to invent, however, demonstrates its power even more among children when there is no specific prompt from an adult. In *MIRACLES: Poems by children of the English-speaking world*, Richard Lewis (1966) included this poem by Danny Marcus, a 7-year-old from the United States:

THE MAGIC FLOWER

Once there was a magic flower.
He lived out in the cold:
He lived in the dark and cold.
So he spun and spun
Until he grew very hot.
The whole world grew hot.
Then,
Out came the magic flower!
It was spun out,
Just as I am telling you.

The child combined his firsthand observations and knowledge of flowers with a strong sense of cause and effect and of the tremendous amount of heat energy he imagines is created by the flower and then transferred to the earth, perhaps to bring about spring and summer, which are the seasons for the flower to appear. Quite clearly, this child has gone beyond mere pronouncements or observations to reflective thought and to a novel idea.

As the foregoing examples of children's inventions tend to suggest, and as we know from science generally, observations or data on phenomena do not necessarily have a unique explanation; there is always the possibility of multiple logical explanations for the same set of observations. This point poses tantalizing possibilities for responsive curricula offerings in schools; the possibilities are curricula and implementations that provide ample opportunity for learners to grapple with the exigencies of their world, to engage in purposeful trial-and-learn activities that enable them to come to terms with the challenges posed by that world, and to create habits of thoughtful abstraction and of invention of ideas regarding its nature.

But that is not all. Since children's explanations will not necessarily coincide with those generally accepted by scholars in a given discipline, the teacher has a distinctive interactive role that creates a greater likelihood of children's inventions having demonstrable viability. Eleanor Duckworth (1987) gives an example of a classroom situation that made room for a child's invention, drawing on scientific principles the child had learned. She wrote about a fifth grader named Hank who had been learning about electric circuits using dry cells (flashlight batteries), bulbs, and a variety of wires. His teacher later made "mystery boxes." Each box had two wires coming out. Inside the box, and unknown to the children, the wires were attached to a bulb, a dry cell, a wire of certain resistance, or not connected at all. By trying to complete the circuit outside the box, the children were expected to figure out the configuration of the wires inside the box, and more. After the children found out which lightbulbs lit, the teacher asked them to devise ways to find out which of the boxes was connected by a lightbulb. The teacher herself did not think that there was a way of finding out. The children were faced not just with the problem of deduction (which they could solve by following procedures they had learned) but also with the task of "inventing" a way to distinguish between different types of connectors inside the boxes. Hank solved the problem by connecting the wires through six batteries instead of through the lightbulb he had been given. If the connector inside the box was a lightbulb, the six batteries would burn it out and a lightbulb connected to the outside wires would not light. If, however, the connector was a wire or a battery, the lightbulb would still go on. He tested his ideas and solved the problem. Fortunately for Hank, his teacher did not just create a situation that made it possible for children to be inventive, she also accepted a "wonderful idea" and gave the child the opportunity to test it.

Geri Smith (1993) gives an example of possibility in children's learning of mathematics. In his desire to help the children be mathematical thinkers, he usually presents his class with real-life problems—that is, problems of practical and often immediate relevance to children. In addition to problems such as how many cars are needed to transport the class to the aquarium, he gave the following problem:

> There are four parents who have come to a PTC meeting held at the school library. As each one enters the room, she/he shakes hands with the other members. If everyone shakes hands once with each person in the room, how many handshakes would there be?

He divided the students into groups of four so that each group could act out the activity—some groups actually created such a vignette. Starting with one member already seated, a second member enters and shakes hands—giving the answer of one handshake (the children gave each member of the PTC a name so that they would not have to bother with first, second, and so on). A third member enters and shakes hands with each of the two members already present—totaling one handshake plus two handshakes, or three handshakes. Then a fourth member arrives and shakes hands with each of the three members already present—a total of six handshakes. After arguing among themselves whether this answer was right or wrong, they decided to check it using unifix cubes as members of the PTC and confirmed it. Geri then suggested that they might want to see the results in the case of five and then six committee members. Significantly, this time one of the children first guessed seven, which they tested, and were amazed to discover that the answer was 10! They tried six people, and then went on to seven, getting:

4 people = 6 handshakes
5 people = 10 handshakes
6 people = 15 handshakes
7 people = 21 handshakes

Soon one of the children saw a pattern developing and thought that they could use it to find out how many handshakes for up to 10 members. After some discussion, they saw that the pattern started by adding four, then five, six, and seven. "We found a pattern!" one of them said, "4 + 6 = 10, and then 5 + 10 = 15, then 6 + 15 = 21, and 7 + 21 = 28." "Oh, awesome! I didn't notice that," said another. The children had discovered a mathematical pattern and used it to predict for 10 and then for 11 members. They were excited to realize that their discovery actually worked; they then undertook the joyous task of finding other patterns. Geri built on this discovery and excitement to engage the students deeper and deeper in mathematical thinking. Of course, not every child in the class undertook the evolution and power of the discovery of the pattern.

These two examples are wonderful, except that they occurred in spite of school curriculum rather than as a central part of learning in school. So the question remains: What can be done to cultivate the children's invention in school while ensuring their progress toward knowledgeable acceptance of scientific or mathematical frames of reference as bases for explanations of observed phenomena?

In England, where primary (i.e., elementary) school teachers have considerable freedom in determining their curricula, teachers have provided numerous opportunities for children's inventions. Stephen Rowland (1984) gives a number of examples in this effort. In one case he wrote about two students who were learning mathematics using the Fibonacci series as a starting point. The series has the following sequence: 1 1 2 3 5 8 13 21 34, etc. The series grows by adding the two last numbers to obtain the next number: 1 + 1 = 2, 1 + 2 = 3, 2 + 3 = 5, and so on. The children soon saw this pattern, but the problem was that the series reaches large numbers very quickly. Interesting features, however, can emerge if the series is modified, as Rowland did, to remain in single digits. This is achieved by adding the two digits in numbers above 10. In the example above, 13 would be entered as 4 (1 + 3 = 4); we would then have 1 1 2 3 5 8 4 3 7 and so on. The second 3 is arrived at by 8 + 4 = 12, then 1 + 2 = 3. When the series progressed this way, children were able to handle all the additions without using calculators. They discovered that when done this way, the series repeats after 24 entries and that if the next set of entries beginning with 2 2 (instead of 1 1) is arranged in corresponding columns in the next row, a matrix of numbers can be created. This arrangement is continued until the last row begins with 9 9. Upon close examination, children can realize that they have created interesting mathematical patterns, for example, multiplication tables. Children can use the matrix to make numerical inventions or to discover mathematical properties of numerical arrangements with which they are familiar.

In a statement entitled *Curriculum with a Difference*, Eleanor Duckworth (1974) discussed an African science program she was associated with that attempted to achieve this goal through science curricula in which "the unexpected is valued." That program produced teachers' guides, but

> instead of expecting teachers and children to do only what was specified in the booklets, without missing anything, the aim of the program is for children and teachers to have so many un-anticipated ideas of their own about what to do with the materials that they never even use the booklets. The point of developing materials at all is to get teachers and children started in producing their own ideas and following through on their own. (p. 16)

What runs through all the examples given above is what Duckworth (1987) referred to as having "so many unanticipated ideas" or, as Richard Frazier (1990) pointed out, to begin without a conclusion. This notion of beginning without a conclusion is what creates opportunities for students to exercise their ingenuity. When practiced well, the notion makes it essential to learn science and mathematics directly by handling objects of phenomena and to keep the details of the learners' actions in full view. In other words, making efforts to build upon children's capacity to think visually and to be highly aware of their own thinking helps cultivate frames of reference that are not just believable to children but also scholastically valid. Making room in the curriculum for the kind of teaching and learning illustrated above is a formidable challenge for a teacher of, say, science at the precollege levels. School science curricula have been carefully constructed to encourage teachers to "cover" specified facts, concepts, explanations, and theories in their lessons; teachers' knowledge of science is inadequate; teaching schedules leave little or no room for flexibility; and resources for science teaching are meager. In other words, neither the usual curricula nor schools nor most teachers can be regarded as inventive. But there are promising efforts in science and mathematics curricula that have been developed nationally. Both the mathematics standards and the emerging national science education standards will buttress ongoing efforts, but curricula and standards alone cannot do it. A change toward making the building of children's ingenuity the central task of schools is essential.

REFERENCES

Bronowski, J. (1974). *The ascent of man*. Boston: Little, Brown.

Chittenden, E. (1990). *The assessment of hands-on elementary science programs* (G. Hein, Ed.) (Monograph of the North Dakota Study Group on Evaluation). Grand Forks: University of North Dakota.

Duckworth, E. (1974). *Curriculum with a difference: Science in the open classroom*. New York: City College Workshop Center, City College.

Duckworth, E. (1987). *The having of wonderful ideas & other essays on teaching and learning*. New York: Teachers College Press.

Frazier, R. (1990). Beginning without a conclusion. *The Science Teacher*, 55(5), 38–40.

Lewis, R. (1966). *MIRACLES: Poems by children of the English-speaking world*. New York: Simon & Schuster.

Rowland, S. (1984). *The enquiring classroom: An approach to understanding children's learning*. London: Falmer Press.

Smith, G. (1993). How do you know what to teach if you don't follow a book. *The Constructivist*.

Wilson, P. (1980). *Man, the promising primate: The conditions of human evolution*. New Haven, CT: Yale University Press.

CHAPTER 13

Democratic Classrooms, Democratic Schools

Bruce Kanze

During 24 years of classroom teaching, I've learned many lessons. The most important has been that children are always thinking and constructing their particular views of the world. They develop meaning from the tiniest interactions. They also struggle with the larger picture. A question I've often come back to in my thinking about classrooms is, How do children translate the discussions, the rules, and the structures we present them with in school into a coherent picture of the world? I present several experiences here, one in my own classroom and others as an observer in a new and developing school, in order to explore the meanings they hold for the children and adults involved.

The first experience took place in my class in Central Park East, an alternative public school in East Harlem, where I've taught for 13 years. More than half of our students come from the immediate community; the rest come from other parts of New York City. My combined fifth- and sixth-grade class had 32 children, ages 10 to 13. It was a multiracial classroom: about one third African American, one third Latino, and one third white. One child came to the United States from mainland China when she was 6.

We'd been discussing fair and unfair situations. We began by talking about what is fair and unfair in school and at home, in our personal relationships (how we're treated), in games, in rules, and in the law. This brought us to the larger perspectives involving considerations of race, gender, and culture. We looked at the different ways historical figures have handled situations they thought were unfair. One of the people we looked at was Dr. Martin Luther King.

What follows are notes I wrote to myself after a discussion we had in class:

> We watched a movie today about the civil rights movement; it was called "I Have a Dream," and it documented a segment of Dr. King's life. It was very powerful. At one point, the film detailed the various false charges that were brought against Dr. King (driving with an illegal license, tax fraud, etc.) and mentioned that President Kennedy intervened on Dr. King's behalf and got him out of jail at least twice. In our class discussion, a child asked, "If the president is so powerful, then why can't he just fix things?" It is a very telling question, because it gets to the heart of right and wrong, power and change. Some of the other students responded to the question intellectually, by talking about the ways in which laws are made and that Congress has to approve a law. These responses spoke to the limits of the president's powers: S/he can propose laws but has to depend on the support of Congress in order for ideas to become law.

I think that the child's original question asked something different. It asked about the relationship between "right" and reality: If something isn't right, and someone has power, shouldn't that person use her or his power to make things right? I remember, as a child, wondering why our government couldn't just arrest everyone who was "bad" (which to me probably meant anyone who was "different"—with different values and beliefs—even more than someone who broke the law).

In our class discussion, I drew a comparison (maybe a little presumptuous on my part, but certainly related) to my position as a teacher: I see things that I think need to be changed, but the kids in the class don't necessarily go along with what I think. I can say, for instance, that everyone should be nice to everyone else, but I can't make people be nice. And who's to say that my view of what constitutes "nice" is the correct one? I'm reminded of the line in Bertolt Brecht's play *Galileo*: "Sad is the country that needs a hero." People make mistakes, but they have to be trusted with the power to govern, or else horrible errors will be committed in the name of doing what is right for them. Doing right, after all, is a social process and not just an end result.

Children do right in class because they have a commitment to the structure and process in the classroom, and they accept a part in that process. What makes citizens do right? It is exasperating to think that something *should* be done, and to see that you can't simply force everyone to do the right thing. In children, a sense of the needs and differences of others develops gradually. How do we nurture in children a sense of fairness and an acceptance of rules that are mutually shared? What happens when they see other children show that they don't accept the rules? What happens when everyone isn't treated equally? And how does the school help children develop a flexible yet strong sense of themselves with respect to the group? To see themselves as people who have to live by rules, but who can also change rules that are somehow harmful?

Schools can promote a sense of power in children, or they can stifle that sense. During my current sabbatical, I'm recording the birth pains of a new alternative public school. This school is being developed in a school district that until now has been exclusively hierarchical. Previously, all decisions about structure, class organization, curriculum, whether to allow parents to see teachers face to face during the school day were made at the top and trickled down through the school administration to the classroom. Parents who rebelled sent their children to schools in other districts or to private school. The tiny new school of just five classes that I've been observing grew out of persistent efforts by parents in the district. When the new district superintendent asked parents of children in private day-care centers in his district, "What would it take for you to keep your children in our district?" their organized response was that they wanted real decision-making power: the power to set up a school that they thought would help their children learn, the power to hire a program director, and then the power to support that director in decisions about who was hired, about what was being taught in the classrooms, and about how it would be taught. So a tiny "experiment" in democracy was started, and new questions and problems started pouring out.

One aspect that interested me was how conflicts between the traditional approach that exists throughout the district and the more open approach that was becoming the defining character of this new school would play out for children. The following incident developed over 3 days: Hope, a second grader in the school, had been struggling to make a castle. She used oaktag, which she couldn't get to stay up. I looked at it with her on Wednesday afternoon, but there hadn't been time to work on it. I thought about it on Thursday and came back on Friday and asked her teacher if Hope and I could work together on papier-mâché. We arranged a time right after lunch and decided to work in the hallway just outside the classroom. Hope picked a friend to work with us. We got the ingredients for the papier-mâché and started talking about what we would need to do. But other students from the class kept coming by, insisting that they wanted to learn to do the papier-mâché too and that to exclude them would be unfair. One child said, "If you're not going to teach everyone to do it, then you shouldn't teach anyone."

I had to stop to think about that concept, so clearly stated. On the surface, it sounds so democratic: Treat everyone the same. But is it a valid concept educationally? It challenged everything I had come to believe about the joy and challenge of teaching, which begins for me with discovering what excites each child especially. I explained to the child that sometimes in a classroom two or three students might learn something first because they are particularly interested or ready or lucky, and then they can teach what they've learned to other students, and so on, until everyone who is interested can learn a specific thing. We talked some more about this child's feelings about being left out and her fear that if she didn't get to do it at that very moment she would never get to do it. She thought that she would be forgotten. She didn't trust promises that her time would come.

This experience suggested more questions: How do you structure a classroom so that children can pursue their interests, even if that means that everybody might be doing something different? How do you build trust so that children will accept that if they don't get to do something in one activity time their turn will eventually come? How do you acknowledge the specialness of one child's work or process without making other students feel left out? Much of the conflict in this particular situation was the result of the students' prior experiences with school. It isn't a coincidence that this incident involved the oldest children in this school (second and third graders), because they are most likely to have experienced school in a different way prior to coming to this new school. In school as they have known it, all students in a class did the same thing at the same time. The exceptions were for misbehavior.

This was probably not always the case, however. Early childhood teachers often pay a great deal of attention to structuring the room and routines so that sharing occurs naturally. I've observed the way teachers set limits by asking children to think of three activities they would like to do, so that if their first choice is filled up, they can get their second or third. They also check with the children: If four children can work at the sand table, and two have already chosen it, how many more can work there? This is intended to help children learn to count in a meaningful context, but it also builds sharing into the curriculum. It happens in classrooms where children are expected to be able to make choices. It's important to point out that classrooms that are built around student choice don't sacrifice the teaching of skills in favor of letting children do what they want. Instead, skills are learned as part of activities that the children themselves help select, plan, and develop. False dichotomies have been set up between learner-centered and skills-oriented classrooms. The inaccuracy of this separation is exposed any time students in a learner-centered classroom are observed hard at work on a task that challenges them to learn, or when one walks into a classroom where the teacher imparts skills and the students ask, "Why are we learning this?"

My question about democracy grew more complex. A democratic classroom is not necessarily one in which the children and the teacher share in decision making equally. That can be a recipe for chaos. Instead, the teacher provides an environment in which children are constantly making choices and in which their interests are reflected in the activities and the curriculum. But the teacher is constantly structuring and framing activities, watching closely as the children grow, supplying books and other resources, asking questions, developing materials based on what that teacher observes as the interests and needs of each child. As the children make choices, the teacher becomes a learner along with the children.

Rules and routines are dynamic; the children's role in setting limits grows as they become more aware of the complexities of community, fairness, and justice. After several months, a teacher of 5- and 6-year-olds recently had a dilemma: A child who was given to tantrums when he didn't get his way wanted to be the third child to work in the block area, which was restricted to two people. The teacher asked the children how they wanted to handle the problem. She felt that the class had learned to work in the block area well enough that they were ready for a third child to come in, but she wanted the children to express their ideas and feelings. After much discussion, they decided that the limit on the number of children allowed to work in blocks could be raised to three. But so that the children would see that other changes were possible and not just this one to appease a potentially upset young man, the teacher asked the children about other areas of the room that could be changed. She was consciously helping the children to see how rules develop and their role in changing the rules that affect them. In classrooms where everyone does the same thing at the same time, and where the choice of study isn't made even by the classroom teacher but by someone higher in the educational hierarchy, students and teachers miss out on opportunities to direct their own learning and to participate in community.

The new school I've been observing is a program inside a much larger school (the school has a total of 1,104 children; the little program I'm looking at has about 120). As part of my job as documenter, I interviewed the building principal. I asked the principal about curriculum and suggested that a difference between the larger school and this smaller one might be that teachers in the smaller program create their own curriculum. She quickly assured me that her teachers create their own curriculum as well. With the passion of a committed educator, she explained that she has been involved in developing curriculum in the district for 26 years. She pulled out two programs she had worked on that she hoped to implement in her school. One is a hands-on science program, the other a literature-based reading program. Both are highly structured and lay out for the teacher exactly what is to be taught, in what way, and on which day. These packages take away from the classroom teacher the need to interact with each student. The teacher is no longer an information gatherer; there is no need to find out about each child's interests or needs or abilities or preferences. This step is superseded by a well-developed set of activities or reading lists, complete with dates when everything is due and letters to parents asking them to sign contracts agreeing to follow through at home. The program developers provided everything thoroughly and completely—nothing is left to chance, to impulse, to possibilities unseen. The principal talked about how exhaustively they had searched for books that would meet the reading levels and address the interests of children in general (the assumption is that children who are the same age with similar backgrounds will have the same interests). So many problems have been solved; all the teacher has to do is open the package and administer it—very tempting.

Many of the parents in the small school I've been documenting chose to send their children there either because of its newness or because of the commitment and friendliness of its tiny staff. But these parents also have a picture in their minds of what a good school looks like, which they learned when they were children in school. They want textbooks, tests, repetitive homework—the things that are familiar to them and that say, "My child is learning. I know that because I can see the neat writing in her workbook." Instead, in this new school, their children's homework is often a discussion or a survey or a suggestion that they cook together. Many parents have said, "I want to help my child, but I don't know what you're asking me to do." This complaint then becomes, "I'm not sure that my child is learning anything. When I ask him what he did all day, he says, 'We played and we drew.' When are they learning?"

Teachers have a responsibility to explain to parents what they are doing with their children on an ongoing basis. We cannot ask parents to accept everything we do on the basis of blind faith. Explaining, convincing, exploring, and illustrating to parents a way of looking at their children's learning, particularly a way that is different from their personal experience, is hard work. On the surface, it seems that a democratic response to the parents' concerns about learning and growth, which can look confusing in the classroom, might be to implement one of the neatly packaged learning programs. But that would be doing exactly what the child in my class wanted the president of the United States to do when she asked why he didn't just fix things that were wrong.

Encouraging children to reveal their thinking and ideas and to follow their interests and preferences leads to children doing different things, studying different topics in different ways, and this is bound to be confusing. The teacher's job becomes helping to identify interests and collecting materials to assist the child in exploring these interests, connecting skill development to deep interests, and then providing opportunities for sharing that learning with other students. A 6-year-old who falls in love with the classroom bunny can spend all day reading and drawing about bunnies. This interest will follow the child around the school, home, and back again. Those skills that teachers and parents are concerned about building can be developed through the selection of reading materials and the activities the teacher works out with the child. And the sharing of discoveries will help the child develop interpersonal skills. The curriculum becomes the children and their ongoing learning. The teacher doesn't deliver learning in neat morsels; instead, the teacher facilitates learning. It is a commitment to this kind of teaching that has excited the teachers in the new small school. But these teachers also have accepted their responsibility to share with parents how they see their children learning, telling parents about the choices their children are making, and earning parents' confidence in what is a new way of doing school.

This is hard work; it requires the teacher to think about children's choices and to be able to talk with parents about these things. One parent explained that her child was becoming more difficult at home because the child wanted reasons for everything. Encouraging the child to question things in school had carried over to home. This is the kind of change that can cause problems between the school and the family, but through ongoing dialogue and mutual respect, this parent was able to see her child's attitude as positive, and she came to support it. What if this hadn't been what the parent had wanted for her child? The school has a duty to meet parents more than half-way, to listen carefully to parents' concerns, and to consider parents' suggestions. The school must explain and then explain some more in order to invite parents into the process. And when communication breaks down, it is the school's responsibility to reach out to families and explain its reasons. Sometimes misunderstandings occur because of cultural differences; when this happens, it is important that the school learn about and find ways to acknowledge the cultural values of the families of the children it teaches. Learning should never be only from school to home. The school is strengthened as parents and school staff become more aware of each other's needs and viewpoints and as the school articulates its reasons for the way it structures learning.

Prepackaged programs change the student-teacher relationship from one of mutual exploration—with all its doubts and errors—to one of linear certainty. Teachers aren't consulted; instead, experts choose books and set up schedules. Students aren't asked about the books they love to read or why they choose to read certain books. Instead, they are given a list of books to read, chosen by faceless, unapproachable experts. It may be that the kids and their teachers would have chosen the very books on the lists, but they are never asked. So the teacher rarely learns what really excites a child about a particular book. Parents are enforcers at home, and this certainly makes things a lot easier, but it bypasses the need for a school to make clear what it sees as learning. It makes the intellectual highway between home and school one way. The school tells the parents what to do, and the parents see (or fail to see) that it's done. Expectations are sometimes written into a contract, perhaps to get current (the parents) and future (the students) workers used to the irrevocability of contracts that are passed down by nameless, faceless management. And in so doing, it kills the generative interaction between the child and the teacher that makes learning individual and special for the teacher, the student, and the parent.

Democracy is sloppy. In the classroom, it begins with conditions that say to a student, "I expect you to have ideas and to make choices, and therefore I'm going to structure our classroom experiences in ways that encourage you to make real choices." Equity doesn't mean everyone doing the same thing at the same time, but everyone doing things that hold meaning for them and being able to share that meaning with others. In a school, it establishes procedures that say to parents, "You are your child's first teachers; you know more about your child as a learner than anyone else; we want to be able to share our knowledge in ways that will support your child's growth." This is a slow process because it involves building trust, trust that is often withheld in public schools that are typically anonymous and too large. But it is by building trust and opening up the school community to all its voices that real learning can take place. In New York City, as in many other school districts, the schools are often battlegrounds, where people in education fight their clients. Often the battle is fought over little differences that belie larger cultural, racial, and class differences. Around the little school I'm documenting, the community is working class and poor; most of the residents are recent immigrants (specifically Dominican) and people of color. The teaching staff of the school is racially and culturally mixed. The staff is careful to issue all its literature in Spanish and English; this includes everything from school notices to homework and invitations to come to school. Meetings are always conducted bilingually, whether they are parent association meetings or family conferences. At family conferences, the staff begins by inviting the family to talk about how they see learning; much of the conference is devoted to learning from the parents about their child and from the child herself or himself. One parent explained her apprehensiveness before a family conference. But 10 minutes into the conference, her 6-year-old son said that he had to go to the bathroom and instructed everyone, "Don't say anything while I'm gone. This is about me, and it's important." Expertise is shared. The parent's and the child's knowledge is celebrated, along with the staff's. This is a slow process, but it is the process of building a popular culture within a democratic school in which everyone is supported and valued.

CHAPTER 14

The Complexity of Teaching

Rita Tenorio

School reform continues to receive attention from all levels of government, from various public officials and policy makers. Yet as we move into the 21st century, we can no longer be satisfied with empty rhetoric and the lack of real commitment to children. We must expect and demand a renewed focus on education. As educators, we can take the discussion into a new era, one that is based on the reality of the students we serve, and one where the voices of those closest to the process of teaching and learning will be heard.

I am particularly concerned about the discussion of national goals as they relate to children starting out in school. One goal that continues to be put forward is that by the year 2000, all students will enter school "ready to learn." If this goal alerts us to the importance of early health care—children's physical, dental, and nutritional needs—I have no argument. I'm anxiously awaiting the day when we have adequate health care for all children so that our students come to school with healthy bodies. Unfortunately, this goal also implies that we set certain norms or standards for young children as they enter school. With this I take serious issue. I question the whole notion of what "readiness" really means and how it is defined.

Education writer John Holt (1965, 1967) got at the essence of what school readiness ought to be when he argued that schools are supposed to work for children, not children for schools. As educators, we must ask ourselves if *we* are prepared to meet the goal of having our schools "ready" to teach the children who come to our door.

We face an incredible challenge each and every day teaching children whose lives are diverse and complicated. Increasing numbers of children live in poverty. Children are the largest group of poor people in our country—20% overall, and double that for children of color. The wave of immigrants from various parts of the world continues. Children of all economic levels are subjected to daily stress as well as various forms of abuse and neglect. In many ways children grow up too quickly, exposed to a range of difficult images, experiences, and circumstances through the media and our society. They see more violence around them; they see more carelessness.

There are some who would say that ecologically we are facing a grim future and that we have only a few years to save our planet. Our society is suffering from increasing crime, and families face intense pressure on a daily basis. The gap between rich and poor widens each year, and we've experienced a sharp increase in the number of poor and homeless people. In our modern, wealthy, and highly technological society we find many people without jobs, without health care, without the resources they need to survive.

All these issues walk into the classroom along with our students. The culture of stress, violence, drugs, and poverty pervading our society permeates our schools as well. Sometimes these problems walk in the front door, in the form of gang violence or cocaine-affected children; more often they come through the back door in the form of mistrust, low self-esteem, or the hopelessness mirrored in the faces of children who experience adults in their lives who are trapped in structures of racism, oppression, and exploitation. For many students, school is the calmest and safest place to be.

We educators view our role as preparing children for their future. As I hear people discuss the future, there is one clear idea that emerges: We really don't know what the next century will bring; there will certainly be change, and we must be prepared to accept and respond to that. We do know that the future lives and work of today's kindergarten children will include things that are not yet known.

We also know that our nation will continue to become increasingly multicultural and multilingual, increasingly technological, increasingly complex. There will no doubt be a critical need to recognize and come to terms with our global interdependence. To be successful, our students will have to be literate in a range of ways: verbally, numerically, technically, socially, politically. But they must also be skilled planners and organizers, skilled communicators, and analytical and global thinkers. We will want them to be self-managers and active, open-minded learners.

What an incredible challenge. Yet I will tell you that I see the future every day in the faces of my students. And despite all the negative things one hears about our schools or our students, there is a different side as well—one that is diverse, positive, creative, and resourceful. We have bright, motivated, and, yes, challenging students. And there are many people—teachers, administrators, parents, and community members —who keep our schools alive and well on a daily basis.

In 20 years of teaching kindergarten, I have never met a child who was not eager, anxious, and "ready" to experience the world around. Despite the crisis we face in our communities and the challenge we face in the future, our hope, our promise is in the investment we make in our children. Young children are ready to take on schooling. It is our responsibility to see that our schools are ready for them.

Curriculum must be conceived as a dynamic process that is the sum total of what is taught and learned throughout the school experience. It is more than books and lesson plans—it is relationships, interactions, feelings, and attitudes. The curriculum reflects our values as teachers, parents, and communities, so we must become explicit about large goals and overriding purposes. For me, deep thinking, equity, and multiculturalism are critical, even at the earliest levels. We must be aware not only of the "academic" goals that we want children to achieve but also of all the other messages, values, and expectations that children are learning in school. Children learn quickly, for example, whether their way of speaking is acceptable. They see if their families are welcomed and encouraged to participate. They look for themselves in the images in the classroom displays, the books they read, and the projects they are asked to do. It is our responsibility to see that they find what they are looking for— something to nurture their souls, something to challenge their minds.

At my school, the vision of curriculum is broad. We have a "two-way" bilingual program, the only one in the state. As opposed to traditional bilingual programs, African American, Latino, and white students are learning together in the same classroom. Spanish and English are equally valued. All students are learning a second language—native English speakers learn Spanish, native Spanish speakers learn English—and all students serve as language models for others. Every child who enters our school comes with the strength of a first language, a skill that another child from a different background wants and needs.

Our two-way program fosters cross-cultural interaction from early on—beginning in kindergarten. Children become sensitive to the difficulty of learning a second language. Bilingualism is an important skill for the future, and in our program, there is reason and purpose for learning another language beginning very early.

It is important to note here that our program was not given to us by a benign administration. It is entirely the result of teachers finding one another, building common cause with parents, and then struggling to overcome a host of obstacles to bring our collective vision to life. It was neither automatic nor easy.

Our program strives to recognize the strengths of children as they enter school; to provide an atmosphere of respect and acceptance for both parent and child. Our curriculum is designed to reflect the experience and culture of the children in the program, provide opportunities for children to build on the strengths of their experiences, and involve the parents in the process. We want to build trust between home and school and show children the connections between their own lives and the larger school experience.

We're proud of the vision we have at La Escuela Fratney. From its inception, parents have been an integral part of the development, governance, and daily experiences of our students. We have sent a strong, recurring message that parents are needed and wanted in our school.

Parents sit on our site-based council. Others meet once a month on our curriculum committee. We've allocated precious dollars of our budget to hire a parent organizer, and soon we will begin the fourth year of a parent project convened by two of our teachers as a study and support group on parenting issues. Parents have given direction and input to our report card, our homework policy, and a statement on multicultural and antiracist education for our school. They work on our newsletter, and they help shape our schoolwide projects such as our Family Day and our No-TV Week.

Every quality program must understand that parents are the first teachers of their children. Parents know how their children learn. We simply need to ask them. What a valuable resource we have in parents, a resource that is typically underused. When teachers and parents can view each other as "equals" we will have achieved a great thing, and we can begin to learn from one another. The time and commitment made by teachers and schools to maintain a parent connection will pay off in the long run. For example, Fratney School parents helped lead the struggle in our district against budget cuts. Three years ago they were instrumental in acquiring city funds to build a new tot-lot that serves all the kids in our neighborhood. I'm proud to say that the parents at Fratney School have a reputation of being vocal and involved and active. And we helped it be that way.

As we make our schools ready for children, we must provide an environment that is both nurturing and challenging to children, with activities that are multisensory, experiential, and hands-on. I said earlier that I'd never met a child who wasn't ready to learn. I need to qualify that now by saying that there have certainly been times when children have been resistant to learning what I wanted to teach. Thus, we must speak to the importance of quality programs being child centered, with appropriate activities meeting a range of interests and abilities, offering children choices, giving them success.

At Fratney School, our curriculum has multicultural and antiracist education at its core, with schoolwide themes each year, for example, "We respect ourselves and others," or "We make a difference on planet Earth." It is here that we can show children how they are connected to the things they learn, that they can see their own strengths and have the opportunity to learn about the things that are interesting to them, relevant to their own lives, and important to their futures.

We want the program in our school to go beyond preparing students academically by teaching them about the serious nature of combating racism in our society. Our schoolwide themes offer students and teachers the opportunity to explore issues such as prejudice and stereotypes. As students learn about history and the experiences of various groups of people in our country, they are encouraged to connect the struggles of the past with the problems of today. Many of our students have firsthand experience with issues of violence, crime, and racism. They bring their experiences with them to the classroom. It is our role to provide the opportunity for children to share their concerns, to explore the options they have as they respond to their world. Through their writing, the stories they read, and the projects they develop, we strive to connect their lives to what they learn in school.

In our policy statement on multicultural and antiracist education, we state: "La Escuela Fratney teaches children to not only understand the world but to help change it. . . . We encourage [our students] to combat racism, discrimination, and injustice wherever it is found." Our goal is to equip our students with the skills and strategies they will need to counteract the negative forces they face, whether it be in the classroom, on the playground, or in their neighborhood. We want them to recognize stereotypes and racist practices when they encounter them and actively discourage others from using them.

Because of the mixture of cultures in our schools, we have a prime opportunity for children to learn from one another and from their families, to build the bridges necessary for true multicultural understanding. One such experience we had at Fratney was a monthlong project under our schoolwide theme "We share the stories of the world." We invited the mothers of our kindergarten students to come in and share with us their first experiences in school. We heard the colorful stories of a mother who grew up in Puerto Rico and slid down the mountains on rainy days, mothers who went to Fratney School when the neighborhood was very different and many kids went home for lunch, a mother from Jamaica who had had the beach as her playground, and a mom whose experience down South included being held accountable to everyone in the neighborhood as she walked back and forth to school.

Not only did we hear the stories, but during one of the first days of the project, a mother shared her favorite kindergarten song. After that, the children requested a song from each guest. This multicultural repertoire was an unexpected bonus of our project. Children were proud to see their mothers in front of the group. Moms were impressed with the children's questions. Teachers gained insights into the backgrounds and cultures of the kids in an authentic way. Trust among parents, teachers, and children deepened with this experience, and we took a small step in helping students learn more about their own cultural heritage and that of their peers.

Yet even with a clear vision and strong motivation to provide a quality program to our students, there are many other obstacles that teachers face, both within and outside the four walls of our schools. Teachers face daily struggles and incredible challenges linked to funding and resources. Meeting individual needs is difficult in large classes conducted in two languages. Our budget was cut, yet we have more students. Implementing a curriculum with thematic units, team teaching, and shared decision making takes time and requires collaboration. We never seem to have enough time or sufficient resources to do all we want to do or could do. We're trying to teach holistically in a system that still wants to measure and assess our students in a linear, standardized way with multiple-choice tests. We're struggling to implement a strong Spanish component with limited resources and materials and the ever-present "English pull" that is so strong in our society. We're continually looking for more and better ways to involve the community and parents in our school— an invitation alone does not automatically bring people into our building, especially those who have traditionally been excluded and alienated from our schools.

Some things begin to seem almost impossible. While we are in our school promoting cooperation, democratic discipline, and open-mindedness among our students, the society is pulling the other way. Our students live in a world that is increasingly violent, racist, and oppressive. They confront it daily, and their lives and their experiences flow into the classroom with them. As hard as it is, those things cannot be ignored. It is here that we must come back to our vision of a "decent" school—one where we use the experiences of our students as the basis for our curriculum; where time is taken to address the real-life problems they face. The vision is one of teachers and parents working together to deal with the hard issues facing us; a vision where time and resources are given to teachers to make school a meaningful, productive place for all involved.

We face incredible challenges that go way beyond what any of our university courses taught us to do or prepared us to face. We must come out of our cubicles and go beyond the walls of our schools to advocate for the children we teach. Each of us must take a stand, and together we must look for hope, for the solutions to the problems we face.

Teachers must learn to respect their students and see first and foremost their strengths and not their deficits. They must learn how to promote a dynamic approach to multicultural education, not just for children of color but for all children, so that they will be equipped with the skills to live in a diverse, multilingual future. Teachers must fight for meaningful professional choices and opportunities for decision making. They must find ways to build trust and support with one another. At the same time, the voices of parents in the school community must also be heard. Parents must have knowledge about our schools and true and meaningful involvement in their governance. Teachers can set the climate and send a message of welcome to parents and community.

Teachers will also be in the thick of the budget wars. They must learn how schools are funded and become leaders in developing equitable and adequate alternatives. Unless we address the money issue, we will never have the quality programs that we want and that our students deserve.

There is an African proverb that states that you can predict the future of a society by the way in which it cares for its children. We must help people throughout our communities to recognize that they too have a role to play in improving education. Each of us has a stake in seeing that the future leaders of our cities are well educated; we each have a practical interest in knowing that our future will be a positive one. Beyond that, I believe that each citizen has a responsibility to promote the notion of the "good common school," one of the few places left in our society where democracy and the issues we face as a democracy can be explored and nurtured. We will have no future without a citizenry of critical and creative thinkers who are able to function in a diverse and technical society. As flawed as our schools may be, they are one of the few public institutions that survive in our nation. They deserve our involvement in making them better.

Those of us inside our schools must work to inform others about the positive things happening. Taking our students out into the community is important, as is exploring ways for community members to come into our schools and give practical support through sharing their experience and expertise. When community members are involved on school councils and districtwide planning and curriculum committees, they can begin to share the complexity of our work with others, and we can help them see the effects that our economy and society have on our students.

Working in coalition with parents and other community members will be critical in the days ahead as we strive to find the solutions to the critical problems facing our schools. Together we must find the resources needed to implement significant reforms inside our schools, such as lowering class size, providing students with technological tools, and providing time for teachers to plan and collaborate on curricular reform. Schools and communities must face the contradictions, the barriers that often keep us apart, such as the lack of trust between teachers and parents (particularly when they are of different races and cultures), the perception of schools as "closed communities" that exclude parents and other "outsiders," and the struggle for power on school governance issues.

Those in the professional or business community have a particular role to play in helping to improve our communities through economic investment, jobs, neighborhood development, crime prevention, and support for reform initiatives in our schools. We'll see improvement in our students and in our schools as we see the revitalization of our communities as a whole. Finally, we must work together to demand that our state and national priorities be focused on the needs of our people. Investments in education are investments in all our futures.

The question, of course, is, do we as a nation really have a commitment to all our children? Do we really view our schools as public places that demand our commitment? Do we really believe that it is the civic responsibility of all citizens to support public education? It will take the conviction of all educators to go forward, to promote change, to take up the challenge to implement programs that will inspire our children, to find ways for parents and communities to be meaningfully involved in our schools, and to empower educators to be decision makers in their schools. We must demand the resources we need: from changes in the funding laws to new priorities at the national level, where infrastructure funding should include dollars for our deteriorating public schools.

There is a specific challenge to those of us in the classroom, a challenge to understand that the job of a teacher is much more than delivering a set of materials to a group of children. Our role is to provide a place for our students that nurtures their strengths and motivates them to live up to their potential as future leaders. We must be willing to leave the traditional notions of curriculum, one "right" way, or "recipes for success" at the door and be ready to use every possible creative resource we can tap to get the message across. We must be willing to risk by sharing our own experiences and being open and accepting of the students' experiences and those of their families. We must open our doors and take the time to build trust between school and community, with the goal of, together, helping students to learn.

Most important, if the voices of those closest to the process are to be heard, we must be willing to stand up and advocate for our students. Ours is a most stressful and difficult job, but we must never forget that we touch the future every day. As difficult as it is to find that extra bit of energy to speak out in a public way for our students, we have to do it if we are to make a real difference in the lives of the children we teach. Institutions will not change on their own. We must use whatever power we have individually and as a collective force to work for positive change. The complexity of teaching is captured in these lines passed on to me by a friend. "Enable me to teach with wisdom, for I help to shape the mind. Equip me to teach with truth, for I help to shape the conscience. Encourage me to teach with vision, for I help to shape the future. Empower me to teach with love, for I help to shape the world."

REFERENCES

Holt, J. (1965). *How children fail*. New York: Pittman.
Holt, J. (1967). *How children learn*. New York: Pittman.

CHAPTER 15

How to Write a Lesson Plan

Susan Huddleston Edgerton

PROLOGUE

Before I get to the main body of this chapter, I want to share some acknowledgments and contextualizations. I've had the privilege of participating in an extended electronic mail correspondence with Laura Bentz, a particularly perceptive and introspective student of elementary education. As one who has often been suspicious (and with good reason, I think) of the expansion of technological tools for "teaching," the richness of this dialogue and the possibilities it fosters in my imagination have pleasantly surprised me, though I remain conscious of the risks. In addition, I had the privilege of receiving a more traditional letter from one of my students, John Toman, in response to a piece I had written about Toni Morrison called "Teaching the Interminable." In lieu of an assignment to write a "response paper" on any of the day's readings, my student wrote:

> Dear Susan:
>   I've recently read (and reread) your piece on Toni Morrison and teaching the interminable and instantly understood a letter response was my only option. Relying on the cough syrup prose of a "formal reaction" would only serve to paralyze the dialogue we began back in August and, in the process, demean much of the "stuff" that dialogue has been about. It seems to me (as I'm guessing it must to you) that academic papers retain a curious knack for rigidity that letters adamantly refuse. Papers are written, read, and marked. Then they die. For students, the internment usually takes the form of a well-meaning, moth-balled trunk. For

professors, if they're lucky, it's an anthology—a fancy, moth-balled trunk.

But letters . . . they're only written to be answered, to set in motion the fluid give-and-take of discussion, to live and relive with each new postmark.

I responded in kind (with a letter) because I think he is right. There is something about a letter, a sense of "intended audience" and of ongoingness, that makes it significantly different from ordinary academic narrative. I suppose that's why I felt sad, for example, when I found a lost or discarded letter from an apparently scorned lover (yes, I read it; I couldn't stop myself) in the mud of a New Orleans street. It's why I felt some loss of hope when my grandfather, post-master in a small north Texas town, showed me the "dead letter of-fice" one day. Such expressions are not supposed to end that way. They should "live and relive with each new postmark."

Another privilege I enjoyed was that I was able to read Joseph Featherstone's chapter for this volume before I wrote my own con-tribution—a piece that is a lovely and loving letter to a student who would be a teacher. He wrote of *hope* and of *romance* as being the basic "stuff" of education. What better place to find hope and ro-mance expressed than in a letter?

Indeed (and another privilege for me), the day before I read Featherstone's letter I received a letter from a friend, through elec-tronic mail, with a special New Year's greeting included—a "letter" from playwright and former Czechoslovakian president Václav Havel about hope. Havel wrote of having fallen, in the dark of night, into a sewer well where for about 30 minutes he gave up all hope of surviv-ing, assuming that he would drown, absurdly, in shit:

> What was striking about the sewer experience was how hope had emerged from hopelessness, from absurdity. I've always been deeply affected by the theater of the absurd because, I believe, it shows the world as it is, in a state of crisis. It shows man having lost his funda-mental metaphysical certainty, his relationship to the spiritual, the sensation of meaning—in other words, having lost the ground under his feet. As I've said in my book, "Disturbing the Peace," this is a man for whom everything is coming apart, whose world is collapsing, who senses he has irrevocably lost something but is unable to admit this to himself and therefore hides from it.
>
> Complete skepticism is an understandable consequence of discov-ering that one's enthusiasms are based on illusion. This skepticism leads to a dehumanization of history—a history drifting somewhere above

us, taking its own course, having nothing to do with us, trying to cheat
us, destroy us, playing out its cruel jokes. (Havel, 1993).

Finally, with his nose just above "the dreadful effluvium," "this fundamental mud," "this strange vegetation," Havel was saved by a long
ladder dropped down. Three months later he was president. That is
the stuff of romance, of course.

For me, as for Featherstone, the themes of hope and romance
are essential ones for the process of becoming a teacher. For me, as
for Václav Havel, I'll presume to suggest, they are also essential
themes for living well. So I too chose to write a letter to a particular
student in my elementary education classes—a student I don't actually know, but one I know very well. Writing a letter to a student is
not a foreign genre to me, but having that impulse so beautifully and
multiply validated in synchrony with the work I wanted to do for this
collection was unexpected, serendipitous, urging me on. I *hope* that
this letter conveys my hope to my students and for them. I hope that
it will not be a dead (or drowned) letter.

THE LETTER

Dear Lucy,
When I hear you voicing concerns about your teacher education
program, I am sympathetic. I know how deadening that institutional
process can be, how hard you work, and how frightening the prospects for your future as a teacher, an authority, sometimes are. But
when the *primary* concern becomes, for example, that you have not
even been taught to do a "lesson plan" in your classes, I am hard-
pressed to sympathize. I hear this sort of concern every semester from
many in your classes, my classes. Because of that, I should take such
concerns seriously, I know. And I *want* to take you seriously. But the
trouble is, I think that you are mistaken when you pin so much of
your anxiety and energy on such technical and often trivial aspects
of teaching. So I'm asking you now, and myself, how do I learn to
take this and similar questions seriously?

I've complained that too many of my students don't know how
to read the world well, by which I mean *interpret* or *read critically*
and *deeply* the written word as well as all other manner of signs and
symbols—to read people, to read children. This, I suppose, has been
the greatest concern for me as a teacher educator, especially as a
preservice teacher educator. But now I'm finding myself, as I *read*

what I just wrote to you, unable to adequately *read your concerns*. That is, I'm aware that I must listen and take seriously such a common, persistent, and earnest complaint. But if I believe that the literal rendering of the question is based on mistaken priorities, then I must interpret it. I'm finding that I do not know how to interpret it, to really read it. Am I capable of listening, of doing for you what I ask you to do for your own students? I have to learn to read better. What do you—as one who expresses this sort of anxiety—need from me, and in what order? How do *I* write a "lesson plan" for our class together?

So you see, Lucy, I write this letter to you, but it is also for me as a teacher educator. Indeed, since you're not here right now to help me, I guess I'll proceed by thinking about a plan for the lesson I need to learn. Then I'll see how far that takes me toward writing a "lesson plan" for my class with you. That is, I have to read "me" to read "you"—so I can read me and you together and then, with luck, read you well enough to be of help. (To *read* is perhaps the same here as to *listen, interpret,* and *respond*.)

Maybe a good beginning for me is to return to that famous, fundamental question framing the study of curriculum: *What knowledge is of most worth?* I think it's a good question, and I remembered it aloud to you, as is my habit, last semester. But to stop there is not helpful. Questions like *What knowledge is of most worth to whom? For what purposes? In which places and times?* naturally (should) arise. And just posing the question doesn't seem to get many juices flowing when it comes time to *decide* what materials to use, in what order, how to use them, when to be silent, and so on.

Recently, I began ruminating over a new question for framing curriculum and thus for teaching and learning: *What knowledge best enables us to care for ourselves, one another, and our environment?* Or, another way of phrasing it: *What knowledge will best assist us in minimizing the violence we do to ourselves, one another, and our environment?* By the way, Madeleine Grumet taught me "that [the word] 'read' is lodged in the very guts of the word 'ruminate,' which means 'to think things over'" (1988, p. 132). Ruminate also means, she goes on, to chew for digestion a meal that was hastily grabbed earlier. So I am ruminating over this question, curious still about its effects on the "student and teacher body"—its "outcome."

Maybe this doesn't clarify or concretize the curriculum question much, but it certainly seems to have a different *feel* to it—for me, at least. I hope you'll be patient with me as I take some time and space to digress from my original question and to ruminate—to chew a few of my own childhood memories of schooling, and of children at school, in light of this new question. I want to do this in order to explore the different feeling I get from my reformulation of the curriculum question.

Recall that children do love, crave, and need adult attention and affirmation. They need the things adults offer such as a sense of safety, someone to read to them, to teach them about those myriad, necessarily confusing, ways of the world. At the same time, remember that as an adult you will be seen as something of a different species. What child can possibly understand folks who'd rather sit around and talk to one another than go out and play! It's that last comment, that sense of difference and antagonism even, that most renders my childhood memories of adults and my adult memory of childhood suspect. Nonetheless, although no one should hold me to absolute accuracy, I am making every effort to be honest about my memories as sensibilities. And maybe in that way my memories can inform us both.

I grew up in a small north Louisiana town where I went to public schools. Those schools were racially segregated until I reached middle school (which we called junior high). Even so, there were differences among children that often seemed directly related to hurts and pains we had suffered. I've been thinking about kids who I imagine suffered at school a lot—some simply because they were poor, others because they in some other way deviated from white southern middle-class propriety or "norms." I suppose I remember differences in children in these ways through the only logic available to me at the time—the logic of a child who compared others to herself in particular ways.

My family was in the middle of the white middle class. But I think we enjoyed a bit of status beyond that because my father taught at the local university (special education). At the same time, we too were "different" because we didn't go to church (in the Southern Baptist Bible Belt), and my parents were "liberal Democrats." So I used to think that my own life was tough because of all that, along with the ordinary crises of childhood. For example (an ordinary crisis), I recall going home on the bus once with my sweater tied around my waist by the arms to hide the fact that I'd wet my pants—I'd been too frightened to ask the teacher to allow me to go to the bathroom. She always seemed to think that we were bad, as I recall. Or at least that's what I thought she thought.

But I want to turn away from my own bodily experiences to the

experiences of those I remember (through childhood lenses mediated by my present ones) as possibly suffering more. I remember
Richey as always having visible ear wax and thick-lensed glasses. He
seemed studious, though, in contrast to other "working-class" boys
like Ron, for example. I saw Ron, even then (in sixth grade), as angry
and defiant but insecure. He vacillated between seeming to want real
contact with me and some of the others and wanting to do violence
to us. Neither of these boys received much teacher validation in my
memory. Richey's quiet and studious manner was scarcely more
affirmed than Ron's belligerence. But the girls, the girls who were
so poor—I suspect they had only mothers at home—are the ones I
remember most.

Trisha was red-haired, loud, and sometimes rough. And Becky
had curly dark-blond ("dirty blond," some of us probably said) hair
and a funky smell. Bodies are so close for children in schoolrooms
and school yards. We knew one another with an intimacy rarely
matched in adult group life. It seems that I even remember the smell
of their scalps and hair—Trisha and Becky—and it was funky, like a
wet dog, and slightly musty and, along with the old clothes they wore,
both disturbing and comforting.

I remember with horror and embarrassment one day as Trisha
was standing at the board in sixth grade and there was blood on the
back of her skirt. No one bothered to explain it to any of us, probably her included. I don't remember if she was taken aside, sent home
to change, or anything at all.

I remember Becky in second grade, maybe at around Christmas
or some other holiday, after she had been given a pack of gum by
someone (maybe the teacher). She ran around the room loudly pro-
claiming "Juicy Fruit gum!" over and over as if it were some cry of
triumph, some delicacy that she'd discovered. I remember feeling
embarrassed, repelled, and quite puzzled at her behavior.

Another poor girl-child I recall from those years is Sheila, a "pie-
faced," pale, soft, and quiet child. I invited Sheila to my home one
day. As I recall, I felt self-righteous in my sense of my own generos-
ity—that I would defy the rules of popularity and condescend to
entertain, take care of even, a poor, sour-smelling little girl. I think
she came home from school with me on the bus, and my mom and
I dropped her at her house later, which was not far from ours but
further out in the country. The house was unpainted, and it seemed
that the screen door was barely hanging on. The yard was bare of
grass and had one large tree in front. My mother and I didn't go in—

we weren't asked. No one came out to greet us or Sheila. She just ran inside. And I never had her over again, perhaps feeling that I'd done my duty, perhaps feeling repulsed, ashamed, afraid.

There were other children who weren't quite so poor but who clearly had less than we did. There was, for example, always a group from the Methodist Children's Home, a home for orphaned children: Sandy (whose entire family of siblings was eventually adopted by a prominent family and who were all quite successful in school), Bobby (a small boy with curly blond hair and a persistent glint of mischief in his eyes and behavior; he reminded me of Danny Kaye), and Tewana (a red-haired, fast-talking girl who I always assumed would do wild things one day, if she wasn't already). I never visited the children's home but was always curious. The thought of ever having to live there terrified me for all its implications. Kids had to share all their belongings, I imagined, with all the other kids. There were no "real" parents to run to for love, reading, hugging, crying. Yet the three I just described were radically different people. How did Sandy and her siblings fare so well when others clearly didn't—at least in school? I didn't know then and I don't know now. One thing seemed apparent: Sandy's siblings were "beautiful" children, they stuck together, they were always "polite," and they worked very hard all the time. I never heard any more about any of the other children from that place.

I recall Liza in second grade. Her mother went through a divorce then, which, at that time, was always a big secret to keep. But to add to this pain for Liza, she evidently started her period in second grade. Her mother made the request, which was granted, that Liza be excused from physical education activities frequently. I don't know why exactly—if it was a mistaken, old-fashioned, belief in the fragility of menstruating women or if she had some truly threatening health problem or if, perhaps, it was so as not to expose her body to other girls who did not have the features of maturity that Liza (obviously) was already developing. Of course, all us other girls whispered and giggled and speculated on what was going on. I think we actually figured it all out, but I don't know a soul who was informed about the process by her parents or anyone else. Children know their worlds better than adults often imagine.

In junior high I remember a guy named Saul who kept getting in fights with other boys all the time. His father was a lawyer who might have been a public defender or maybe even a civil rights lawyer. I do vaguely remember someone taunting Saul with words about his father's "defending niggers," but I didn't at the time connect that with his fights. I thought that Saul was obnoxious (maybe he was) and that that was why he was always having to fight. He was arrogant, but maybe he was that way as a preemptive defense. I remember his getting into a fight with Matt, my first boyfriend (at 5 years of age), and I never knew what the fight was about. Matt, I think, got up with a bloody nose. He was losing badly. But as I recall, both boys were crying. This was seventh grade, and I can recall my own horror and my own gratitude that I was not a boy.

Of course, these vignettes are generally about children's lives in a world over which teachers, or others, have little control. But in all these accounts of children's traumas or difficulties, I never once *recall* any teacher intervening, attempting to explain important stuff to the rest of us, or even broaching difficult topics at the most surface of levels. No, they remained "neutral" as they systematically tracked students in reading groups that were roughly synonymous with a child's socioeconomic class or social situation more generally. And they often "played favorites" in ways that seemed obvious only to us students. For example, I recall that in the early grades, Sandy—smart as I thought she was—was always in the middle reading group. Was it because she was an orphan, and a shy one at that? I was excruciatingly shy too, but my father was a professor of education. That *must* mean that I should be smart, right? (I wonder if my father's particular occupation in a university education department ever intimidated any of my teachers.) And in the first grade I remember the teacher saying to another girl (who already seemed to dislike me), "Why can't you act more like Susan?"

What I'm saying to you, Lucy, is that I didn't feel that I learned in school enough about caring for anybody, myself included, or about many things that I now believe are crucial for a decent quality of life for myself and others. You say to me that you are entering the field because you love children, and I believe you. I imagine most of my teachers did too (and it's possible that my memory is ungrateful and unkind). But I suppose I want you to recall your love of children every day and ruminate over it each time you begin to wonder how to pass the school day with children. You have similar memories, don't you? Now and then you've shared them with me, so I know you *know*. I suppose much of our most difficult work is accessing what we already know. Then we must continue, interminably, to learn what we don't know and to connect it to what we do.

What *does* it mean to really love children? I've recalled and written about events here that would mostly be slotted outside the purview of academic concerns. I haven't begun to relate the horrors of actual class work that I recall—rote memorization, repetition of "dead letters" (textbook "knowledge"), and so on. Actually, I think I've forgotten the details of such stories in favor of a blur of discomfort. Maybe such a memory is a kind of self-protection, maybe a reflection of how unimportant the "lesson plans" were to me. But the stories I've just shared are related to the more overtly academic ones *through* the notion of teacher caring. Seeing the child as someone with her or his own special, individual, and collective needs does not end at the end of a "formal lesson." Nor does it end at the end of recess or lunch or with social interactions that seem to have little to do with academic lessons. Seeing and respecting children pervades all those areas. And I'm suggesting that maybe when we think of curriculum in that way—as searching for and through the knowledge that best enables us to take care of ourselves, one another, and the environment—then, and only then, can we *not* avoid dealing with the difficult issues that arise when we work, play, and live with children.

In fairness to my former teachers, I'll add that maybe they weren't unaware of these things so absolutely, and probably they did the best they could. For example, maybe we weren't told about menstruation out of a very realistic fear on the part of the teacher of parental and other repercussions. Maybe they feared harming certain children more than helping any child. You will face these sorts of difficulties in your daily life as a teacher too. I face them as well teaching at the college level. It's not always easy to make judgments that are compatible with one's own beliefs and sensitivities and with institutional and social forces. Teaching can be difficult emotional, intellectual, and physical work. But I know that you also know that teaching is extremely important and often rewarding work.

Now, back to the problem of writing a lesson plan. You've seen the diagrams in your textbooks. Here is one (there are other formats, of course):

    Lesson:
    Objectives:
    Procedures:
    Materials:
    Evaluation:

The teacher fills in the blanks and does the lesson accordingly. Let's see what happens when I fill in these blanks for myself, here, for what I'm trying to do for myself in this letter to you.

Lesson: "Seeing the student" (you)
Objectives: The student teacher (in this case, me) will "demonstrate" an appreciation for the uniqueness of each student in the classroom (and today that student is *you*!)

(I put *demonstrate* in quotation marks because this is the language expected for "behavioral objectives." One cannot, with this language, *become* appreciative or sensitive or whatever. One can only demonstrate those qualities.)

Procedures: The student teacher will recall children from her own childhood and memories of her own relations with them and will write her thoughts. At the same time, the student teacher will be thinking about her relationship to her students (you) and, through her memories of differences among children in school, by analogy, will try to recognize what she is not seeing, not understanding, about you.

(You see, this doesn't really fit procedural language *or* behavioral objective language. But how would you describe what I'm doing? That's the problem with "lesson plans." They tend to avoid the larger, more meaningful questions. So I might have to change my language for the plan to be turned in, if such is required, and write a different one for myself. Maybe I would just leave it at: "The student will engage in exercises such as looking at old photos, letter writing, discussing with others, after which she will write about her childhood memories.")

Materials: A warm, well-fed, rested body. A mind freshly stimulated by reading others' thoughts, memories, and accounts as well as any of her own earlier written memories. (So, by implication, I will need books and other written materials as I can find them.) Old photographs, if necessary. A phone for conversing with parents, siblings, and old friends, if possible and if necessary. Tools with which to write and rewrite.

(Obviously, this particular "lesson plan" is also "homework.")

Evaluation: In this case, writing to you as a composite and thus "imaginary" person necessitates that evaluation be deferred as it awaits your letter in response to mine. But when

I get your letter, I will reevaluate *this* part of my lesson plan
as well as the rest of it. I will use your response to make
judgments about my success—judgments derived from my
teaching and other interpersonal experiences that are much
too lengthy, complex, and inarticulable to enter into a simple
daily lesson plan.

(Again, this language would not do for certain expected forms of
lesson plans. It must be more concrete, such as: "The student teacher
will take pretests and posttests in order to measure the success of
the lesson." But how would one write up such tests? How would *they*
be evaluated? Philosophically, of course, that is another big problem. But such problems needn't enter our "official" lesson plans.)

All right, so I've tried to write up the "lesson" I just worked on in
the formal manner described by so many methods texts. But what
about the "lesson" that will take place in a class period with you in a
university classroom, a lesson that might at least begin to address
your concerns? And, by the way, I don't intend to simply set up an
antagonistic relationship at the outset between a future you, the
teacher, and "them," the administration. It's quite possible that that
won't be the case. But isn't that the worst-case scenario you are, in
part, so concerned about? It is an understandable concern.

Lesson: "Writing a lesson plan"

(Maybe we should say one for you and one for "them.")

Objective: The student (you) will learn to write a lesson plan
for a day in a classroom—one that incorporates the implications of her (your) love of children into work that will also
satisfy institutional requirements.

(That is what you're concerned about, isn't it? But for "them" I'd
probably just say that "the student will write a lesson plan for a day
in a classroom." I might even mention a content area that the lesson
plan could address, or a topic.)

Procedures: (There are many ways to do this. What follows is
one suggestion for a way to proceed.) Look at Chicago public
school curriculum guides and select an objective for a particular content area and for a particular grade. Find something
within that particular area about which you feel passionately

and would like to learn more. Think about a child you have observed and imagine that child in your classroom. Learn something about the topic you've chosen by reading about it for, say, an hour. Learn something about the child you have chosen by recollecting, or maybe even calling someone to ask questions. Maybe you could even talk to the child! Think about the materials you will need in order to explore that topic with that particular child. Write it all down. (It's only a bare beginning! It's only one day!) Write the objective from the guideline in large letters on a piece of butcher paper (this will be posted in your room on that day in the future for any supervisor to see), then forget about it. Begin to think about the impact of this procedure on many other, unknown, children. (For future reference: Maybe each child will have her or his day. Maybe you could concentrate on one or two children a day until you have come to know every child in your class that way.)

(I hope that you're getting the point: This would not do for the lesson plan to be turned in to "them," depending on who "they" are and what they require. I must keep it simple and concrete and, most likely, relatively empty.)

Materials: Curriculum guidelines. Observation experience. A variety of written resources on a variety of topics that can be found in the guidelines: books, articles, essays. This letter and other similar works. Possibly, access to a telephone. Butcher paper. Tools for writing.

Evaluation: Self-evaluations shared at the end of class. Does this sound like a viable lesson plan to others? (On another day, perhaps, we can practice the lesson plans with one another. You might choose one student in this class to focus on as you would a child in your own classroom.)

(For "them," maybe another pre- and posttest.)

Lucy, do you notice how my learning seems to leak into yours, which would, if you were writing a plan for your classroom now, also leak into your prospective students' learning? Our lesson plans are not, in fact, separate, are they? At least that's my perception. I'd like to hear your thoughts about that. I hope that you can come to see the typical *institutionalized* lesson plan for what it is: an instrument of surveillance and control. If you are forced to reduce your grander ideas into behavioral terms, you are easier to control—not only by "them" but also within yourself. That is, you *internalize* the values implicit in those plans such that your thoughts about teaching get squeezed into smallness. By this I don't mean to posit some conspiracy theory about "them." "Them" is an abstraction, after all, impossible (usually) to pin on real human beings. But this is also what makes my message one of *hope*. Such formal formats *are* trivial, small, easy to fill out. Then you can go about your business as you see fit, more or less. That is, you don't *have* to internalize these things. You can consciously work against it with daily reminders to yourself of your reasons for being there.

I would never say, however, that what I'm suggesting to you won't take courage—just the contrary. I imagine, too, that you may be having difficulty with a word I used earlier—*passion*. Other students I've known have seemed unable to make the connection between that word and what they are doing in a lesson plan. No, passion is not measurable or particularly tangible. Maybe in our next letter we will more fully explore that word and its implications. For now, I will simply leave you with the suggestion in this question: How can you expect a student to feel passionately—that is, to care—about a lesson that *you* don't feel passionately about? I know that, like me, you are passionate about your students.

Sincerely and with great hope,

Susan

REFERENCES

Grumet, M. (1988). *Bitter milk: Women and teaching*. Amherst, MA: University of Massachusetts Press.

Havel, V. (1993, October). Never hope against hope. *Esquire, 120*(4), p. 68.

CHAPTER 16

The Scary Part Is That It Happens Without Us Knowing

Helen Featherstone
Patty Gregorich
Tricia Niesz
Lauren Jones Young

One day is very vivid in my mind. I had been teaching only two mornings a week for a month or so. Jenny, my field instructor from the university, was observing me teach. I had had Jenny as a field instructor during another term, and I can think of no time that she intervened while I was teaching. We talked after I was done teaching but never during. Fortunately, however, Jenny stepped in during this particular lesson. Students were working during writing workshop when I was about to signal for silence. I was getting nervous about the noise level. Jenny stopped me before I signaled and she softly said, "Patty, wait. Look at what they're doing." I looked and realized that all but one or two students were completely engaged in some stage of the writing process. Then Jenny asked me to listen. I did. It wasn't noisy. It was wonderful. All the talk that I heard had to do with writing. It wasn't loud. I couldn't believe it. I was already beginning to internalize the messages of "school." According to my previous standards, things were going perfectly. However, according to the strong messages about what school should be, something was wrong because the students were too loud. It didn't matter what the talk was about. It was too loud, and that was the only fact that needed to be considered. I went into this field experience

feeling strongly about my convictions, yet I was already
beginning to think in these terms.

Patty Gregorich
July 1993

Patty is reflecting on the changes she saw occurring in her thinking and her behavior toward children in the months she spent as a
student teacher in an urban elementary school. Both she and Tricia,
close friends and 1993 graduates of a teacher education program in
which Lauren and Helen teach, found that their apprenticeship in
urban elementary schools challenged many of the beliefs that they
had felt surest of as students, beliefs that seemed fundamental to their
new identity as teachers. As their teachers—during student teaching, Tricia and Patty took an independent study with Lauren and a
seminar with Helen—Lauren and Helen were troubled by what Patty
and Tricia wrote in their journals and by the stories they told. They
had taught these two young women before and knew them to be
exceptionally thoughtful and articulate and exceptionally committed to creating classrooms in which *all* children learn, classrooms
that did not recreate or reinforce the inequalities—of race, class,
gender, language, or disability—of American society, what we all
came to call teaching for social justice.

Lauren and Helen knew that the first years of teaching can challenge the convictions of idealistic young teachers who leave the university with nontraditional ideas about schools and classrooms (see
Featherstone, 1993; Veenman, 1984). But the conversations they had
with Patty and Tricia both during student teaching and in the months
that followed helped them see more clearly how the reality of schools
can eat away at the ideals and convictions that novices have so recently developed.

This chapter grew out of our shared belief that in these conversations we learned some important lessons about the work to which
we are all committed—the work of learning to teach for social justice. We have organized the chapter in such a way as to preserve some
of the separate voices and individual stories. The first section begins
with some excerpts from the journal that Tricia kept during and
immediately after student teaching—excerpts that describe some of
what she was experiencing at the time and some of what she was
thinking and feeling about the experience. Three months later, Tricia
revisited her journal and her memories of her student teaching; her
reflections conclude this first section of the chapter. In the next section, Lauren and Helen reflect on Tricia's experience. Then Patty
describes her involvement with one of her students, telling a story

that extends through her entire senior year, and Lauren and Helen respond to Patty's story. In the final sections of the chapter, we draw together some of what we think we have learned from Patty's and Tricia's experiences and from our conversations and collaboration.

TRICIA: A STUDENT TEACHING JOURNAL

Day 1

Today was nice. The children were amazing—it was like they sensed my apprehension and stress level. They were terrific. It made me feel good and happy. Yet I really didn't teach today. I realize how much I would love to sit and listen and talk to them. Pressures make me feel like I have to be the "boss" (that word that disturbed me from the kids). I hate that feeling. Perhaps I could find a way to be a friend and listener and still teach effectively. It sounds kind of crazy to put it that way, but [my cooperating teacher] especially thinks I need to get tougher. I'm sure I'll feel more comfortable with that soon. When I have my own classroom it would be easier to keep my quiet manner with kids than jumping into this situation—I think!

Week 2

Student teaching is a strange thing. Unfortunately, it is a very quick jump into reality. And for me and my friends, it is a jump that hasn't been pleasant. Our wonderful TE [teacher education] classes were inspirational and very interesting, but the reality of school and teaching [in many elementary schools] is much different. There are daily problems, interruptions, politics, restrictions, and situations that make it nearly impossible to teach the way we believe. Actually there is probably a way, but it is very difficult to see.

Being in a school 5 days a week, all day, it chases away some of the idealism. At least it has for me. Our classes made teaching seem rewarding and fun. But it is hard to keep that attitude in the reality. Needless to say, it has been disheartening.

Week 3

This week a new concern has come up. It is a concern that others (and I guess myself) have been talking about. It is my "style." I have been encouraged to be more interested (interesting?). My CT [cooperating teacher] really draws them in with the way she dramatizes things. That really isn't me. And therefore the kids don't respond to me. Part of the problem may be that I haven't been real interested in some of the things I have been asked to teach. The kids can sense that. But I don't think that dramatizing everything I teach is as necessary as my CT seems to think, if only because I have seen some wonderful teachers who were quiet, calm, and other adjectives that have been used to describe me. I'm not convinced that I can't be a good teacher with my style. Actually [my field instructor] has encouraged me to find my style. I agree that this is a very important step. There is also the question of the age level of the kids. Perhaps first grade isn't the best place for my "style." I have decided for other reasons that I might like to teach a higher grade. And perhaps the kids are just not used to me.

I'm concerned about the difficulties I've had. They are hard to pinpoint. I'm just not very happy—I don't like it and I don't feel I am doing a good job. Being a perfectionist it is difficult to go into a situation where you don't have control and you can't make things perfect. Unfortunately, I haven't even made the best of things because I'm not happy with the situation. I do realize I need to work harder at making this a better experience. I was even doubting my desire to teach. But then I think about how things will be different in my own classroom. Then I worry about if, again, I'm being more idealistic than reality allows.

The article about the importance of learning about ourselves [Featherstone, 1993] is all a part of this. For some reason I realize that I don't work very hard at things that I can't do my way. I realize I should do what I can. I have a goal for next week to figure out (a) how to learn from this experience and (b) how to make things better for the kids and myself.

Week 4

I have figured out a way to keep my motivation (inspiration?) up. . . . I reread old articles and textbooks from my classes; one class in particular—Debbie's literacy class. It was helpful for two reasons: (1) It made me excited about teaching again! (2) It reminded me that there are ways of teaching that I could probably be successful at.

The ways of teaching and classrooms that made me become fascinated with the field of education, those from our classes, are in a different world than the one I'm in now.

That day I also reread a field log of last winter term. I was in an incredibly exciting classroom in Oak Ridge. This document helped me even more in thinking about how I wanted to teach.

The lesson learned . . . (well, I have been learning this for a while): I can't ever afford to stop learning. I have no desire to. I not only need to keep learning for the sake of my teaching, but also for the sake of being interested in teaching. The new perspective I have from a completely different angle certainly cheers me up. Teaching is less scary when you realize you can always keep learning.

I was thinking about how last week I wrote about having to be perfect. Well, I thought of some goals to help me not worry so much about it. If I keep these things in mind, it will take some of the pressure off. I want to:

1. Have a positive influence on kids' lives.
2. Have a positive influence on kids' learning.
3. Have a positive influence on the field of education.

I realize I haven't been writing specifically about instances in the classroom much lately. Perhaps it is because I haven't had many good days yet. (Yet, they are coming soon!) But in realizing that I haven't been writing about interesting incidents, I have realized I am missing an important aspect. I should be more specific about the instances that go "wrong" and reflect and learn from them, documenting more specifically what or why I am unhappy. I need to be learning more than I am from this experience.

Week 5

Well, I finally see that I have learned something! And it took me a while to learn. For first graders, at least these first graders, the learning activities need to be intensely fun, like a game, contest, or challenge, for these kids to learn. I have been fighting that knowledge for a long time. In all of my classes I have always learned that the kids need to be engaged and interested. I haven't been fighting that. I have been fighting the "tricking" aspect. It seems so much like I have to trick them into learning with a gimmick or game. That is not what I imagined teaching to be. It felt like bribery or something—maybe condescending is the word.

To be honest, I have to admit that a lot of the stuff I have planned wasn't interesting to 6-year-olds—it wasn't "hands-on" enough. It is a scary thought but I wonder this: Even though I have had 2 years of great TE classes, I may be planning things very similar to what I thought school was before becoming a teacher. Perhaps this lesson about extremely interactive learning for first graders is one I should've known. Yet it didn't carry over from my own learning to teaching. I don't know why but I am remembering a paper written by Jenny Denyer and Susan Florio-Ruane (1991) about TE undergrads who excel in courses and seem to really "get it" (I always thought I did) reverting to their growing-up experience with education. Things aren't carrying over.

After Reading Herb Kohl's *36 Children* (1967)

On page 3, I was struck by another feeling I've been struggling with that Kohl writes about: "For a while, as I learned to teach, the me in the classroom was an alien and hostile being. But nevertheless it was me, terrified, showing my terror to everyone but myself."

Kohl just put into words what I have suspected but didn't know how to say. My fear of losing control turned me into a person I didn't want to be with the kids. Therefore, I wasn't really able to teach. It all goes back to the "comfort level" that I've talked about before. The fear of chaos changed my teaching style (in a negative way). It's great to know that Kohl felt that same way and overcame it and became a good teacher. The challenge is to stay aware of the problem and the pull to change this way (into a "suppressive" teacher). This stress caused me to stop listening to children at times and responding to their needs since I was so concerned with keeping order. I hope to never stop listening again.

I was struck by how Kohl was able to realize and accept normal human relationships between teacher and students. I think it is rare to find teachers who are human with students. Perhaps this idea (of acting human with kids and accepting natural responses) is where I am trying to go with my thinking. . . . It is such a shame that teachers are conditioned and encouraged to develop an inauthentic role with children.

I was also struck by how teaching . . . seemed like a *fight* against society's idea of what teaching is supposed to be. Kohl "fought" against teachers, administrators, etc. just to get the opportunities to truly teach.

Three Months Later

It has been almost 3 months since I finished student teaching, and I have recovered, but I've done so by locking it all away somewhere in my mind and avoiding opening the door at all costs. People ask me about student teaching all the time: "How was it?" I answer: "I didn't have a very good experience." Then I try to change the subject. They then ask "why?" (what could be difficult about teaching little kids?), and again I reply vaguely and try to squirm out of it. Anything not to have to open that door. At the risk of sounding melodramatic (and this probably won't be the last time), student teaching was an agonizing experience. Recently, Helen attached the word "depressed." It scared me at first and then relieved me, because depressed is exactly what I was during those 10 weeks.

Not only does it feel yucky to try to remember student teaching, I actually probably don't remember a lot of it. I started blocking things out during the experience. I became so detached that I am surprised I remember anything at all. This will probably make more sense if I describe what my teacher education experience was like.

I am incredibly thankful to have graduated from the Learning Community teacher education program.[1] I'm thankful for the size and closeness of the cohort, for the quality of the educators, for the well-chosen reading materials, and for the attention and experience in classrooms. Learning Community didn't just introduce me to the field of education. Through the program I became a learner for the first time in my life (or so it felt). Through 15 years of doing school and being called a "gifted" student, I had never realized that I could contribute to and participate in learning. I never realized how much I could learn from my peers. Teacher education was exciting, inspirational, and, above all, empowering. Our teachers trusted us to find our own way into the field of education while providing us with the best possible material and modeling. It was an exciting time. I was constantly amazed by the company I was in—by the brilliance of my mentors and peers. (I would come home from class and talk the ears off my roommates trying to relate what and how I was learning.) From my experiences in the Learning Community program, I developed a vision of what my own classroom would be like, once I graduated and started to teach.

My best memories of student teaching were when I could listen to and talk to the kids. Of course, I couldn't do that when I was "teaching." Earlier in my teacher preparation, my field experience actually focused on listening to kids. But my role had completely changed. Being "teacher" in this environment meant that I needed control. The pressure to manage was so strong, it became the first priority. I couldn't balance management and pedagogy. Philosophically, I didn't want to be *in control*, but I had to find a way to do that to succeed in student teaching.

I was failing miserably. It felt terrible. I would wake up every morning nauseous, with my heart racing. Probably the worst part, though, was my feeling about teaching. I began to actually believe that *this* was what teaching was. I hated it as much as children "hate" school. Soon I decided that I would never teach. Then I felt better.

An obvious question is why didn't I try to create some of what I had imagined when I began full-time student teaching. I wonder that myself, although I have a list of excuses a mile long. During those agonizing days, I didn't try to change things. The thought of it was completely overwhelming and very scary. I didn't feel confident enough to rock the boat. I didn't have the courage or the energy.

Perhaps it was too discouraging because I knew that I couldn't transform this class into the learning environment I wanted. The culture was in place; the norms were set up. The little efforts I did make didn't work and didn't make sense in this classroom. The fear of violating my cooperating teacher's practice (which I now believe was almost completely self-imposed) also held me back. I began to realize that I wasn't teaching, and the kids weren't learning. The children sensed my apprehension and terror. My unhappiness and discomfort were obvious to everyone in that room. It probably even made the children uncomfortable.

Soon the survival instincts took over: Given the "fight or flight" choice, I flew! I numbed myself to the situation, all the while thinking one of two things: during the darkest days it was, "I'm not going to teach"; during slightly better times it was, "This is nothing like how my classroom will be." This was how I coped. I avoided student teaching in my mind. I avoided it in my actions and began to be less and less prepared.

Fortunately, I employed some more positive survival techniques. Talking to Patty revitalized me. We'd go out to dinner or the bar and end up talking about teaching the entire time. We needed to! We talked about things we saw, about how we'd teach when we had our own classrooms, and about issues that mattered to us. Those talks were so important because teaching became interesting again.

Melissa taught down the hall from me. One day we realized that we were both very unhappy, and we began to visit each other regularly. We talked about how we felt, how we'd never been told that teaching would be like this, and what we were going to do now that we had this new knowledge. We were also both there when the other broke down. The moral support we provided was necessary.

Writing in my journal and actually analyzing what was wrong was also helpful. The best I felt was one day when (instead of planning) I sat down and looked through old readings from my teacher education classes. I found the pieces that had most inspired me and reread them. I felt alive again—that's the only word that accurately describes it. After student teaching ended I visited three classrooms that I knew would interest me. In all of these instances, I was attempting to show myself what teaching could be!

The professional relationships with my field instructor, Helen, Lauren, and others eventually led me back into teaching. Helen's seminar and the books and articles we read provided me with the inspiration I needed. The independent study (an ongoing conversation about teaching and social justice with Lauren and Patty) helped me figure out why I was feeling so bad. Through our discussions, Patty and I realized that we felt as if we'd lost our idealism. Actually I think we were teetering between feeling that our ideals were being squashed by the "real world" and feeling like we were losing our own idealism.

Through the independent study I got the input I wanted. Patty and Lauren helped broaden my perception of diversity. I was having trouble with the children who were behavior concerns. We'd been discussing creating classrooms that welcomed diversity of all kinds. Diversity in behavior and energy level was something that had never occurred to me. I needed to learn this, and I needed Patty and Lauren to teach me. I had probably begun to see these children as "bad kids."

Another time we were discussing our expectations for kids. It hit me that I had been lowering mine for some children because I was trying to be nice. I'd never have realized that without our talk. Many times Patty and I felt "saved" by revelations we'd had during these discussions. So often our subconscious dictates our action. The interaction of professional learning and growth with actual experience is how we can improve teaching. When learning about gender bias in Lauren's TE 350D, I had no doubt about where I stood on the issue. Yet, in the midst of trying to teach, it was far from my mind. It took discussion with other educators about education for me to realize that I was unknowingly paying more attention to the boys in the class. Isolation is the biggest culprit of stagnant teaching. We need people!

After we had been student teaching for 4 weeks, the 25 students in the Learning Community program met as a group. This meeting was devastating. The things people were saying about students and teaching showed me that I wasn't the only one affected by the "realities" of schools. We sounded just like the frustrated, hopeless teachers we'd consistently lamented. I wondered if everything we'd be-

lieved, discovered, learned, and said so eloquently for 2 years had
been a dream! Had we internalized anything? One of the best teachers among us even said, "We just can't do everything we thought." I
remember searching Helen's face that day for clues to what she was
thinking. I wanted to tell her, "This really isn't us. We're usually incredible! We don't really believe what we've been saying." But that's
where I got stuck. What do we believe now?

Can we really teach like we thought? Can we keep our idealism?
Can we hold on/hold out in the view of opposing forces like school?
Are our ideas unrealistic? I may still be very naive, but it seems like
not having hope is what makes schools the way they are.

I've been told that first-year teachers turn quite conservative, and
now I can see why. But I never thought we would. It has been said
that we are the hope for education. I used to hear that with pride
and with confidence that things will soon be better. Now I'm much
more cynical.

By its nature, student teaching is a difficult time. The children
have adjusted to a teacher (the real one) and a way of doing things
(the right way). One can't underestimate the power of an established
environment or the lack of power in not having one. A change in
control is an invitation to test it. I was encouraged to find "my style."
Yet I felt the only way to succeed in someone else's classroom (and
get the children to respond) would be to adopt her style. It was a very
uncomfortable feeling.

Teaching is much more complex than teacher education. Discussing an isolated topic isn't difficult compared to dealing with the
30 people and hundreds of things going on. Issues don't come one at
a time anymore.

Knowing what we believe in theory doesn't mean we are
equipped to carry it out. More likely, we'll fall back on what we
"know." Two years of intense learning has to contend with a life of
living and doing school. New teachers are pressured to give up ideals either to fit in to a school or because they don't know how to rec-
oncile idealism, theory, and learning with the real world. The scary
part is that it happens without us knowing.

LAUREN AND HELEN REFLECT ON TRICIA'S STORY

As a student in elementary and secondary school, Tricia had always
succeeded in doing what teachers asked of her—she had, indeed, been
labeled "gifted"—but in college classes she discovered that she and

her fellow students could create knowledge as well as absorb it. She watched herself taking new roles as a student; she read about and visited classrooms in which teachers thought about learning in new ways and offered their students experiences that she had never had, or even imagined, as a child in a schoolroom. She entered the setting in which she was to student teach with a vision of teaching that was very different from anything she had encountered as a child. As she tried to imagine creating a classroom community like the ones described by Vivian Paley, Kathy Short, and Herb Kohl, she felt enormously excited.

Her big hopes made her vulnerable: She had set her heart on a goal that would be hard to achieve even with a great deal of support. To make matters worse, elements of her vision clashed with the ways schools often work.

Watching Tricia sink into depression, Helen was reminded of her own experience as a student teacher 25 years earlier. Like Tricia, she had been animated by a vision of teaching that was very different from what she had experienced as a student in a very traditional elementary school and very different from most prevailing practice. Like Tricia, she had felt depressed and inadequate while student teaching in the classroom of a teacher who was highly competent, eager to be helpful, and well regarded both by parents and by the university. After reading Tricia's journal, Helen reflected on her own student teaching:

> My lessons bored me and they bored the first graders, but I don't think that I ever seriously contemplated trying anything radically different. I prayed for a snow day every night and drove to school every morning with butterflies in my stomach. I wondered why I had ever thought that I wanted to teach.
>
> Fortunately, every student in my teacher preparation program moved to a new classroom after 7 weeks. My second placement was in the first grade of a tiny alternative school in Roxbury, Massachusetts. Here I saw children choosing their own activities, reading real books alone and with partners, building things, painting and drawing wonderful pictures, writing their own books, and glowing with pride in their own accomplishments. Although a number of the children had been labeled behavior problems in traditional public school kindergarten, I never saw Nancy, the teacher, raise her voice; her enthusiasm for her students and their learning seemed to inspire them as much as it inspired me.

I fell back in love with teaching. Of course, I knew that I wouldn't be able to create a classroom like Nancy's for a long time, but that realization did not discourage me. The important thing was that I had reconnected with a vision of teaching that excited me, and I had learned a little bit about what it looked like in practice.

It is hard for a beginner to stay clear about what good teaching looks like and what sorts of inadequate approximations are the right ones to strive for. As countless numbers of beginners have found, the alternatives are rarely between excellent progressive classrooms, where children are productively engaged in a variety of developmentally appropriate activities, and classrooms in which all are silently doing seatwork. Not all children in the "progressive" classroom will appear to their teacher to be productively engaged; not all conversations will have a positive, supportive tone; often when two children are "working together," one is doing all the work and the other is watching—or worse. Revisiting her first months in her own classroom, Helen recalls:

> I knew what I wanted—I had seen it in Nancy's classroom. I knew what the school valued: I could see it across the hall and on the expressions of colleagues. I would have been ready to die to defend my students' right to have an experience like the one that Nancy's students were having, but I wasn't always sure how much they were learning in the afternoons when the Cuisenaire rods and the sand unit and the building stuff came out. Was building a tower really so much better than practicing penmanship? I wasn't sure of the answers to a lot of questions. And there was no one to ask. No one who knew, or even valued, what I was trying to do.

The problem, then, is partly how to live with not being very good at doing something different from what others in the building are trying to do. The surprise is that one powerful enemy is yourself.

Tricia helps us see how difficult it is to figure out what you really do want when your goals do not match those of your colleagues. She shows us how hard it is to muster the energy and hope needed to create a community that is quite unlike anything your students have seen in school.

But she also identifies strategies that she used to stay afloat during the darkest days of student teaching: talking to friends and teachers who shared her vision, writing about what was happening and why it troubled her, reading books and articles that had inspired her in the past, visiting other classrooms. All these activities helped her see her environment and her alternatives more clearly. In one way or another, all nourished hope and awareness.

And awareness, Tricia insists, is much more at risk during these early months of immersion in teaching than either novices or their university mentors realize. When a novice who has spent 13 years as a student in traditional schools joins a traditional faculty, she is tugged powerfully and insidiously toward familiar images of the schoolroom and old ways of thinking about learning.

As Patty's story demonstrates, the culture of the school can overwhelm even personal experience with an individual child.

PATTY: KEITH AND HIS SILENCE

"What is wrong with Keith?" That was my question when I began teaching in the third-grade classroom in September. Keith did not talk. He sat expressionless. When I asked Keith a question, other students would jump in. "Miss Gregorich, Keith is shy. He doesn't like to talk." After a few weeks, I began to feel that Keith was not just shy. He seemed entirely withdrawn. I rarely, if ever, observed Keith making eye contact, and he often had a very far-away, dazed look on his face. When I asked my cooperating teacher what was wrong with Keith, she told me that he was a "selective mute."

"Selective mute?" What does that mean? "He chooses not to speak," was the answer to my question. I decided to try to reach him.

I realized that Keith was not writing, so I talked with many people to get ideas for ways to motivate him. I considered keeping him in for recess if he continued to write nothing for the 45 minutes of writing workshop. However, I quickly realized that this might cause him to feel negatively about writing. Instead I chose the cheerleader approach. I tried everything. I offered suggestions about what he could write. That didn't work. I told him I wanted to see words on his paper. "Keith, you need to write." That didn't work either. Then one day I noticed that he wrote the date and made pictures out of the letters. I wrote him a note and left it in his writing folder: "Wow! It's neat how you can make pictures out of the letters! I want you to write and get your wonderful ideas down on paper!" This didn't work immediately, but in retrospect, I believe that I was making progress. A friend suggested that I offer him the option of either writing or drawing. I told Keith, "You have a choice, you can either write or draw. It's your choice, but you must either write or draw." It worked! He drew. I cheered and praised his picture. It was a monster. Now I wanted words!

I talked to more people. They suggested showing him comic strips. I decided to bring in comics from the newspaper. I also brought *The Mysteries of Harris Burdick*, which had captions for each picture but no story. I told Keith that his picture was a mystery to me. I didn't know what the monster was doing. I explained that the pictures in my book were also a mystery. "You could write a sentence about your picture or make it like a comic where the monster is saying something." I left him alone, and when I returned to his desk 10 minutes later, he had written words! The monster was saying, "Yum, Yum!" I asked Keith if the monster was eating something. I guessed what the monster was eating, but my guess was wrong. Keith told me that the monster was eating toys. He said only a few words, but I understood. Wow! He spoke to me about his picture. I was ecstatic! I told the world about the triumph.

For the next few months, Keith continued to write—sometimes entire stories. He was quite sporadic in his writing. I would encourage him to write, but some days he would not. However, days when I saw Keith writing nothing, I would open his writing folder later in the day and find a story or a picture. Was he communicating with me? Did he have to feel safe enough before he would share words with me?

As I look back and try to examine what was happening, I am sad. I did not continue to give Keith as much attention, and it is difficult to wonder what would have happened if I had continued to do what I was doing. Keith continued to write, but it was still sporadic. I realized that he would sometimes write but not put it in his writing folder where I would see it. I am afraid that some of the trust I had built was lost, and he ceased to feel as safe with me.

In late November, I needed to choose a student to conduct a math interview with. I decided to interview Keith and Anthony. My cooperating teacher discouraged me from interviewing Keith. She expected him to sit silently. This is also what I expected, but I wanted to give him a chance. I wanted to build a relationship with Keith while also learning about communicating with someone who does not use many words. The interview was incredible. I was able to understand exactly what Keith understood about fractions—as well as I understood what Anthony knew about fractions. The two students are completely opposite in communication styles. Anthony talks often, and Keith rarely speaks. I explained to Keith that he did not have to talk. He could draw, write, point, and show me in order to explain his thinking. He used very few words, but he did talk. He usually answered my questions with a word or two. I was very surprised. I expected him to sit silently and say nothing. He showed me that he had a pretty good grasp of fractions.

But even after Keith had told me about his picture of the monster, had written stories, and had clearly communicated his thoughts to me during the math interview, I still expected Keith not to speak. I continued to label him as a selective mute even though he was without a doubt communicating with me. I am scared by the use of labels and hope not to use them again. Describing Keith as a selective mute is like describing me as a girl from the Upper Peninsula of Michigan. Both of us are much more complex. When I thought of Keith as a selective mute rather than as an individual child with unique characteristics, I created certain expectations for him. I expected him to sit silently, to prefer to work alone, to avoid answering questions or reading aloud.

So, who is Keith? (I feel frustrated that I am just now forcing myself to put into words who Keith is.) Keith is a child who is quite intelligent. He is a good writer. His stories are interesting and make sense. He is a good speller and seems to enjoy drawing. He is also good at math. He can add and subtract and quickly caught on to the idea of multiplication. He understands what a fraction is and how to divide a group into parts. He communicates with other children more than he communicates with adults. Sometimes he joins the games during gym and recess and sometimes he walks around the gym or playground. He doesn't usually make eye contact and doesn't volunteer answers to questions. However, he does answer some questions that adults ask him and sometimes communicates with other children.

For my 3 months in his classroom, I labeled Keith and had low expectations, but I tried desperately to reach him. I showed interest in him by interviewing him and encouraging and praising him about his writing. Yet when I began my student teaching experience in January, I forgot about Keith.

After a month and a half of student teaching, I realized what a disservice I was doing to Keith. I read Ray Rist's (1970) article on teacher expectations. I had always believed that if a teacher expects a student to fail, the child will likely fail, but if a teacher expects a child to succeed, it is likely that the child will succeed. Yet somehow, in the confusion of teaching, I had forgotten this. When I read what Rist had witnessed in the kindergarten classroom, I was infuriated.

How insane that such a crime could happen to children. Then I realized that I was doing the very same thing.

As I reflected on my treatment of Keith, I realized that I did not call on him to answer questions, ask him to read aloud, or even invite him to write answers on the board. I did not intend to be cruel. I was afraid to put Keith on the spot by asking him to speak in class. I didn't want him to feel uncomfortable. What I am realizing now is that I was the one who was uncomfortable. If I did ask Keith a question, I often immediately asked him if he would like to pass.

I was heartbroken when I realized how neglectful I had been and how I had gone off track in my own thinking. However, I planned to set higher expectations for Keith. One day, when the class was reading aloud, I asked Keith to read. I asked him if he would like to read, but I just called on the other students to read. Keith shook his head that he didn't want to read. I never let any other child refuse to read unless he or she seemed on the verge of tears, but I allowed Keith to refuse to read. I remember the encounter vividly. I asked Keith if he wanted to read, and as I asked him, I was shaking my head. The look on my face clearly said that I did not expect him to read. I remember each of us looking at the other—in a state of limbo—neither sure what the other wanted. Did he want to read? Did I really want or expect him to read? Keith looked confused, as if he were trying to find the "right" answer. He then shook his head that he did not want to read.

I am grateful that I realized that I had sent Keith all the wrong messages. The next time our class was reading aloud, I called on Keith to read just as I had asked the other students to read. I kept my eyes on the book and simply called his name. After a few moments of silence, I told Keith the page number and had Peter show him where we were. *He read aloud!* I was almost unable to speak. I was so grateful, so excited, so proud of him. I tried to hide my amazement as I said, "Keith, please continue, you did such a wonderful job reading the last paragraph."

When I expected him to read aloud, he did! It is such a sad and beautiful thing at the same time. If we set high expectations for students, we can witness extraordinary accomplishments. Yet so sad and frightening is the fact that if we have low expectations for students, they may live up to those expectations and fall far below their potential.

LAUREN AND HELEN REFLECT ON PATTY'S STORY

Like Patty herself, we revisit the story of her work with Keith with mixed feelings. Patty's experience seems to say an immense amount about what is involved in moving from the role of university student and participant observer in an elementary classroom to that of acting teacher.

As a college senior who was spending two mornings a week in Keith's class, Patty was in a good position to raise questions about Keith and to investigate the results of rejecting the little boy's definition of his own relationship to school. In her first months in the classroom, she was an outsider still in the process of defining her role and her responsibilities. She had more time available to her—time to give Keith extra attention, to talk to him—and she saw the children and the classroom with fresh eyes.

She used her opportunities well, and Keith responded to her optimistic and caring attention by communicating his ideas in a number of new ways. Had the story ended there, it would have been an uncomplicated success, a victory for persistence, energy, and hope. In fact, however, the situation took a less satisfying turn: Patty remained in Keith's classroom, but as her role changed and her responsibilities expanded, multiple problems—and children—vied for her attention. As her focus shifted from Keith, the little boy relapsed into silence.

When Patty stepped out of the role of teacher, into the role of university student or observer, she found ways to communicate with Keith and to draw him into the life of the classroom. But when she assumed the mantle of the teacher and the complex responsibilities that went with that mantle, everything changed. Certainly she had less time to devote to Keith's needs, but Patty insists that there was more to it. As she moved into the role of insider and teacher, she began to think differently about Keith. The label that the school had offered (and that she had once questioned) now overwhelmed even her own experience. Her description is both eloquently simple and full of remorse.

Like Tricia, Patty found that taking on the role of teacher creates unexpected difficulties. Matters that looked unambiguous in teacher education classes—for example, the importance of holding high expectations for all students—seem murkier. Some issues and imperatives sink unnoticed beneath the bubbling surface of classroom life.

Because Patty and Keith managed to find their way out of the maze of labels and low expectations, their story seems to us more of a victory than the defeat that Patty felt it to be as she searched her journal remorsefully for mentions of Keith. It is, however, surely a cautionary tale: Had Patty not talked about Keith with Lauren and Tricia and then revisited Ray Rist's article, she would never have connected Keith's silence to her expectations of him. As Tricia observed, "Teaching is much more complex than teacher education. . . . Issues don't come one at a time anymore."

Surely the complexity of Patty's new responsibilities distracted her attention from Keith. But there were other pressures as well: As she became the teacher, she left the world of the university and entered the world of the school full time. And as that happened, she began to see more of the life of the classroom through lenses that the school offered. The label "selective mute" helped school staff explain Keith's puzzling behavior; how natural that she should adopt it as their world became hers.

All through her senior year, Patty struggled with the contradictions between what she had learned as a student in teacher education classes and what she was experiencing. Sometimes she saw herself behaving in ways that did not fit the beliefs she had brought to student teaching and wondered whether her ideals had changed, whether her earlier ideas had been naive. But often she flinched in dismay, feeling that she had absorbed through osmosis ways of thinking—and acting—that ran counter to her deepest beliefs. One such incident occurred in the fall, when Jenny prevented her from calling for silence during writing workshop (see the epigraph). Something similar happened near the end of student teaching:

> We were having a "read-in" during my eighth week of student teaching. I had invited a variety of individuals to visit our classroom and read one of their favorite books to us. Students were bringing blankets and sleeping bags in order to sprawl out on the floor while listening to the stories. As I was talking with April, another student teacher, before school, I looked out the window and saw several students carrying their blankets and sleeping bags. I thought aloud, "Oh my goodness. It's going to be total chaos this afternoon!" April jumped in immediately, asking, "Do you mean that you are expecting them to fail before they even walk in the door?"
>
> Wow! April clearly set me straight. I would never have expected students to fail 2 months ago in the way I was doing now. What had happened? Had I come to believe these things? Deep down I don't think I had—yet my actions did not fit what I firmly believed about teaching and learning. As soon as April confronted me, I knew that the statement I had made was wrong and that it was absolutely *not* how I wanted to ever think about students.

When I began student teaching I felt extremely aware. I was unshakable in my beliefs about social justice issues. My convictions were strong. Students must be respected. I must have high expectations for all students. Learning is noisy and not always neat. What happened? I found myself teaching in ways that I did not believe. When someone reflected back to me what I was doing, I was shocked, ashamed, heartbroken.

I had been *so* confident that I would hold on to my ideals in the face of any obstacles and always act as I believed. . . . Telling my stories has helped me to piece together transformations I underwent. It's helpful for me to examine what happened and why.

Both Patty and Tricia are telling us about what can happen when bright, thoughtful young women bent on reform take on the mantle of "teacher" in traditional and bureaucratic schools. They show the powerful tug of colleagues and of school norms. Patty and Tricia were exceptionally committed college students. They *wanted* to student teach in urban schools because they wanted to make a difference in the lives of poor kids. But as their ties with the university loosened, as they became student teachers and spent more time in charge of the class and took on more of the duties and responsibilities of teachers, they found themselves thinking and acting more and more like teachers whose attitudes they had deplored in the past. In student teaching they had hoped to learn more about how to create classrooms where *all* children would read, write, and engage with one another and with powerful ideas. Instead they found themselves coming to see these ideas as visionary and impractical. Only by maintaining contact with voices outside of their schools were they able to keep alive their original vision—and the selves who had embraced that vision.

GETTING OUTSIDE THE SITUATION

What's involved in learning from the experience of teaching? Teachers say that they learn most of what they know in classrooms, with and from children, rather than from, for example, their teacher preparation programs (see, e.g., Lortie, 1975; Johnson, 1990). Although this is partly a commentary on the abysmal quality of much that passes for teacher education, it also reflects the enormous complexity of teaching and of classroom life and the immense difficulty of teaching—or learning—about the dance that is teaching in the relatively simplified environment of a university classroom.

Given that all teachers can expect to learn most of what will eventually make them good teachers after they leave the university—Frances Hawkins, a masterful teacher of young children, once told Helen that it takes at least 10 years to learn to teach well—novices need to think hard about what they can do to make sure that they learn *what they want to learn* from experience. Patty's and Tricia's stories show how easy it is to learn the wrong lessons, the ones that convince you that teaching is not for you, that "attending to the needs of individual children" means not expecting or asking the very shy child to talk, that being an experienced teacher means noticing the decibel level in the classroom even before you notice what the children are actually doing.

But if their stories show that even the most committed novice is in grave danger of learning all the wrong things from the type of experience they are likely to get in a city school, they also show the power of conversation. The stories that these young teachers tell are of novices who felt powerless and who often seemed about to go under. Their excitement about teaching and their belief in classrooms that accommodated, celebrated, and educated all the different children assigned to them were more than at risk. But because they maintained vital connections with other voices and perspectives—with April, with Jenny, with the articles that had ignited Tricia's excitement in the first place—they managed to keep themselves and their visions of good teaching alive.

Most people need communities in order to learn. For Patty and Tricia, being part of a community of adults who valued what they valued, and who could help them see what they passively observed, was an answer to being sucked into the quicksand of public schools. The beginning teacher, particularly the beginning teacher in a rigidly bureaucratic urban school, needs such a community even more than other people do, because she is trying to manage a complex world that she has only just begun to make sense of and because her work makes immense demands—emotional and intellectual. Unfortunately, not all communities promote inquiry. Although some teachers support one another in asking and answering hard questions about children, classrooms, and learning, many do not. Too often the ready-made community of the teachers' lounge encourages the novice to blame students and their families for the inevitable difficulties or offers formulas for simplifying her understanding of a complex issue.

And so, the teacher who wants to stay intellectually alive needs to find or create, and then nurture, communities and connections that support her learning. This is no easy task: Having been brought up to be "nice," most of us would hesitate, for example, to ask the kind of hard question that April asked Patty; whatever we thought of her comment, we would be tempted to smile and agree that a classroom full of 8-year-olds in sleeping bags is a frightening prospect. Yet Tricia and Patty showed us over and over how much they learned about their students, their options, their environments, and themselves from others who held up a mirror that reflected their ideas back to them from another angle, who challenged their way of seeing and acting.

FINAL THOUGHTS

The need for learning opportunities does not evaporate when the prospective teacher completes her degree. From Patty's and Tricia's experiences in student teaching, the four of us learned—or re-learned—how vital it is for teachers to connect continually with other people who share their faith that all children can learn and that the learning that matters most is often best nourished in classrooms that look very different from those valued in most city school systems. Our own collaboration has allowed us to imagine more fully the kinds of learning communities that can be created to support good practice, for it has introduced us all to new possibilities for collaborative work. Just as Patty and Tricia had not, before today, written with their teachers, Helen and Lauren had not collaborated in this way with their undergraduate students. Yet this collaboration is simply an extension of what we try to do in the classroom: to listen carefully to those we teach, to try to learn well what their stories tell us, and to reflect these stories back in ways that offer students new opportunities for seeing and sense making.

NOTE

1. The Learning Community program was one of four thematic teacher education programs at a large Midwestern university; its aim was to prepare elementary teachers to teach school subjects effectively while focusing on the development of personal and social responsibility among students. Twenty-five to 30 juniors entered the program each year and took all their teacher education courses together.

REFERENCES

Denyer, J., & Florio-Ruane, S. (1991). *Mixed messages and missed opportunities: Moments of transformation in writing conferences and teacher education*. Paper presented at the annual meeting of the American Anthropological Association.

Featherstone, H. (1993). Learning from the first years of classroom teaching: The journey in, the journey out. *Teachers College Record, 95* (1), 93–112.

Johnson, S. M. (1990). *Teachers at work: Achieving success in our schools*. New York: Basic Books.

Kohl, H. (1967). *36 Children*. New York: New American Library.

Lortie, D. C. (1975). *Schoolteacher: a sociological study*. Chicago: University of Chicago Press.

Rist, R. C. (1970). Student social class and teacher expectations: The self-fulfilling prophesy in ghetto education. *Harvard Educational Review, 40* (3), 411–451.

Veenman, S. (1984). Perceived problems of beginning teachers. *Review of Educational Research, 54* (Summer), 143–178.

CONCLUSION

Ten Alternative Classrooms

William Ayers

John Taylor Gatto (1992) taught in New York City public schools for 26 years and in 1991 was elected New York State's Teacher of the Year. At the awards ceremony—the ritual in which the happy-face sticker is placed on the honoree's chest—Gatto put a pie in the face of the self-congratulatory assembly by saying, in effect, that schools murder the souls and minds of children *by design*, and that he has been fighting a guerrilla war against genocide in the classroom his whole life—a war that he believes he is losing badly.

Streetwise and blunt, Gatto pulls no punches: "The lesson of report cards, grades, and tests is that children should not trust themselves or their parents but should instead rely on the evaluation of certified officials" (p. 11). "Children will follow a private drummer if you can't get them into a uniformed marching band" (p. 12). "It is the most important lesson, that we must wait for other people, better trained than ourselves, to make the meanings of our lives" (p. 8).

Gatto outlines in excruciating detail the real lessons of American schooling, things like hierarchy and your place in it, indifference, emotional and intellectual dependency, provisional self-esteem, and the need to submit to certified authority. For many students, the experience of schooling is just this: Nothing of real importance is ever undertaken, nothing is ever connected to anything else, nothing is ever pursued to its deepest limits, nothing is ever finished, and nothing is ever done with investment and courage. This may not be the intention of policy makers, politicians, or administrators; it is certainly not the hope of most parents and teachers. Yet it is often what children live and learn.

John Taylor Gatto is not alone in his condemnation of American schooling, nor in his search for positive alternatives. Rita Tenorio,

Wisconsin Teacher of the Year in 1990, Adela Coronado-Greeley, Illinois Teacher of the Year in 1994, and thousands of thoughtful, experienced teachers whose names are not in the newspapers share a deep belief that the structures of schooling stand in the way of teaching and learning. Bell schedules, tests, grades, the press of time, the large numbers of students expected to do the same things at the same time—all these and more reduce teaching to monitoring and controlling and make school a kind of large sorting machine. This was not what most of us had in mind when we chose to become teachers.

There are endless approaches to creating alternatives to this dismal picture. Here, for example, are 10 sketches of what could be done by teachers today:

1. *Classrooms could be lived in the present tense.* Teachers could provide opportunities for rich experiences and powerful interactions *right now*. Teachers could decide that the best preparation for a meaningful future life lies in creating a meaningful present life. Further, teachers could realize that the best way to entice youngsters to participate positively—to show up and to engage fully—is to provide opportunities for relevant and vital experiences every day. The work of school, then, would not be constructed as bitter medicine, hurriedly swallowed on someone else's promise that it will be profitable to you "someday." In fact, "preparation" would no longer frame issues of teaching and learning; preparation would be bracketed, and school work would not be justified by reference to it. The work of school would be valuable in its own terms.

2. *Classrooms could become workshops for inventors.* Children are human beings (not human becomings), and human beings are by nature inventors. Of course, only some of us invent famous machines or technologies or institutions, but all of us create works as an expression of our consciousness. The young child learning to speak, the older child working at an easel and discovering the color purple, the class inquiring into employment and neighborhood housing and finding revealing patterns based on race—these are all examples of inventors at work. Since everything is on some level a human invention—literature and the arts, of course, math and science, but also racism, sexism, and even childhood itself—school could become a place in which people would be expected and encouraged to be inventors, where participants would regularly explore together the consequence of human inventions both for the growth of children and for the society we want to build.

A classroom for inventors would look more like a laboratory than an assembly line, more like a workshop than a factory, more like a discovery center in a museum than a mini-lecture hall. The focus would be on activity, experimentation, problem solving, and surprise. There would be multiple entry points into an adventure in learning, depending on the knowledge, skills, know-how, and experience students bring with them to school. There would also be a wide range of media, materials, and literacies available to challenge students to attend to broader horizons and to different (perhaps deeper and wider) ways of knowing. In these classrooms, big questions would be followed to their outer limits because the pressure to "cover the curriculum" would be pushed back, and the *pretense* of coverage would be rejected. These are places that would encourage curiosity and engage mystery.

3. *Classrooms could become fearless.* School should be made safe—both physically and emotionally—because we know that fear destroys intelligence. But classrooms could also be designed for risk taking. School could be a community that discourages *acquiescence*, the passive dullness that is the hallmark of most schools, in favor of building collective *consent*. Teachers here would likely believe that although you can have compulsory schooling, compulsory education is an unworkable contradiction. Education and learning require assent, some personal act of courage and will and affirmation, and so teachers would struggle to construct a place where matters of paramount importance are developed and pursued in a compelling way, a place that draws students' interest, attention, and consistent presence on its own basis.

4. *Classrooms could honor diversity truly and fully.* Although diversity has many dimensions, consider race as a central example. In a good school, race and racial differences would not be the basis for privilege and oppression, but neither would they be ignored or dismissed. Rather, race, racial differences, and racism would be explored and studied. They would be studied because these constructions have defined so much of our history and continue to motivate and power so much of human thinking and action today.

The assumption in this school would be that racism hurts all people and is a force that can degrade education and stunt growth; that stratification along racial lines blocks progress and the fulfillment of potential; and that simply because grown-ups can't talk or work sensibly around issues of race doesn't mean that it can't be a schoolwide focus of inquiry and action. To the extent that this focus draws people of different races together in a common cause, the school would also attend to internal questions: What expectations do we have of one another? How do we work in a way that acknowledges and respects the contributions of each? What are the formal and informal "rules of the house," and who decides what they are? How do we create a productive tension between comfort and discomfort in our process and in our study?

5. *Classrooms could begin with high expectations and standards for all.* Standards would not be reduced to immutable laws or benchmarks for testing but would be construed as principles and values around which to reflect and raise questions. In fact, standard-setting would become part of the conscious, stipulated work of the school. Standards, of course, would be developed close to the classroom, by the students and the teacher, and close to the family, by the children and the parents. They would not be held outside or above the concerns of those most intimately involved in the growth and development of children, and therefore they would not easily be thoughtless, lifeless, or disfiguring.

A core question, one that is dynamic, ever-changing, and alive for each person and that guides much of the work of a good school, would be this: What knowledge and experience are most worthwhile? In order to adequately grapple with this question, teachers need to know each student well, to know how each is doing in terms of growth, development, and the acquisition of skills or capacities or dispositions of mind.

In this school, teachers would acknowledge the human impulse to value and to express preferences and, further, would treat values as if they matter.

6. *Classrooms could be places where adults tell children the truth.* Most schools live on half-truths and lies, and dissembling is the sad, often exhausting, always deflecting norm of behavior. One pervasive example is the notion that standardized test scores are a fair measure of student intelligence, achievement, or worth.

Think what would happen if students were told that the single most powerful predictor of academic success, including scores on these tests, is family income and class background. Furthermore, think what would happen if students were told that the scoring of tests is structured so that half of all test takers *must* fail. Suddenly the all-powerful Oz would be revealed for the old fraud that he is. This could lead to a range of interesting investigations, projects, and activities—all based on simply pushing back the hidden screen and looking at who's pulling the strings.

7. *A classroom could be an intimate community where children find unconditional acceptance.* In many schools, nothing about children—not their lives and experiences, nor their families and communities—is deemed valuable. Their very presence is seen as a burden, an encumbrance, an obstacle. And their presence is always contingent: Students are sorted, classified, graded, moved along. By contrast, a good school would be a place where students feel that they have a right and a responsibility to be present, a place that could not function without the contribution of each particular kid. Teachers in this school would challenge themselves to see each student as a fellow creature with his or her own experiences, knowledge, skills, dreams, expectations, and hopes. Seeing the student as complex, changing, dynamic, and worthy would guide teachers to avoid easy summary evaluations in their search for the next teaching question: Given what I know now, how will I teach this child? This would be a touchstone for trust and hope.

8. *Classrooms could become thoughtful places that honor the thinking and work of teacher and students.* They could also become places that consciously provide opportunities for the community to enact its values: compassion, curiosity, justice, openness, humor, or creativity. In this school, teachers would resist the pressure to push out all that is most important and worthwhile in learning and living in favor of a narrow, instructable, and easily testable agenda. Rather, they would struggle to create the conditions that would allow the entire community to experience and enact its values and to recover a language of valuing that has been weakened through disuse.

9. *Classrooms could be places that breathe biography and autobiography.* Reading about lives, writing about lives, and collecting life-history narratives are all powerful ways to understand and participate in the great human story unfolding all around us. Biography and autobiography live at the crossroads of individual lives, history, and culture. They are all about the big, enduring issues: love and passion, freedom and control, society and identity, the personal and the political, life and death, you and me. Reading and writing biography could be the essential core of an educational experience, providing opportunities to take intellectual stock, to develop a sense of agency and embeddedness, to create an empathetic, responsible culture for learning.

10. *Classrooms could be fair places where people make a difference.* Citizenship would be considered a practical art here, and it would therefore be practiced rather than ritualized. Students would struggle to extract knowledge from information, to consider the com-

mon good, and to link consciousness to their own daily conduct. This
school would be characterized by activity, discovery, and surprise
rather than passivity and rote repetition.

A good school would stand in critical opposition to much of the
schooling we see all around us today. Based on a different vision of
human life and potential, such a school would be a radical alternative. And radical alternatives are desperately needed for the lives of
our children today and for the hope of creating a better tomorrow.

Teachers capable of creating these kinds of classrooms begin by
rejecting the notion that teaching is something simple or settled,
something easily grasped in a college classroom, painlessly practiced
with 30 students, and (if there are problems) quickly remediated by
some supervising expert. They begin then to conceive of teaching as
fundamentally ethical, political, and intellectual work, the task of
people willing to plunge in alongside their students and search for
ways to nourish a wide range of interests, needs, and aspirations.
They recognize teaching as a creative act that, like all creative acts,
is characterized by uncertainty, mystery, obstacle, and struggle.

REFERENCE

Gatto, J. T. (1992). *Dumbing us down: The hidden curriculum of compulsory schooling.* Philadelphia: New Society Publishers.

APPENDIX A

Getting a Life:
A New Teacher's Guide

Joseph Featherstone

Here are some suggestions about how to develop yourself intellectually as a beginning teacher and also create a life for yourself outside the classroom. Both are necessary for vital, creative work. What interests and pleases you is an important thread to follow in finding what will lure students into learning. One step toward being interesting to students is to develop some interests of your own. New teachers end up discovering themselves, but discovery can also be a way of making and inventing. You choose—no one could do everything that follows, but someone who doesn't develop any cultural interests at all will probably be a dull teacher and may end up covered with aluminum siding.

Your aim should be to become a practical intellectual, able to show students the uses and pleasures of culture and help students learn to make ideas and meanings. You can think of culture as a series of conversations you want to be part of, as habits and practices, and as a series of tools for inquiry, thought, and entertainment. By simplifying culture to such basics, you can begin to make cultural development practical for yourself and your students. There's nothing mysterious about developing cultural interests. One of the best ways to develop them is through talk—because whatever else teachers may teach, they are always working with words and language. If you expect kids to talk in class, you should learn how to speak well about subjects that matter and are interesting. Conversations include current and past debates: Did you see *The Age of Innocence*? Who killed JFK? Is *Huckleberry Finn* racist? Is this movie better than the book? The main thing is finding conversations to be part of in some way, either directly or indirectly. Habits and practices include any regular activity that keeps you making thought and culture for yourself—watching serious movies and television offerings, reading books and reviews of books in an area you are interested in, going to a lecture, keeping a notebook or a journal about teaching or some other cultural interest, and perhaps above all finding and cultivating some people who share your interests. Doing things—going camping or taking up a musical instrument—is the way to begin developing active culture as opposed to passive, received culture. Tools include things like dictionaries, encyclopedias, museums, galleries, universities, libraries and bookstores, television sets, VCRs, books and materials, and knowledgeable people in fields where your interests lie.

Writing

Telling a story involves enacting meaning, reflecting, and posing problems. Jerome Bruner (1990) says that human cultures organize knowing in only two ways—the practice of scientific thinking, with logic and evidence, and telling stories. Work on both, for they are the essential human building blocks of culture. Start telling stories of your own. You would be foolish not to begin a journal for noting down thoughts and reflecting on issues, including doubts and negative thoughts and the poetry of becoming a teacher. You could also start a folder with a portfolio of your work from courses and the like (useful in many ways, including job hunting), and a notebook in which to jot down ideas in the area of curriculum and pedagogy. The main things a writer needs to develop are practice and an audience. If your college has e-mail, get an e-mail number and start an e-mail conversation. Find out about INTERNET. If you expect kids to write, you should work on your own writing. Make your classroom into a place where writers get the audience they need.

Reading

Collect course books and books on teaching, especially the firsthand accounts by teachers, ranging from Herbert Kohl's to Vivian Paley's works. Start collecting classic children's books and films. Make a point of expanding your taste in reading. If you don't read novels, start now. If you don't read nonfiction, sample some. You are in training to become a culture guide for students, so broaden your own experience of literacy. Build a new teacher's personal library. Look at book reviews—the Sunday *New York Times Book Review*, for example—and when you read a rave review, go out and read the book. Find a friend who likes to talk about reading. Some publications that review literature and poetry and cultural matters generally are *The New Yorker*, *The Nation*, *The National Review*, *The New York Review of Books*, *The New York Times Book Review* (which can be subscribed to separately from the entire newspaper), *American Poetry Review*, and *Poetry*.

Check out local university and public libraries and local bookstores. A good bookstore in your region can give you an idea of the many ways a teacher can use such a resource—get the list of public events like readings, story hour, or book-signings for a month and go to a few. Hang around and imagine what you would do if you could hold a class in a bookstore or library for a few hours. (They would probably let you.) Librarians are great, often untapped, resources.

Find a few books, essays, poems, or plays that take the top of your head off. One book that changes your mind or your life will let you taste what literature is like at its strongest, and then you will be able to speak to your students on such matters with what all new teachers crave—authority.

Conversation

Arrange your schedule so you have a chance to talk with other students outside of class. Find one or two people who like to talk shop, as well as other things (the mix might be important). Such conversation can be a model for how you think and work together—and enjoy life—with colleagues and students in a school. (Alternatively, without conversation, you can replicate the isolation of many classroom teachers.) Good conversation is at the heart of learning, and you should learn how to take part in it as well as some first steps toward being able to create it in your own classroom. You won't get better at it unless you practice. What are the elements of an intelligent conversation? You now have a professional interest in this matter, so start noticing, beginning with yourself and your friends. Who has intelligent, interesting, educational, funny conversations? How are they created and sustained? Do some informal fieldwork. Form a book club or teachers' group.

Cultural Literacy

The term "cultural literacy" is not well defined, and it is sometimes abused, but it can still be useful. To start with, look at two books, one by E. D. Hirsch, et al., *Cultural Literacy* (1987), and the other by Herb Kohl, et al., *From Archetype to Zeitgeist* (1992). Both try from different political perspectives to give you a way to assess the state of your own learning and, better than that, a short course in how to expand your vision and your vocabulary. Both convey the big idea that people need to learn how to participate in cultural conversation. Kohl has a better sense than Hirsch that there are many cultures in the United States today and that we need bridges and translations, not cultural police, but both are useful in giving you a sense of how students learn to take part in a wider world—without necessarily forgetting their roots.

From the point of view of different areas of the curriculum, two recent books by Daniel Boorstein (1983; 1992) amount to a "kit" for a liberal arts education. They are full of short chapters that a teacher can use—for example, the history of printing, astronomy, medicine, or drama. They might best be used as background and reference books by a classroom teacher or by the kids. They are *The Discoverers* (science and the study of society) and *The Creators* (the arts and humanities).

Get a copy of the new (expensive) *Columbia Encyclopedia*, or buy a (cheap) remaindered copy of an old edition. It is a book meant to guide you and your students to other sources. For example, if you look up the painter Mary Cassatt, it will refer you to a biography. You and your students need to learn some of the basics of how to find things out, and having a copy of such a reference work that you use and have students use is a wonderful thing. Similarly, a dictionary will allow you as a teacher to dramatize the importance of words and to show your students that although no one knows everything, there are tools for expanding their (and your) knowledge. Any good dictionary will do, but I recommend the *American Heritage Dictionary*, especially for roots of words. If you can't afford the big version, use the collegiate version. If your students ever wrangle over words, they are on the way to taking the culture bus and driving it on their own.

Learn literacy by doing it. Promote a variety of literacies for you and for the kids you teach:

Poetry readings. Attend live readings of poetry or literature in your region. On college campuses, most public readings are free, but even the ones that aren't—the celebrity series, for example—sometimes offer ticket returns to waiting students. Find out which publications advertise events in your area.

Do some writing of your own. The Bay Area Writing Project has pioneered the idea that teachers who want to develop students' writing should develop their own, and this idea is catching on. Turn an autobiographical sketch from a course into a poem or a short story, just to feel what this is like. Start a poetry writing group with friends— or kids. Find the kind of writing you like to do. Not everyone thrives on poetry.

Drama. Look for drama classes or local amateur groups to try out for (learning by doing). Look for a good teacher in school or a children's theater group in your area for some hints about how to do theater with kids. Ask if you can watch some sessions. Read a play out loud with a group of friends. Look at the video store selections with an eye to good plays. Drama is the sleeping giant of the curriculum.

Music. Watch the calendar and the schedules for campus and local concerts—many are free. The range of music in the local pop scene is, or can be, educational. While you are a student might be a terrific time to get music lessons—free or paid for in cash or in kind. As a summer project, learn to play the guitar. In your classes, find kids who can provide music at the proper time. Note television specials and concerts.

Films. You can find good films in the mainstream theaters, campus "classic" and dorm series, international series, classic series on cable TV, and video stores. Look at the film criticism in a magazine that regularly reviews movies—*The New Yorker*, for example, or *Time* or *Newsweek*. Take your kids to a movie.

The sciences. Look for science lectures for a general audience. Read a science magazine or the once-a-week science supplement in *The New York Times* and start clipping it for things that will help you start thinking imaginatively. On television, "Nova" still airs, along with many nature specials. And two older series are well worth a look on video: "The Ring of Truth" (Philip Morison) and "The Ascent of Man" (Jacob Bronowski). Sequences from the science and nature shows on TV (available in video stores) can be a terrific addition to a science curriculum. Also, science writing is enjoying a new renaissance these days—check this out in a library or a bookstore. Visit museums and observatories. Do a science project—maybe raise some butterflies. (Get clearance from the landlady first.)

The arts. Take a studio or art history course. Visit campus exhibits, art museums, and local exhibits of art and photography. Buy a sketchbook and some simple art materials. Check out the art books in the library. Survey art videos and slide collections from museums.

Computers. Learn word processing. Learn desktop publishing so that you and your kids can put out a class newspaper or magazine. Learn basic programming. Get an e-mail address. Locate some friends who know about computers and get them to initiate you. Begin collecting ideas about how kids can use computers for real, not as electric workbooks. A classroom or school publication is a fundamental tool for literacy.

Local museums. When you visit, think like a teacher: How is this made interesting? What ideas can I steal? If I brought my kids here, how would I build on this? Where are the powerful ideas? What makes "an experience" memorable and important?

History. Find out local sites and places of historical interest. How much history can you "read" from local architecture and monuments? What does it show, and what would such an approach leave out? How could you make good use of such stuff with groups of kids? Look into the Foxfire organization and Eliot Wigginton's writings. What about you and your kids? Are there people in the area doing oral history? Are there books on big local events—a strike or a flood, for example? Can you find other teachers who might be interested in a project, say, on the Great Depression in your area? Three public television series—"Eyes on the Prize," "The Civil War," and "The Great Depression"—have set a new standard for popular documentary history. Look at them and begin to figure out how pieces of them might be a part of history or literature study. If you could watch the depression or the civil rights series with a group who lived it, you and your kids would hear wonderful stories.

Nature study. Visit state parks and preserves and campus nature areas. When are wildflowers in bloom? In many areas, the Audubon Society sponsors bird and nature walks all spring and summer. Video stores have fantastic material from film and television documentaries. Get involved in a local group working on environmental issues.

Foreign languages. If you don't speak one, why not learn one while you are on a college campus? Spanish alone will be an invaluable asset for U.S. teachers in the 1990s. Read newspapers and periodicals, listen to French or Spanish radio stations. Arrange to swap languages with a foreign student. If you can travel abroad (or better yet, live abroad briefly) try to remember what it is like to be a foreigner and what helps you learn and cross bridges to the new culture. This is useful experience for teaching.

Keeping informed. Get a student subscription to a national news or opinion magazine such as *Time, Newsweek, The New Republic, The Nation, The National Review,* or *The New York Times* (student rate). Listen to the morning or evening news on National Public Radio; check out the show "Fresh Air." Look at public and network television news. Start comparing news sources—TV, radio, newspapers—and thinking about how you would get kids to become thoughtful critics of the news.

Physical education and exercise. Check out tennis facilities, for example, or swimming pools. Running or walking costs nothing. Learning a new sport is not only good exercise but a way to think about learning generally. How would you sell a sport or exercise you like to kids? What about the literature—in books and films—on sports?

Education and politics. A good introduction to thinking and acting like a citizen would be to join a campus political group for a year. Look around in your community for groups doing political work. From a teacher's angle, see the journal *Rethinking Schools* and look into the organization Educators for Social Responsibility (ESR). Especially interesting are the ESR materials on caring for the environment and the work of a curriculum outfit called Facing History and Ourselves, which has developed materials on the Holocaust, genocide, and racism generally. Read Herbert Kohl's *Basic Skills* (1982) and Myles Horton et al.'s *The Long Haul* (1990).

Make a point of finding opportunities to mix with people whose backgrounds are different from your own. You might want to do an assessment of your own experiences and what you think you need to become at home in a multicultural and multiracial world in which schools welcome students who were once barred for being "different." Some campus religious groups provide opportunities for interracial and cross-cultural experiences. Some secular organizations and activities are more diverse than others. There are opportunities in dorms and elsewhere on campus to work on your skills in these areas—and sometimes get paid to do so. Service learning programs, summer jobs with kids in the area, work experiences generally, and your own choice of free-time activities could help you build values and skills in this area that is essential for teachers of the 1990s. No one is truly educated in the United States who cannot cross cultural and racial and handicap boundaries. As a teacher, you need more than a minimal dose of such experiences to help your students learn how to do this. Read Brown and Ling's *Visions of America* (1993) for a sample of the huge and growing literature on the U.S. rainbow of cultures, and, of course, many current books and films (Alice Walker, Toni Morrison, the film and text of "The Autobiography of Malcolm X," the books and films on Chinese American life by Amy Tan, and so on). This literature offers teachers and students imaginative ways to think about the variety of peoples in the United States—materials for a curriculum that speaks and looks like America.

A teacher's job, culturally speaking, is to build bridges between the broad culture of the school or university curriculum and the local neighborhood cultures of the students. The bridges work best as two-way streets, so students can move out to the wide world and back to their own lives and communities. If you yourself have tried to learn about life in the treetops while maintaining your own roots, you may be in a good position to help your students. Maybe seeing this connection is an important step in your own development. Your own autobiography may be a resource for helping students straddle different worlds of class, race, or ethnicity. If not, you may be able to study some figures who seem able to move in different worlds with pride and an intact spirit. There is no formula for how a teacher learns to guide students to an understanding of the wide world and a deeper insight into their own community, but this is the challenge. Look for models and examples in the world your kids inhabit, and invite them into your class.

Look around in fieldwork opportunities for teachers to admire and learn from. Find out where such teachers are getting their ideas. Make them your mentors. Notice how some veteran teachers work to develop their practice. Be politely critical of teachers who don't. Look for interesting speakers and brown-bag (lunchtime) sessions at local colleges. Many offer stories about work that is vital to teaching today. Read the "classic" accounts by teachers, and start collecting your own stories in a journal.

Don't forget that in many fields, parents and members of the community have knowledge to offer. From politics to nature study to sports to culture, there are always some folks who know a lot and would be delighted to come to your classroom and tell some of their stories. Such visitors—like field trips—always make school more interesting and exciting.

Start becoming a magpie in the curriculum areas you are involved in. Shop for ideas, odds and ends, materials, and tricks. Set aside space in a closet and get yourself a file drawer. Find out who is doing interesting things in curriculum in your district and arrange to meet them. On a vacation, take a trip to a library that has curriculum materials from the past—John Dewey's school, George Count's social studies texts from the 1930s, Lucy Sprague Mitchell's *Young Geographers*, the 1960s materials from ESS (Elementary Science Study), the 1960s physics and math and social studies materials. Check out MACOS (Man, a Course of Study), and see what all the fuss was about. Work at becoming a collector and critic of curriculum ideas—a thoughtful consumer making choices for yourself and your students. Keep a sharp eye out for stuff that is open-ended enough to adapt for your purposes. Be wary of material that tries to be "teacher proof" or assumes that a teacher and her kids are just a bunch of ventriloquist dummies.

Continue to make use of your own childhood as a major resource for teaching, but don't assume that it is universal. How we are alike and unlike is one of the great human questions. Teachers work on it for a lifetime. Get to know a few children well, preferably out of school. Try to get a sense of how they learn and what sort of teaching would work with them. Know one or two well enough to have fun with them. Learn enough about families so that you can respect the work of raising children in this country today. Look for teachers who connect to families and communities rather than setting up barriers. Service learning and tutoring opportunities abound. In your school placements, notice the teachers who are students of their students. Take a special interest in how children and youth are portrayed today. Start to read children's literature and look at films and television with a curiosity. Is "Beverly Hills, 90210" an accurate portrayal of teenagers today? How would you compare it with "My So-Called Life"? What do the media images of kids have to do with actuality? When a book or film or TV show portrays kids with imagination and freshness and dignity, notice how and why, and make a note to tell your students about it.

Students need to encounter strong teachers, with minds and voices of their own—speaking up, making choices, developing voice and style and convictions. These necessary qualities for a strong teacher can be developed too. They can be part of your own self-development, but, like the children you will teach, you will thrive best if a social setting encourages you and if you can get some help. If you are shy, think of activities and realms that will help you overcome shyness. If current friends don't take your mind seriously, locate people who will. Development is always social as well as individual. Don't try to do it all by yourself. Don't expect your students to.

A variety of teacher groups and networks exist as models for how teachers can break their isolation. Don't write off your union or association—some are lively and offer real support as well as a link with the wider world of politics and policy. If the union in your area is not really alive, think about becoming an activist and performer in union affairs. New teachers need to find other new teachers to meet with. Perhaps a "Thank-God-It's-Friday" group could meet for pizza and a movie or talk in a bar or café or somebody's apartment. Sometimes people need to socialize before they feel able to bring up real problems. Every school has one or two veteran teachers able to help new teachers out. Try to locate them and begin mustering the support you will need. Beginning and veteran teachers could meet in a study group once a month or so to read something together, or see a film, or to tackle issues of community, curriculum or other problems in the school. In creating and sustaining any of these groups, you will gain valuable experience. Teaching is, after all, mainly the care and feeding of groups. Helping to create a teachers' group will give you essential support and save you from the deadly isolation of the schools; it will also equip you with skills you need to help students balance individual learning and cooperation—two essentials for all intellectual activity. Such groups are part of the social life that keeps teachers interesting and human—shapers of live culture.

REFERENCES

Brown, W., & Ling, A. (1993). *Visions of America: Personal narratives from the promised land*. New York: Persea Books.

Boorstein, D. (1983). *The creators*. New York: Random House.

Boorstein, D. (1992). *The discoverers*. New York: Random House.

Bruner, J. (1990). *Acts of meaning*. Cambridge, MA: Harvard University Press.

Hirsch, E. D., Kett, J., & Trefil, J. (Eds.). (1987). *Cultural literacy: What every American needs to know*. Boston: Houghton Mifflin.

Horton, M., Kohl, J., & Kohl, H. (1990). *The long haul*. New York: Doubleday.

Kohl, H. (1982). *Basic skills*. Boston: Little, Brown.

Kohl, H., Kohl, E., & Garner, D. (1992). *From archetype to zeitgeist: Powerful ideas for powerful thinking*. Boston: Little, Brown.

APPENDIX B

Selected Resources for Becoming Teachers

TEACHER NETWORKS

The Center for Collaborative
  Education
1573 Madison Avenue, Room 201
New York, NY 10029
212-348-7821

The Chicago Forum for School
  Change
College of Education
University of Illinois at Chicago
1040 West Harrison
Chicago, IL 60607-7133
312-413-8066

The Coalition of Essential
  Schools
PO Box 1969
Brown University
Providence, RI 02912

Foxfire Fund
Rabun Gap, GA 30562-0541
706-764-5319

The Institute for Democracy
  and Education
210 McCracken Hall
Ohio University
Athens, OH 45701-2979

The National Coalition of
  Education Activists
PO Box 679
Rhinebeck, NY 12572-0679
914-876-4580

The North Dakota Study Group
Center for Teaching and
  Learning
University of North Dakota
Grand Forks, ND 58201

The Workshop Center
City College of New York
North Academic Center 4-220
New York, NY 10031
212-650-8436

JOURNALS

Democracy and Education
210 McCracken Hall
Ohio University
Athens, OH 45701-2979

Fairtest Examiner
National Center for Fair and
   Open Testing
342 Broadway
Cambridge, MA 02139

Green Teacher
95 Roberts Street
Toronto, Ontario M55 2K5
Canada

Hands On
Foxfire Fund
Rabun Gap, GA 30568

Insights
Center for Teaching and
   Learning
PO Box 8158
University of North Dakota
Grand Forks, ND 58202

New Advocate
480 Washington Street
Norwood, MA 02062

Pathways
Center for Teaching and
   Learning
PO Box 8158
University of North Dakota
Grand Forks, ND 58202

Radical Teacher
Boston Women's Teachers'
   Group
PO Box 102
Kindall Square Post
   Office
Cambridge, MA 02142

Rethinking Schools
1001 East Keefe Avenue
Milwaukee, WI 53212

Teachers and Writers
Teachers and Writers
   Collaborative
5 Union Square West
New York, NY 10003

Teaching and Learning
Center for Teaching and
   Learning
University of North Dakota
Grand Forks, ND 58201

Teaching Tolerance
400 Washington Avenue
Montgomery, AL 36104

Young Children
National Association for
   the Education of Young
   Children
1834 Connecticut Avenue,
   NW
Washington, DC 20009

OTHER CURRICULUM ASSETS

Algebra Project
1603 South Michigan Avenue
Chicago, IL 60616

Anti-Bias Curriculum: Tools for
Empowering Young Students
National Association for the
Education of Young Children
1834 Connecticut Avenue, NW
Washington, DC 20009

Best Practice Network
Center for City Schools
National-Louis University
2840 Sheridan Road
Evanston, IL 60201-1796

Chicago Metro History Center
60 West Walton Street
Chicago, IL 60610

Civics for Democracy: A Journey
for Teachers and Students
Essential Books
PO Box 19405
Washington, DC 20036

Educators for Social
Responsibility
23 Jordan Street
Cambridge, MA 02138

Facing History and Ourselves
16 Hurd Road
Brookline, MA 02146
617-232-0281

Food First
398 60th Street
Oakland, CA 94618

Global Village
2210 Wilshire Boulevard
Box 262
Santa Monica, CA 90403

In Our Own Image: An African
American History
The Peoples Publishing Group
and the Rochester City
School District
800-822-1080

Keepers of the Earth: Native
American Stories and
Environmental Activities for
Children
Network of Educators on the
Americas
1118 22nd Street, NW
Washington, DC 20037

Multicultural Mathematics
PO Box 658
Portland, MD 04104

National Women's History
Project
7738 Bell Road
Windsor, CA 95492

Open Minds to Equality: A
Sourcebook of Learning
Activities to Promote Race,
Sex, Class, and Age Equity by
Nancy Schniedewind and
Ellen Davidson
Prentice-Hall
Englewood Cliffs, NJ

Rites of Passage (a student-written   1118 22nd Street, NW
   journal from Portland, Oregon)   Washington, DC 20037
Network of Educators on the
   Americas

ET CETERA

Defense for Children   Designs for Change
   International–USA   6 North Michigan Avenue, Suite
210 Forsyth Street   1600
New York, NY 10002   Chicago, IL 60602

About the Editor
and the Contributors

William Ayers began teaching in 1965 in an experimental free school associated with the civil rights movement. He has been involved in community and adult education, prison education, and a variety of school reform projects and movements. He has taught preschool through graduate school, lived in a residential home for "delinquent" youngsters, and founded and directed three separate alternative schools. His own children, now teenagers, have been a major source for thinking and rethinking the issues of teaching and learning. He is the author of *The Good Preschool Teacher* (Teachers College Press, 1989) and *To Teach: The Journey of a Teacher* (Teachers College Press, 1993) and coeditor (with William Schubert) of *Teacher Lore: Learning from Our Own Experience* (Longman, 1991). He is currently associate professor of education at the University of Illinois at Chicago and director of the Small Schools Workshop.

Nancy Balaban is director of the Infant and Parent Development Program in the Bank Street College Graduate School of Education. She is an expert on the development of infants and toddlers, early childhood curriculum, and the study of child behavior through observing and recording. Her articles on early childhood education have appeared in several publications including *Working Mother*, *Young Children*, *Good Housekeeping*, *Day Care and Early Education*, *Thought and Practice*, and *Parents Magazine*. She is the author of *Learning to Say Goodbye* (New American Library, 1987), *Starting School* (Teachers College Press, 1985), and (with Dorothy Cohen and Virginia Stern) *Observing and Recording the Behavior of Young Children* (Teachers College Press, 1983).

Suzanne C. Carothers is associate professor of elementary education at City College of the City University of New York. As Adult Literacy Program director in the Office of the Mayor, she coordinated the ground-breaking New York City Adult Literacy Initiative. She has taught 3-year-olds and has done extensive teacher education and staff development for more than 18 years. A chapter from her Ph.D. dissertation, "Catching Sense: Learning from our Mothers to Be Black and Female," was published in *Uncertain Terms: Negotiating Gender in American Culture* (Beacon Press, 1990).

Monroe D. Cohen has extensive experience in teaching (nursery school through graduate school), editing (10 years as director of publications for the Association for Childhood Education International and editor of its journal *Childhood Education*), and consulting (overseas tours with the U.S. Agency for International Development in Afghanistan and Brazil; and project director of Magnet Schools Assistance Program grants). Currently he is extending his lifelong interest in education through art as director of the Queens College Children's Program. He is also a practicing painter.

Lisa D. Delpit is a full-time researcher with the Institute for Urban Research at Morgan State University in Baltimore. Her work has focused on the perspectives, aspirations, and pedagogical knowledge of teachers of color, and she has used her training in ethnographic research to spark dialogues between educators on issues that have an impact on minority students. She has spent time studying multicultural issues in Alaska, Papua New Guinea, Fiji, and various urban and rural sites in the United States. Her background is in elementary education, with an emphasis on language arts. She has taught elementary school in an urban community in Philadelphia and preservice and in-service teachers in many communities across the United States. Her work on school-community relations and parent involvement was cited as contributing to her receiving a MacArthur Award in 1990.

Hubert M. Dyasi is professor of science education and director of the City College Workshop Center. He is an internationally known science educator with 25 years of postdoctoral experience in the United States, Africa, and England. He holds degrees from the University College of Fort Hare (Rhodes University) in South Africa and the University of Illinois, Urbana-Champaign, and has done further studies at Yale. He has taught at the University of Sierra Leone, All Souls College at Oxford University (England), and the University of Illinois. His work has been published in various journals, including *The Journal of Environmental Education*, the *Cambridge Journal of Education*, and *Prospects*. He has also contributed chapters on science inquiry to several books.

Susan Huddleston Edgerton is an assistant professor of education at the University of Illinois at Chicago, where she teaches courses on curriculum, instruction, and evaluation; diversity and difference; and curriculum and the politics of identity. She has written extensively on issues of race, gender, identity, autobiography, love, and pedagogy.

Helen Jencks Featherstone is an associate professor of teacher education at Michigan State University, senior research associate at the National Center for Research on Teacher Learning, and founding editor of *Changing Minds*, a bulletin on school reform. She is a former lecturer at Harvard University and founding editor of the *Harvard Education Letter*. Her book, *A Difference in the Family: Life with a Disabled Child* (Basic Books, 1980), examines the ways in which a child's disability affects parents and siblings. It won the 1981 Educator Award from the Delta Kappa Gamma Society International.

Joseph Featherstone is a professor of education at Michigan State University, where he has created an innovative teacher education program. He is a journalist, activist, poet, and former school principal. He is the author of several articles and books, including *Schools Where Children Learn* (Liveright, 1971) and *What Schools Can Do* (Liveright, 1976).

Artin Göncü is an associate professor of educational psychology and coordinator of early childhood education at the University of Illinois at Chicago. He has numerous publications in Turkish as well as English. He has written extensively on issues of children's play, cultural variations in play, play dialogues, and the role of play in growth and development.

Maxine Greene is professor emerita at Teachers College, Columbia University, where she has been on the faculty since 1965, holding the William F. Russell Chair in the Foundations of Education since 1975. Her courses have dealt with the philosophy and history of education, social philosophy, aesthetic education, ethics, literature, and phenomenology and existentialism. She has also taught at Montclair State College, New York University, and Brooklyn College and has lectured widely at universities and educational associations. She is author of many journal articles and chapters as well as *Existential Encounters for Teachers* (Random House, 1967), *The Public School and the Private Vision* (Random House, 1965), *Teacher as Stranger* (Wadsworth, 1973) (winner of the 1974 Education Book of the Year from Delta Gamma Kappa), *Landscapes of Learning* (Teachers College Press, 1978), and *The Dialectic of Freedom* (Teachers College Press, 1988).

Patricia Gregorich is a 1993 graduate of the Learning Community Teacher Education Program at Michigan State University. She is currently a second-year teacher of sixth graders at Jason Lee Middle School in Tacoma, Washington. She is passionate about growth—for herself, her children, and the educational system.

Patricia Redd Johnson is an education consultant, former teacher and lecturer at Harvard University, and former director of development at the Efficacy Institute. A school reform activist, she has lectured widely on issues on educational change, race and racism, and the arts.

Bruce Kanze is a fifth- and sixth-grade teacher at Central Park East I, an elementary school in El Barrio, a Latino community in East Harlem, New York. For 25 years he has struggled as a classroom teacher with questions about the many ways in which children learn and how to support that learning in the classroom. He has worked with other teachers to restructure schools and to create networks that help teachers and parents learn about children. He has lectured at City College and Lehman College in New York City and has worked with the various teachers' colleges in the New York City area. He is currently on sabbatical and is documenting the formation of a learning-centered school in northern Manhattan.

Tricia M. Niesz is a master's candidate in educational foundations, policy, and practice at the University of Colorado at Boulder. She is deeply committed to helping to dismantle the financial inequities among public schools.

Mary Anne Raywid is a professor of administration and policy studies at Hofstra University, where she also directs the Center for the Study of Educational Alternatives. She has published widely in the areas of school-society relationships and the politics of education. School reform, restructuring, and choice are her current major interests. She has taught high school and adult education as well as university graduates and undergraduates. She has been active in education organizations, having served as president of the Philosophy of Education Society, the John Dewey Society, and the Society of Professors of Education. She has also served on the editorial boards of more than a dozen professional journals.

Mara Sapon-Shevin is a professor in the Teaching and Leadership Programs at Syracuse University. Her work focuses on the establishment of inclusive, cooperative classroom communities, and she works actively with preservice and in-service teachers to support their efforts toward full inclusion of children with disabilities. She has lectured extensively throughout the world and has had articles published in *Educational Leadership, Teachers College Record, Phi Delta Kappan, Journal of Education, Cooperative Learning, Holistic*

Education Review, *Educational Foundations*, and *Exceptional Children*. Her book, *Playing Favorites: Gifted Education and the Disruption of Community* was published by SUNY Press (1994).

Rita Tenorio is the program implementer at La Escuela Fratney in Milwaukee. She has been a kindergarten teacher for 18 years, the last 13 in Milwaukee public schools. She played a major role in helping to establish La Escuela Fratney, the only school in Wisconsin with a dual immersion or "two-way" bilingual program in which native speakers of both Spanish and English learn in two languages. She considers herself first and foremost an advocate for children. She is an active member of the Milwaukee Teachers Education Association and the National Coalition of Education Activists and is a coeditor of the educational journal *Rethinking Schools*. In September 1990, she was named Wisconsin's Elementary Teacher of the Year.

Lillian Weber was professor of education at City College in New York City. In 1972, after several years of work in the public schools of New York making changes intended to better support children's active learning process, she founded the Workshop Center for Open Education at City College. She was a founding member of the North Dakota Study Group on Evaluation, served on the board of directors of the National Consortium on Testing, and was a member of the board of the Prospect Center. She authored numerous books, articles, monographs, and chapters focusing on the child as an active learner and on teaching as an activity that can support the child's growth and development. She lectured throughout the world, and continues to be widely regarded as the leading voice of the late 20th century in showing teachers how to accept children as lusty and inquiring and how to create environments that stimulate children's outreach to make sense of the world. Lillian Weber died in 1994.

Lauren Jones Young is associate professor of teacher education and educational administration at Michigan State University. She is senior researcher with the National Center for Research on Teacher Learning, and is leader of one of MSU's teacher preparation teams. Her teaching and research interests include race, gender, class, and educational equity in teaching practice.

Index